SERVICES IN TRANSITION

SERVICES IN TRANSITION
The Impact of Information
Technology on the
Service Sector

Edited by
GERALD FAULHABER
ELI NOAM
ROBERTA TASLEY

Ballinger Publishing Company • Cambridge, Massachusetts
A Subsidiary of Harper & Row, Publishers, Inc.

Copyright © 1986 by Ballinger Publishing Company. All rights reserved. No part of this publication may be reproduced, stored in a retrieval system, or transmitted in any form or by any means, electronic, mechanical, photocopy, recording or otherwise, without the prior written consent of the publisher.

International Standard Book Number: 0-88730-092-8

Library of Congress Catalog Card Number: 86-7918

Printed in the United States of America

Library of Congress Cataloging-in-Publication Data

Services in transition.

   Papers presented at the Conference on the Impact of Information Technology on the Service Sector, held at the Wharton School, University of Pennsylvania, Feb. 7-8, 1985.
   Includes bibliographies and index.
   1. Service industries—United States—Communication systems—Congresses. I. Faulhaber, Gerald R.
II. Noam, Eli M. III. Tasley, Roberta. IV. Conference on the Impact of Information Technology on the Service Sector (1985 : Wharton School, University of Pennsylvania)
HD9981.5.S44 1986   338.4'6'0973   86-7918
ISBN 0-88730-092-8

CONTENTS

List of Figures ix

List of Tables xi

Introduction xiii
Gerald Faulhaber and Eli Noam

Chapter 1
Services: Certainties and Uncertainties 1
Eli Ginzberg

Chapter 2
Information Technology and the U.S. Health Care Industry: A New Direction 7
Richard M. Scheffler

Discussion of Chapter 2 21
Mark V. Pauly

Discussion of Chapter 2 26
Kenneth E. Thorpe

Chapter 3
Technology Impacts on the Structure of the Insurance Industry — 31
David Young

Discussion of Chapter 3 — 44
Howard Kunreuther

Chapter 4
Technology and Financial Services: Regulatory Problems in a Deregulated Environment — 49
Almarin Phillips and Mitchell Berlin

Discussion of Chapter 4 — 73
Peter Linneman

Discussion of Chapter 4 — 76
Robert P. Shay

Chapter 5
The Impact of Information Technology on Trade in Services — 81
Geza Feketekuty and Kathryn Hauser

Discussion of Chapter 5 — 98
Donald A. Hicks

Discussion of Chapter 5 — 106
Gérard Pogorel

Additional Comments on the Impact of Information Technology on Trade Services — 110
Ronald Kent Shelp

Chapter 6
Information Technology and the United States Economy: Modeling and Measurement — 119
Charles Jonscher

Discussion of Chapter 6   132
Dennis A. Yao

Chapter 7
Information Technology, Demographics, and the Retail Response   137
George Sternlieb and James W. Hughes

Discussion of Chapter 7   175
Peter Linneman

Discussion of Chapter 7   178
Mitchell Moss

Chapter 8
Information Technology and the Service Sector: A Feedback Process?   183
William J. Baumol

Chapter 9
Conclusion   195
William J. Baumol

Index   201

About the Sponsoring Organizations   207

About the Editors   209

About the Contributors   211

LIST OF FIGURES

2-1.	Hospital Information Systems Market (by type of application)	14
2-2.	Hospital DP Expenditures per Patient Day (by hospital size)	15
5D-1.	Computer Software and Data Processing Services (SIC 737): Target Market for Major Project	102
6-1.	The Inputs and Outputs to Production and Information Labor Processes	122
6-2.	Chains of Production and Information Activity: Case 1, A Manufactured Product	123
6-3.	Chains of Production and Information Activity: Case 2, Banking Services	124
6-4.	A Two-Sector Model of the Macroeconomy	126
6-5.	Information and Production Sector Data: United States, 1960 and 1983	128
6D-1.	Size and Productivity of the Information and Production Sectors, 1950–2000	133

8-1.	Shares of Labor Force by Sector, 1800–1980	185
8-2.	U.S. Total Factor Productivity Annual Growth, 1844–1969	191

LIST OF TABLES

2-1.	DP Expenditures as Percentage of Total Hospital Expenses	12
2-2.	Electronic Data Processing Is Only a Fraction of Total Operating Expenses	13
2-3.	Hospital Information Systems—Estimated Sales Breakdown by Principal Vendor	16
4-1.	GNP, Selected Money, and Asset Aggregates and Turnover Rates, 1968 and 1984	53
5D-1.	International Export Orientation of High-Technology Firms in the Dallas–Fort Worth Regional Economy	101
6-1.	Information and Production Sector Input Coefficients for the U.S. Economy, 1960 and 1983	129
7-1.	Total Population Age Structure, U.S. Total Population (Including Armed Forces Abroad): 1970 to 1983	142

7–2.	Population Projections by Age, U.S. Total Population (Including Armed Forces Abroad): 1990 and 1995	144
7–3.	Estimates of the Resident Population of States, July 1, 1983 and 1984 (Including Armed Forces Residing in Each State)	146
7–4.	Population Change, Selected Cities—1950 to 1980	151
7–5.	Projected Household Growth Increments: By Age, Type, and Tenure: 1983 to 1995	153
7–6.	Owner and Renter Households by Age and Type, U.S. Total: 1983	154
7–7.	Household Projections by Age, Type, and Tenure of Households, U.S. Total: 1995	155
7–8.	Total Civilian Employment in the U.S., Four Largest European Nations, and Japan: 1970 to 1981	156
7–9.	Civilian Labor Force, by Sex, Age, and Race, 1970–1982, and Middle Growth Projection to 1995	157
7–10.	Total Civilian Employment in the Selected European Nations, and Japan, by Economic Sector: 1970 to 1982	158
7–11.	Overseas Message Units	170

INTRODUCTION
Gerald Faulhaber
Eli Noam

The last two decades have witnessed two profound changes in the U.S. economy: the extraordinary revolution in computer and telecommunication technology and the transformation to a service economy. While both these changes have been discussed before, seldom have the effects of one change upon the other been studied. Indeed, the application of information technology holds the promise of substantial productivity increases in services, our fastest growing sector, while at the same time spurring rapid development in advanced information technology. This interaction can form a new basis for economic growth, as well as provide an international competitive advantage for the United States, but is that potential being realized?

The scholars and practitioners who gathered at the conference on the Impact of Information Technology on the Service Sector at the Wharton School, University of Pennsylvania, heard and discussed papers from a broad array of disciplines and viewpoints on the topic. The conference was jointly organized by the Fishman-Davidson Center for the Study of the Service Sector, at the Wharton School, and the Center for Telecommunications and Information Studies, at Columbia University. The conference was sponsored by the United States Census Bureau and the National Science Foundation.

If there was a single common theme that emerged from the papers and discussion, it was the role of information technology in improving service sector productivity. Traditionally a victim of the "cost disease" (in William Baumol's words), the service sector has been perceived by insiders and outsiders alike as resistant to technical change and doomed to low or no productivity growth. As labor costs rise, so must the prices for services (the traditional view would have it) in the numerically dominant sector of our economy.

A somewhat different view emerges in the papers of this volume, however. With the help of the new information technology, industries are beginning to put in place the kind of productivity improvements needed to cure the "cost disease." No astounding breakthroughs, but solid progress in insurance, banking, and health care.

The technology not only affects the production and distribution of existing services, however; it also changes the nature of those services and creates new opportunities, and problems, that were largely unanticipated. For example, the ability of computers and high-speed data links to move "money" at the speed of light from one bank to another, from one form of asset to another, from one country to another, may have all but wiped out the ability of governments and central banks to have an effective monetary policy, as Phillips and Berlin's analysis indicates.

What is ahead for services, and how is information technology shaping that future? Eli Ginzberg, from Columbia's Graduate School of Business, a distinguished observer of secular trends in the economy, presents an overview of what we know, and what we don't know, about services. His contribution takes a long look at the past twenty-five years of service industry research at Columbia University and the University of Pennsylvania.

From this historical view, Ginzberg sets forth a number of certainties and uncertainties. The seven certainties are (1) the increasing scale of services in advanced economies, (2) the weakness of the term "services" as an analytic device, (3) the confusion of economists in dealing with services, (4) the contribution of services to the increasing employment of women, (5) the greater mobility of service jobs, (6) the differential impact of information technology on services, and (7) the restructuring of firms as a result of information technology.

Less certainty emerges from the facts that (1) information technology effects involve both space and time, (2) it is difficult to distinguish among data information and knowledge for decisionmaking, (3) much service advance is based on complex cross-national information flows, (4) access to data is limited by concerns for privacy, and (5) the ultimate effects of information technology on the basics of life are very unpredictable. Acknowledging that both "services" and "information technology" are soft concepts, Professor Ginzberg predicts that, by this century's end, information technology will be the leading industry in all developed countries.

The paper by Richard Scheffler of the University of California-Berkeley presents his insights into information technology in the U.S. health care industry, an industry that accounts for 10 percent of U.S. GNP. Greater productivity has become an imperative in the increasingly competitive for-profit hospital market. Improvements in information technology are being heavily relied upon to meet the new demands of cost control, excess capacity, and a rapidly changing regulatory environment.

While almost all hospitals use computers for routine billing and accounting operations, the advent of DRGs and prospective payment policies have increased pressure for management control of case-mix. New software systems promise to deliver that control to facility administrators. The implications of these developments are explored in the comments of Professor Kenneth Thorpe.

The new technology, however, has hardly touched the patient-provider relationship, which remains highly labor-intensive, as well as knowledge-intensive. Professor Mark Pauly's comments address this failure and question just how much information technology can affect health care, if providers' skills and motivation to use the technology remain low.

Turning to the insurance industry, David N. Young, president of PARTNERS National Health Plans, emphasizes the speed of change in his sector. In this case, however, automation of the industry involves providing agents with their own information accessing equipment—that is, decentralizing functions instead of centralizing them. This effort will greatly improve productivity by reducing the size of the insurance work force.

Computers and communications have also facilitated the strong trend in insurance markets to unbundle the risk transfer function from the pure service function (claims administration, risk assessment). Professor Howard Kunreuther, in his comments, notes that increasing automation in this industry could result in major carriers increasing their market power over both agents and customers.

The University of Pennsylvania's Almarin Phillips and Mitchell Berlin identify technology change in the financial services industry to have been a major source of market innovations that have accelerated deregulation.

Radical productivity increases in the transactions technology involved in asset switching underlies the enormous growth of assets other than bank demand deposits. This blurring between demand deposits and other deposits of banks has limited the effectiveness of the traditional forms of regulation. From this, they conclude that neither monetary policy nor deposit insurance is likely to work well without basic changes. Comments by Professors Peter Linneman and Robert Shay disagree with the contention that the new technology makes monetary policy by the Federal Reserve difficult or impossible; they focus instead on other instruments available for monetary control.

The contribution by Geza Feketekuty, Senior U.S. Trade Representative, addresses the international trade consequences of information technology. After identifying four causes for the increase in international trade in information- based services—advances in microelectronics, demand created by multinational corporations, the substantial service inputs required by automated production processes, and the emergence of international networks—Feketekuty singles out two key requirements for such trade. First, in order to ensure an efficient communications network, it is essential to maintain open international flows of data. Second, international networking, including the establishment of network services in the country within which trade is to take place, must be encouraged by an international agreement governing trade in services.

Comments by Professor Donald Hicks distinguish between new technology and the diffusion of older technology. He suggests that the spread of international trade in services owes more to the spread of the older communications systems than the development of new information processing systems.

Comments by Professor Gerard Pogorel focus on the potential for the new technologies to internationalize and centralize key services, and the natural resistance and protectionism that may arise as a result. The comparative advantage of the United States in these new technologies may extend into the global service sector.

Ronald Shelp of American International Group (now of Celanese) discusses the concerns regarding establishing trade rules for services. He mentions several reasons why trade in services has developed outside the framework of GATT: (1) lack of economic understanding of the role of services in international trade; (2) lack of data on services; and (3) fear of other nations that the United States has an overwhelming comparative advantage in services. Several governments, including the United States and Japan, actively support including service trade under GATT; others, such as Brazil and India, actively oppose it, taking a protectionist, "infant industry," stance toward their own service sectors. As the new technology makes more and more services tradable, the author foresees continuing dissension among the developing and developed nations over the free trade issue.

The papers from the second day of the conference address issues that are more general to all service industries. The paper by Charles Jonscher of MIT notes the increasing demand for information technology as a fraction of all technology, and the increasing demand for white collar (information) labor as a fraction of total labor. He then addresses whether this fundamental shift in the economy is occurring because consumer tastes are changing to be more information-intensive (e.g., entertainment, education) or because our economy now requires greater information resources in order to manage and coordinate production. The author finds that it is primarily the latter, using a highly simplified but insightful model of the U.S. economy.

Professor Dennis Yao's comments urge caution in the use of any empirical predictions from such a stylized model. He goes on to suggest bases in modern organizational theory of firms that offer some explanation as to how information can be used to improve the efficiency and effectiveness of firms.

George Sternlieb, director of the Center for Urban Policy Research at Rutgers University, tackles the implications of information technology on future demographics. His speculative inquiry touches many aspects of future spatial patterns, labor force characteristics, and retail sales patterns, all of which will be markedly different from the present, in considerable part because of information technology. In fact, Sternlieb believes that the pace of change will accelerate because demographic and economic parameters associated with the aging of the "baby boom" generation will create a far more receptive environment for technological innovation.

In his comments, Peter Linneman cautions against "surprise-free" projections. He points to the role of technology in the Sunbelt development—for example, irrigation, pest control, air conditioning, and improved communications.

Professor Mitchell Moss also notes that the new technology will affect demographic trends in unexpected ways, leading to the decentralization of some industries, such as mail-order retailing (dependent on "800 Service" and the credit card), while perhaps centralizing others, such as financial trading.

Princeton University's William Baumol presents a fascinating, and disturbing, theoretical result. His main thesis is that highly variable, "noisy" data on productivity in service industries does not necessarily imply that the underlying economic forces that drive productivity growth are uncertain. Indeed, Baumol shows that very simple economic feedback systems can behave as if random. Observing productivity patterns that appear quite noisy, therefore, does not allow us to conclude that these patterns are the result of randomness in the underlying economic forces. He cautions academics and practioners alike that this problem is inherent and that measurement of effects should take this into account.

Collectively, the contributors to this volume analyzed central themes in the evolution of the economy in the United States and other developed countries. They point to a blurring of the concepts of industry and services, with services increasingly intensive in information capital, and industry more and more reliant on information services such as programming, data bases, internal communications, automated purchasing, and distribution. General Motors, which has recently diversified heavily into information technology, is a telling example. For America's traditional industry, the enhancement of products and production by a strong information service component that permits rapid change and customization is one important way to keep up with low-cost mass production countries.

At the same time, service providers, traditionally decentralized and often small-sized, are being linked through communications technology and can be organized on a national scale. The global provision of services is becoming a reality, spearheaded by financial services and followed by information provision, data processing, and engineering. Because the United States is a leader in both the design of information technology and its applications, it is able to make the combination of services and information technology a key for export strength. This threatens other countries' industries that have not been accustomed to compete internationally, and it raises global issues of protectionism and national sovereignty in information.

For America, too, trade-in-services is a two-way street; stock exchanges in Singapore, data bases in Korea, and program syndicators in Paris may well begin to provide services that are concentrated today in New York, or Chicago, or Los Angeles. Domestically, the changes towards information-based service industries cause shifts in regional and urban work distribution and residential patterns. They help absorb well-educated new workers but threaten traditional skills. They decentralize organizations but make them instantaneously accountable to the centers. They raise productivity of services but at a slower rate than in the industrial sector. And they create a vast new labor-intensive service industry—information creation, processing, and transmission, as the brain and nervous system of the economy.

All this affects society: economically, socially, technologically, psychologically, and legally. Can this country live on the export of services? How can the monetary system be stabilized? How can privacy be protected? What are property rights in information and its uses? A long agenda for academic research and public policy debate is emerging. It may require a reorientation of traditional categories of analysis. For example, economists have classically used as factors of production capital, labor, and land, corresponding to the social classes of nineteenth century Europe. These classifications may be useful for the analyses of agriculture or manufacturing but not necessarily to the service sector. Perhaps a more useful trinity, as Kenneth Boulding has suggested, would be material, energy, and information.

The role of information, in particular, is a key issue for assessing the development of the service sector. This volume attempts to provide research on several of the industries that are affected; the authors hope that it will spark fruitful further work.

Unfortunately, a conference proceedings volume cannot capture the conflicting opinions and spirited discussion that characterized this conference. If the papers in this volume lead the reader to question and probe, as they did the conference participants, then the organizers will view it a success.

As in all collaborative efforts, thanks are due to more people than can be mentioned. Foremost thanks, however, are owed to Laura Murphy, Rick Hiemann, and Barbara Gittelman of the Wharton School, who ensured the smooth running of the conference by having the right people do the right thing at the right time (but not too long). From Columbia, special thanks are due to Mei Ng, who devoted many hours to the perfection of the manuscript with her ever present skill and good humor.

We are grateful to Charles Brownstein and Lawrence Rosenberg of the National Science Foundation and to James Aanestad of the United States Census Bureau for supporting parts of the conference. Special thanks go to Marilyn Englander for her splendid editorial work.

1 SERVICES: CERTAINTIES AND UNCERTAINTIES
Eli Ginzberg

This book will explore the impact of a major new technology—computer-communications—on services. There are two important aspects of the way in which mainline economists have dealt with the subject of "services." From Adam Smith to William Baumol, who has written the conclusion for this volume, economists have been biased against services on a variety of grounds. They have argued that services are nonproductive, that they are not subject to economies of scale, that in many instances technology cannot be used to replace human labor, that they cannot be readily traded and transported, and, worst of all, that they are subject to "cost disease." Not only mainline economists have taken this pessimistic view of services; the great dissenter, Karl Marx, and our own prominent dissenter, Thorstein Veblen, were also discouraging about services. Both of them had what can be described as a "commodity bias."

My colleagues and I at the Conservation of Human Resources, Columbia University—initially Hiestand, Reubens, Greenfield, Stanback, and later Cohen and Noyelle—began to focus on services in the early 1960s. *The Pluralistic Economy* (1964), which presented our work on the importance of governmental and nonprofit services, was largely ignored by economists primarily because of their market bias. We had pointed out that it was questionable whether the U.S. economy could be considered one that is almost exclusively "private sector" since, according to our calculations, not less than one quarter of the Gross National Product (GNP) and between one third and two fifths of all workers were in the not-for-profit sector. These workers were employed by government; the products they manufactured were sold exclusively to government (such as missiles), or they held jobs in nonprofit organizations such as voluntary hospitals and private colleges.

At that time, American economists simply were unable to accept that much of the dynamism of the U.S. economy was in the service sector, particularly societal services such as education, health, defense, biomedical research, and recreation in which government plays a leading role. It is still difficult for many economists to bow to the figures even with the federal budget in the $1 trillion range.

Although our colleagues ignored us, I was pleased that the then executive vice president of ARA told me that he used our book as a manual to help train that part of his sales force that was focusing its efforts on the not-for-profit sector. He was not encumbered by ideological baggage.

Now, we will consider what "certainties" there are about services. The first important certainty is that the dominant role of services in the U.S. economy is not an abberation; it is characteristic of all advanced economies, from the Canadian to the Japanese. The major exception is the German economy, and this can be explained by the fact that Germans tend to "internalize" many producer services within their manufacturing firms.

In the United States our system of data collection obscures the extent to which services now dominate our economic life. For example, both GE and IBM are classified as manufacturing firms, and therefore all of their employees are classified under "manufacturing"; however, no more than about 35 percent of GE's total work force, according to the corporation's former chief executive officer, is directly engaged in physical production. The proportion is steadily decreasing; with advances in CAD/CAM, it will be still smaller tomorrow.

The difficulty of distinguishing between employment in goods and employment in services calls attention to the softness of the term "services." It is a catch-all category that includes everybody who is not classified as employed in agriculture, mining, manufacturing, or construction. It is not our purpose here to enter into a discussion of the different subcategories into which services can be usefully divided, but we will note that one subcategory, the "producer services"—which include banking, legal, accounting, marketing, advertising, and computerization—accounts for just about the same proportion of the GNP in terms of value added (22 to 24 percent) as all of the manufacturing in the United States.

Here is another certainty. Adam Smith had little difficulty in discerning the movements of grain prices over several centuries since the item—"a bushel of grain"—did not change over time. Consider, in contrast, the "per-diem cost of a hospital day," not over centuries but during the last three and a half decades, between 1950 and 1985. The range and intensity of the care the patients receive—and the outcomes in terms of alleviation and cure—are vastly different.

The strong and continuing increases in the output of services in the post–World War II economy are closely linked to the availability of a large supply of women who were ready and eager to find employment out of their homes and who were well suited in terms of educational background and job preferences (part-time) to fit into many expanding sectors of the service economy. And the more active role of women in the world of work led to substantial increases in the demand for a variety of new services from child care to fast foods.

An important facet of the ways in which changes in services and employment are linked can be found in the dynamics of career mobility. In the past, the internal labor market in large manufacturing firms was the key mechanism through which workers with time and experience advanced to better and higher paying jobs. In the new service economy, career mobility requires workers to move among employers. A waiter in a small restaurant must move to a larger one for additional opportunity and income.

The impact of technology on services varies according to the nature of the technology involved. One certainty is that the computer-communications technology belongs to the genre of basic technological breakthroughs such as the telephone, the railroads, electric power, the automobile. Accordingly, we must anticipate that over time it will result in major transformations both in the types of services that are produced and the ways in which they are produced. The revolution that is occurring in "financial services," and it is a revolution, foreshadows the impacts of the new technology on many other sectors in the years ahead.

It may be useful to consider the evolution of the computer-communications technology so far and what may lie ahead. After three decades of penetration, the computer has been used primarily for "numbers crunching." The next stage of the technology is likely to have a much more pervasive impact by increasing the types of products that will be available and, further, by making it possible to restructure organizations and the ways in which business decisions are made and corporations are managed.

These are the certainties. Now, we will have a quick look at the uncertainties. The concept of impact involves time as well as extent, and when technology is involved, time is hard to capture except in retrospect. I once heard Kuznets explain at some length that at any point in time many embryonic technologies appear to be promising but most of them are stillborn. Only a few will get off the ground and even fewer will be successful. We will know which few do make it only in retrospect.

Let us consider briefly where the computer revolution may be on its expansion course relative to that of the automobile. Is the industry at present at the comparable level of 1915, 1935, or 1955? The answer is elusive, but I would pick 1915!

A second uncertainty is what we mean when we use the phrase "information technology." More specifically, what do we mean by information? I like to distinguish among data, information, and knowledge—and while I admit that one may fade into the other, I believe that in many cases there is nothing but data and more data. One thing is certain—we have much more data than we have knowledge. I would venture the hypothesis that the more we develop technology that is capable of processing large amounts of data at a low cost, the further we get from, not the closer to, useful knowledge. I admit that this may be a rationalization of my ineptness with the new technology because I still prefer to do most of my calculations in my head!

Another area of uncertainty is the issue of access to data bases versus the protection of proprietary property. I remember that a not very radical president, Herbert Hoover, when he served as Secretary of Commerce, considered it important that the U.S. government strengthen its data collecting–data disseminating capabilities since he was convinced that a stronger informational infrastructure would help U.S. business. Today, however, few observers other than Nobel Laureate Leontief ever think about the appropriate balance between public and private data files.

Closely related are the policy issues involved in developing sensible laws and agreements about the transmission of data across national boundaries. The United States insists that such transmission be free and unencumbered or that it be as close to that ideal as possible. A leading expert, Walter Wriston, has estimated that the United States moves about 80 percent of all data across national borders. But what is sensible for the United States does not necessarily meet the goals of other national states that face many challenges from national security to essential record keeping, with protection of confidentiality and other issues in the middle.

I realize that most U.S. economists (and other specialists) can make a strong case for the reduction and removal of government from most regulatory activities affecting the protection and distribution of information. While I acknowledge that some of the evidence they present in support of deregulation is telling, I am not totally convinced. I am impressed with the evidence that my colleague Eli Noam has presented about the "monopolistic" tendencies that have led the European Postal Telegraph & Telephones (PTTs) and their respective trade unions to persuade their respective governments to continue a large number of restrictive policies. At the same time, however, I do not think that dismantling the entire regulatory structure would be sensible for most large or small countries. They have too much to lose, too little to gain.

Here is one more uncertainty. There is no answer to the critical question of how much life and work and leisure will change as the information society continues to evolve. The deputy editor (Norman Macrae) of *The Economist* pointed out some years ago that large cities are doomed and that before long most of us will be working out of our own homes. I am reasonably sure that he will be found wrong on both counts, but we must wait and see. We are told that before long we will be doing our banking with personal computers at home. This is possible, but not for certain. Only a prophet would have been able to foretell in 1915 the impact of the automobile on the structure and functioning of the U.S. economy and society in 1985. And it is my hunch that the computer-communications revolution today is at a comparable point in its growth curve.

I offer this endnote. Both "services" and "information technology" are soft concepts. This is especially true if we consider their usefulness for long-term projections. Nevertheless, I would bet that by the end of this century, which is less than fifteen years away, information technology will be the leading industry in all advanced economies.[1]

NOTE

1. For reinforcement of this forecast, I refer the reader to Stephen McClellan's recent book. *The Coming Computer Industry Shake-out: Winners, Losers, Survivors* (New York, John Wiley, 1984).

2 INFORMATION TECHNOLOGY AND THE U.S. HEALTH CARE INDUSTRY: A NEW DIRECTION

Richard M. Scheffler

A rough estimate suggests that health information systems consume between 1.5 and 2 percent of the Gross National Product (GNP). The health care industry spends over 10 percent of the GNP. Hospitals, the major users of health information technology, account for about 40 percent of all expenditures. Estimates are available that indicate at least one quarter of a hospital's operating budget goes to some form of information collection and processing, which includes electronic data processing and manual information processing (Eralp and Rucker 1984). These costs include the personnel and equipment costs of collecting, recording, retrieving, and disseminating both financial and clinical data. In addition, health insurance companies as well as government payers such as Medicare and Medicaid spend heavily on information processing, as do nursing homes and physicians' offices. If these users spend half as much on health information systems (a conservative assumption), then our estimate that health care information costs consume 1.5 to 2 percent of the GNP is a fair one.

The author gratefully acknowledges the contribution of Randolph Hill to the research and writing of this paper and Allen Cheadle for assistance with the data analysis. The author also thanks Robert Turnage, Otto Stoll, John Nicholas, Jonathan Osgood, Caro Carpenter, and William Kine for providing helpful data and information.

In this chapter we will describe the development and growth of health information technology in the U.S. health system and will detail its uses. We will identify major developments in the health care field, including regulatory, environmental, and organizational changes that are affecting the use of technology. In the conclusion we will make some guesses of where the health care information industry is headed and why. Perhaps these conjectures will serve as the basis for further discussions of the new direction of information technology for the health care sector.

THE USE OF HEALTH INFORMATION SYSTEMS

Health information technology has had an impact on almost every aspect of the health care industry. The major areas are the following:

1. *Medical Education:* access to biomedical data for research and teaching
2. *Patient Care:* automated medical records
3. *Patient Education:* computerized instruments to measure health risks
4. *Business Management:* financial data and billing records.

The rapid advances in computer technology during the last two decades, particularly the increases and quality and reductions in cost of both hardware and software, have paved the way for many of the developments in health care computer use. Smaller stand-alone computers have replaced the large centralized computers that used high-speed batch systems (Waters and Murphy 1983). Today, mini- and microcomputers have permitted the development of in-house turnkey systems that are more flexible and can be tailored to the needs of the individual user.

One can define three distinct levels of health information systems. The first employs on-line, real time, communications-oriented systems with interdepartmental data integration. The user interacts with computers on-line and obtains immediate real-time responses. This level of medical computing is oriented towards the financial functions of the hospital. The second level uses on-line, real-time systems that have been designed to capture and process part or all of the patient's medical record. The third level is very similar to the second, but it combines patient data elements with the medical resources being used on the patient. This third level of medical computing is expanding rapidly because of regulatory changes in the health care industry (Waters and Murphy 1983).

The diffusion of health information systems in the United States has been rapid in some areas of the health care industry and surprisingly slow in others. Automated computer billing systems for accounting have spread rapidly with over 90 percent of hospitals having such a system. The use of automation for diagnosis and treatment such as the analysis of electrocardiographic signals by computer systems has expanded more slowly. Only 15 percent of EKG's used this procedure in 1979. Also, less than one percent of the hospitals made use of the automation of medical information systems with patient information (Lindberg 1982).

Within the hospital industry there are three major uses of computer technology in health information systems (HISs). The Patient Information System is used to insure proper treatment while the patient is in the hospital. The system follows the patient throughout his or her hospital stay. It notes when the patient is treated by a physician, and it keeps an on-going record of pharmaceutical and laboratory uses by the patient. The second type of HIS is used for financial management. It deals with typical business functions such as billing, payroll, and accounts receivable. The third use of an HIS is in the area of strategic management, which is the fastest and growing area in health information systems. The HIS provides information on financial planning and resource allocation, as well as information on the environment in which the hospital is located (Packer 1984b).

AN OVERVIEW OF THE HEALTH CARE INDUSTRY

This overview is intended to highlight several characteristics, especially those that have been affected by or impact upon information technology. As is the case with most overviews, there will be sweeping generalizations, and in some cases the exceptions will be of considerable interest.

The most casual observer of the health care industry is aware of its rapid rate of growth, which has accelerated over the past two decades. This growth is part of the overall increase in the service sector of the economy. Yet, the passage of federal and state programs that finance the delivery of health care to the elderly (Medicare) and to the poor (Medicaid) has stimulated the growth of the health care industry to an even greater degree. The fact that the purchase of health care is now dominated by third party payers such as government payers and private insurance carriers is of particular interest to economists. About 90 percent of individuals are covered for hospital services and about 40 percent for physician services (Arnett et al. 1985). There is some cost-sharing in the form of copayments and deductibles.

Hospitals are the primary not-for-profit sector of the health care field. Community hospitals and university medical centers are set up on a not-for-profit basis. Today about 85 percent of all hospitals are considered nonprofit (Samors and Sullivan 1983). This feature, however, is changing rapidly. For-profit hospitals are growing in their number and influence.

The fastest growing component of health expenditures has consistently been hospital services. An important factor influencing the rate of growth of costs is medical technology. As noted earlier, a number of the technological innovations in hospitals have been geared to improve the state of medical information that is used for diagnosis and treatment. CAT scanners, fetal monitors, and computer-assisted EKGs are but a few examples.

The health care industry employs about six or seven million people, depending on how its scope is defined (Ginzberg 1978). Most significant has been the increase in health personnel, especially physicians. Aided by federal funds and to some extent state funds, the supply of physicians is expanding rapidly. The current supply of practicing physicians is about 400,000 and is expected to increase by about 600,000 in the next five to seven years (Scheffler et al. 1979).

Pressure on government budgets has led to recent developments in the health care industry. In many states, health care is the largest single item of the budget, and the fastest growing as well. In the federal budget following social security, health is the largest component of the social service budget. Within the private sector, health insurance consumes the largest share of the fringe benefit package. The annual rate of increase of health insurance premiums have averaged about 16 percent, and for some industries it has been as high as 30 percent in recent years (Fox, Goldbeck, and Spies 1984). It appeared to many health experts and health economists that the industry was growing out of control and some market discipline was required.

The pressure from government and the private sector has produced some significant trends:

1. Growth in the for-profit hospital sector
2. An increasing number of hospital mergers, including both horizontal and vertical integration

3. Increased concentration in the industry
4. New regulations for the financing of health services

The growth of the for-profit sector of the hospital industry is significant for health information technology. These hospitals tend to be run with more attention to production and cost decisions than nonprofit hospitals. They have a greater need for timely and useful information.

The large hospital industry, with over 7,000 hospitals nationwide, is operating with a great deal of unused capacity. Current bed occupancy rates are in the 65 to 70 percent range (Ermann and Gabel 1984, 1985). To cover fixed costs, hospitals are being pressured in general to expand their markets and to compete with other hospitals for patients. To compete in the market, hospitals are merging into chains and multihospital systems. Market power is increasingly becoming an important factor in the hospital industry.

Cost control is also becoming a real issue. Medicare uses a new prospective pricing system—a DRG system—that has changed the economic character of the hospital. Previously, hospitals were paid their costs and reimbursed retroactively. The diagnostic related groups system (DRG) pays hospitals a set price for treating a patient with a specific diagnosis. There are currently 470 diagnoses in which the patient can be placed for payment. Certain adjustments are currently possible to these prices, and there is a policy covering outliers. For the most part, however, hospitals face a given price for a given DRG. Private payers and states are using this type of payment policy with increasing frequency. Its major impact, however, is on federal payments under Medicare (Wennberg, McPherson, and Caper 1984).

The physician market is also changing. Large supplies of physicians are putting pressure on the market. Purchasers of care such as insurance companies and business firms are using their market share of patients to lower their costs. There is a new financing scheme that is gaining a fair amount of momentum in the health care industry: the development of so-called "preferred provider organizations" (PPOs). These are composed of groups of physicians, or hospitals and physicians, that agree to discount their fees in exchange for the patient base of the insurance company or a business firm (Gabel and Ermann 1985). Organizational forms of PPOs abound, with many hybrids, but the essential feature is discounting by physicians in exchange for guarantees of large patient populations. The small solo or candy store physician's practice is giving way to corporate medicine. Statewide and, in some instance, nationwide

PPOs are being developed. Competition for market shares and the growth of PPO systems is clearly a potentially large and new market for health information systems.

Although the rate of increased concentration of the health care industry is difficult to quantify, its direction is clear. Some believe that within a decade three or four hundred large firms or chains will control a major portion of the health care market. The rate of growth and improvement of health information systems will be an important factor in determining which portions of the system grow and which decline.

TODAY'S HEALTH INFORMATION INDUSTRY

There has been a considerable increase in the size of the health information industry. Much of this growth, as might be expected, is in the hospital industry. Data processing (DP) in hospitals is small in comparison with other service sector industries but is expected to increase at a rapid rate. Although about a quarter of the hospital's budget is used for information collection (about 25 billion dollars in 1984), only about 2.2 percent is spent on data processing (see Table 2–1). Table 2–1 suggests a projected increase of 20 percent per year. Even before the beginning of DRGs (prospective payments), DP as a percent of operating expenses was increasing.

It is interesting to note, as Table 2–2 shows, that expenditures on data processing increases with the size of the hospital. The DP expenses per bed increases from $1,035 for small (100 bed and less) hospitals to almost four times that amount for large (500-plus bed) hospitals. The

Table 2–1. DP Expenditures as Percentage of Total Hospital Expenses ($ millions).

Year	Total Operating Expenditures	Total DP Expenditures	DP as % of Operating Expenses
1980	76,851	1,610	2.1
1981	90,572	1,939	2.1
1982	104,876	2,305	2.2
1983	116,412	2,780	2.4
1984	130,964	3,405	2.6
1985	148,382	4,141	2.8

Source: Eralp and Rucker (1984).

Table 2-2. Electronic Data Processing Is Only a Fraction of Total Operating Expenses.

Size	Total U.S. Hospitals	Total DP Expenses	Avg. DP Expenditures Per Hospital	Avg. DP Expense Per Bed	DP as % of Total Hosp. Expenses
(Number of beds)		($ Mill.)	($ Thous.)	($)	(%)
500+	332	872	2,625	3,805	2.9
400-499	273	350	1,282	2,900	2.5
300-399	423	345	816	2,400	2.2
200-299	738	324	439	1,807	1.7
100-199	1,380	263	190	1,350	1.6
99 or less	2,655	151	57	1,035	1.6
Total	5,801	2,305	397	2,283	2.2

Source: Eralp and Rucker (1984).

Rate of increase appears somewhat less pronounced when DP expenses are viewed as a percentage of total hospital expenses. Small hospitals (less than 100 beds) use 1.6 percent of their revenues on data processing whereas large (more than 500 beds) use 2.9 percent of their revenues on data processing. Reasons for this are many: larger hospitals are more complex, and they provide more technical services; management planning needs are greater; and DP needs require more specific tailoring to the structure of the hospital.

In 1982, almost all hospitals had DP systems for financial billings. This one item accounts for almost two thirds (64.1 %) of the expenditures by hospitals on DP (see Figure 2-1). The other large item is patient care, which accounts for almost 22 percent. These separate areas are beginning to be merged as hospitals respond to DRGs. The market for purely financial services is saturated and little growth is seen in this area. The average data processing per patient for financial management and patient care generally rises as hospital size increases from a little over $5.00 per day to almost $8.00 per day for large hospitals (see Figure 2-2). These costs are small in comparison to the cost of a hospital bed per day, which is in the range of $500.

The hospital data processing market is quite competitive. There are almost two hundred firms—the three largest being IBM, SMS, and McDonnell Douglas Automation (see Table 2-3). Revenues in 1982 approached $1.5 billion and are expected to pass $5 billion by 1987

Figure 2-1. Hospital Information Systems Market (by type of application).

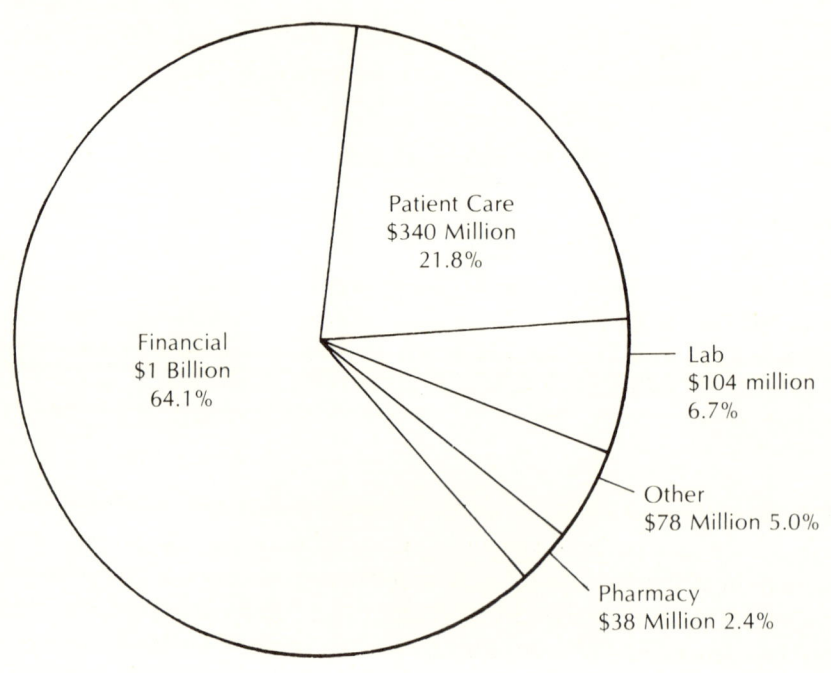

1982 Total: $1.6 Billion

Source: Eralp and Rucker (1984).

(Nicholas 1984). Hardware manufacturers account for the largest portion of sales; IBM has 40 percent of the market for hospitals over 300 beds, with vendors selling shared services accounting for the next 20 percent of the market (Carpenter 1984).

The growing companies, however, are those that can provide either turnkey or in-house systems that can be tailored to individual needs. Rapid turnover and on-line systems are replacing batch systems that were primarily used for billing. Hospitals now need to make timely resource allocation decisions and require data and data-based reports for financial planning. With the advent of DRGs, hospitals have become particularly interested in purchasing software to manage the case mix of the hospital and to help select the most profitable DRG for a given

Figure 2-2. Hospital DP Expenditures per Patient Day (by hospital size).

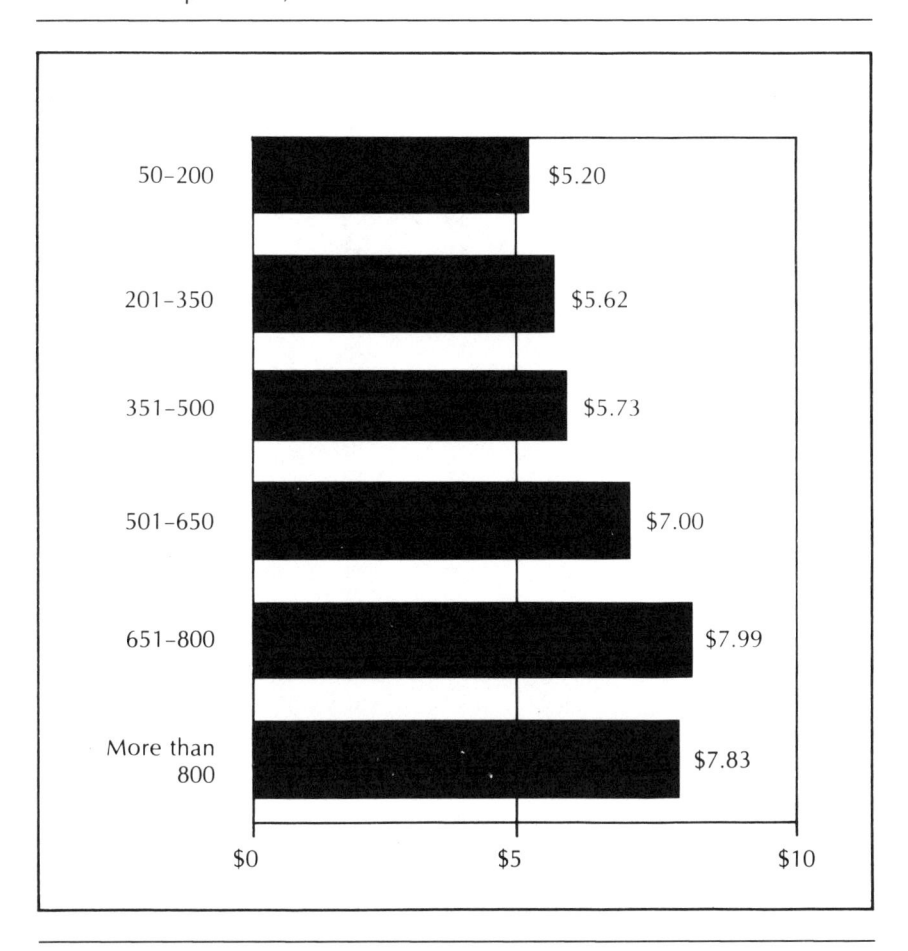

Hospital Size	Expenditure
50–200	$5.20
201–350	$5.62
351–500	$5.73
501–650	$7.00
651–800	$7.99
More than 800	$7.83

Source: Packer (1984).

admission. Those companies in the industry who sell software and turnkey systems are scrambling to develop effective hospital resource management packages. Furthermore, the market has tightened as prospective payment policies have forced hospitals to be more price conscious in the selection of a health information system.

Many of the companies in the market give IBM the hardware portion and develop other services that are compatible with IBM hardware. However, some companies such as HBO are in the process of developing and marketing new software products that are compatible with Data

16   SERVICES IN TRANSITION

Table 2-3. Hospital Information Systems—Estimated Sales Breakdown by Principal Vendor ($ millions).

Vendor	1980	1981	1982	1983	1984	1985
IBM Corp.	310	380	450	540	660	845
SMS	106	132	166	209	255	329
McAuto	95	126	156	198	250	308
Data General	24	32	40	60	90	135
HBO & Co.	23	37	53	66	85	111
Compucare	7	11	21	40	55	75
Technicon	25	31	38	44	63	78
AMI	3	8	12	25	37	55
DEC	64	71	78	92	105	111
Mediflex	10	13	18	24	32	43
Baxter Travenol	0	2	5	12	25	40
EDS	3	7	10	13	20	28
H-P	14	17	19	31	43	46
Amherst	4	7	10	13	17	23
Burroughs	50	54	57	55	63	60
Systems Assoc.	6	9	11	15	20	25
Community Health	7	9	11	14	18	22
Tandem	10	13	15	18	23	26
CDC	14	18	22	26	31	33
NCR Corp.	55	58	60	55	51	47
Four Phase Sys.	48	51	54	60	48	25

Source: Eralp and Rucker (1984).

General equipment. Many industry analysts feel these new products will greatly increase HBO's dominant market share. For example, HBO recently released a system, *Galaxy,* that integrates accounting, patient care, and case mix applications in a single turnkey system for hospitals with less than 150 beds.[1]

Another popular competitive strategy followed by SMS, HBO's most direct competitor, is to purchase licensing rights to software developed by a single hospital or academic institution for its own use and then to sell the product under an SMS name and label. SMS is also attempting to meet the new price sensitive environment through the repackaging of its old systems in smaller and cheaper units.[2]

Also of interest is the increase in mergers among leading companies. Recently, HBO, a fast-rising vendor of hospital computer systems, purchased two of its major competitors, Mediflex and Amherst Associates (Benway 1984). Mergers will have a significant impact on the direction and growth of information technology in the health sector, but the nature of that impact is quite uncertain.

Although health information systems are less well documented in the physician's practice, the increased attractiveness of micros has led to the availability of data systems for individual physician practices. Moreover, the increase in group practices and health care delivery systems such as health maintenance organizations (HMOs) and PPOs has increased the need for all types of HISs and technology. Cost control pressures on physicians require attention to resource allocation and production. Corporate medicine and the trend towards large health systems will be a new and expanding market for HISs.

THE NEW DIRECTION

Information technology is a driving force in the delivery of health care in the United States. It is crucial to the field of medical research developing new medical tests and procedures. Information technology is at the forefront of medical knowledge. Pacemakers that monitor heartbeats, the computer-assisted health risk instruments that assess health needs are some examples. There is even talk of the "hospital on the wrist": a small microprocessor with electronic probes capable of monitoring changes in the body, measuring vital signs, analyzing blood and enzymes (Ruby 1984). The device would network with a hospital or a physician. "Lifeline," which is now operational, is linked to a hospital and will respond if the patient needs care.

The health care data processing market will continue to grow at a prodigious rate throughout the remainder of the decade. The trend is shifting back from decentralized departmental computing (a micro in every office) to more integrated, database oriented systems that can be used throughout a hospital or other major health facilities. The big hardware vendors such as IBM and Data General disappointed many hospitals in the early seventies because their systems, promised to handle all the hospital's data processing needs, proved unable to do so, causing large facilities to resort to using shared systems or purchasing small departmental in-house systems. But such leading companies such as HBO and Mediflex, selling integrated turnkey systems, have caused a reversal in the trend.[3] The wave of the future may be networking of the already purchased smaller systems, especially in smaller health care facilities. For example, AT&T is expected to enter the health care industry aggressively with its new line of hardware and its networking software such as UNIX. Some predict that IBM will follow its age-old strategy of dominating the market by imitating popular software packages and entering the field through aggressive advertising. Thus, the market for information technology in the health care industry could be following the pattern of the health care industry itself: increasing centralization and concentration to meet growing competition and cost pressures, with extremely large firms dominating the industry.

Information technology is helping to change the face of the health care industry. The industry's response to cost control, excess capacity, and the changing regulatory environment will undoubtedly increase the need for information technology. Hospitals are effectively integrating health information systems that link patient data with financial and resource use data. In addition, information technology is being used increasingly to improve financial management and the strategic planning of hospitals and health care systems. There appears to be an ever stronger demand for HISs and information technology in the health care system. We are just at the beginning of an era of expansion.

NOTES

1. Information regarding recent products of health care technology companies came from the author's personal discussions with industry representatives.
2. See note 1.
3. See note 1.

REFERENCES

Arnett, R.H.; C.S. Cowell; L.M. Davidoff; and M.S. Freeland. 1985. "Health Spending Trends in the 1980's: Adjusting to Financial Incentives." *Health Care Financing Review* 6, no. 3:1–26.

Benway, S.D. 1984. "More Feverish Growth?" *Barrons* 44 (December 24): 11, 20.

Carpenter, C.J. 1984. *Company Update: Mediflex Systems Corporation.* Baltimore, MD: Alex Brown & Sons Research.

Eralp, O., and B.B. Rucker. 1984. *The Hospital Information Systems Industry.* San Francisco: Hambrecht and Quist.

Ermann, D., and J. Gabel. 1984. "Multihospital Systems: Issues and Empirical Findings." *Health Affairs* 3, no. 1:50–64.

——— . 1985. "The Changing Face of American Health Care: Multihospital Systems, Emergency Centers and Surgery Centers." *Medical Care* 23, no. 5:401–20.

Fox, P.D.; W.B. Goldbeck; and J.J. Spies. 1984. *Health Care Cost Management*. Ann Arbor, MI: Health Administration Press.

Gabel, J., and D. Ermann. 1985. "Preferred Provider Organizations: Performance, Problems, and Promise." *Health Affairs* 4, no. 1:24–40.

Ginzberg, E. 1978. *Health Manpower and Health Policy*. New York: Universe Books.

Lindberg, D.A.B. 1982. "Diffusion of Medical Information Systems Technology in the United States." *Journal of Medical Systems* 6:219–228.

Nicholas, J.P. 1984. *Hospital Information Systems Update*. Chicago: William Blair & Co.

Packer, C.L. 1984a. "A Comparison of Hospital Data Processing Costs." *Hospitals* 58, no. 15:83–86.

——— . 1984b. "Major Data Processing Systems and Applications." *Hospitals* 58, no. 17:66–72.

Ruby, G. 1984. "Information Technology and the Health of an Aging Population." (Background chapter for paper presented at the Symposium on Computer Applications in Medical Care, Washington, D.C.).

Samors, P.W., and S. Sullivan. 1983. "Health Care Cost Containment Through Private Sector Initiatives." In *Market Reforms in Health Care: Current Issues, New Directions, and Strategic Decisions*, edited by J.A. Meyer, Washington, D.C.: American Enterprise Institute for Public Policy Research.

Scheffler, R.M.; S.G. Yoder; N. Weisfeld; and G. Ruby. 1979. "Physician and New Health Practitioners: Issues for the 1980s." *Inquiry* 16:195–229.

Waters, K.A. and G.F. Murphy. 1983. *Systems Analysis in Health Information Management*. Rockville, MD: Aspen Systems Corporation.

Wennberg, J.E.; K. McPherson; and P. Caper. 1984. "Will Payment Based on Diagnosis Related Groups Control Hospital Costs?" *New England Journal of Medicine* 311, no. 5:295–300.

OTHER REFERENCES

Austin, C.J. 1979. *Information Systems for Hospital Administration*. Ann Arbor, MI: Health Administration Press.

Austin, C.H., and H.S. Carter. 1981. "National Hospital Information Resource Center: A Model." *Inquiry* 18:291–299.

Ball, M.J., and T.M. Boyle, Jr. 1980. "Hospital Information Systems: Past, Present and Future." *Hospital Financial Management* 34, no. 2:12–24.

Dorenfest, S.I. 1981. *A Comprehensive Review of Hospital Computer Use.* Highland Park, IL: Sheldon I. Dorenfest and Associates.

Dorenfest, S.I. 1983. *A Guide to Better Hospital Computer Decisions.* Highland Park, IL: Sheldon I. Dorenfest and Associates.

Fedorowicz, J. 1983. "Hospital Information Systems: Are We Ready For Case Mix Applications?" *Health Care Management Review* 8, no. 4:33–41.

Hospital Financial Management Association. 1981. *Data Processing Information Survey.* Chicago, IL: HFMA.

Menning, W.R.; R.W. Bolek; and D. Mon. 1984. "Microcomputer Use Comes of Age in Hospitals." *Healthcare Financial Management* 14, no. 8:32–37.

Packer, C.L. 1984. "The Four Principal Approaches to Data Processing and the Satisfaction They Provide." *Hospitals* 58, no. 11:88–93.

Packer, C.L. 1984. "Management Information Systems: Key Tools for CEOs." *Hospitals* 58, no. 22:107–109.

"Trends: Computer Review." *Hospitals* 58, no. 7:39–78.

Wiederhold, G. 1982. "Databases for Ambulatory Care." In *Computer Applications in Medical Care,* edited by D.A.B. Lindberg, pp. 79–85. New York: Masson Publishing.

DISCUSSION OF CHAPTER 2
Mark V. Pauly

Richard Scheffler has provided an interesting look at the present and the future of information technology in the U.S. health care system. It is surprising that so little change has actually occurred in medical care as a result of the technological revolution in information. The kinds of structural changes we see in banking and telecommunications are ones that we just do not see in health care. Although there have been some changes, and even more are in the works, the industry structure is not all that dissimilar today from what it was ten or even thirty years ago; information technology has thus far been neither an important cause nor an effect of those changes.

Scheffler provides ample documentation for this sweeping generalization. Data processing expenditures have increased only modestly over the decade as a percentage of hospital expenses—surely at a lower rate than for many other industries. What is more important, even the computerization that has occurred has virtually all been directed at substituting machines for old tasks; there have been few successful attempts at using the new technology to define new products or new markets.

In my comments, I will respond to three questions Scheffler raises:

1. What impacts are current changes in the industry likely to have on the use of information technology?

2. Why hasn't information technology had more of an impact on the structure of the industry?
3. Is technology likely to make much of a difference in the future?

It is especially important to note that the medical market has become more marketlike, and at a fairly rapid pace. Third party payers—beginning with Medicare and continuing through preferred provider organizations (PPOs), Medicaid, and some Blue Cross plans—are moving toward prospective payment and away from cost-based reimbursement, while both for-profit and not-for-profit firms are paying more attention to the financial bottom line.

These changes have had four kinds of effects on the demand for information technology. First, the mere fact of change requires new expenditure, as the old systems become inappropriate to the new (and often perplexing) environment. This surge, however, will obviously be temporary. Second, incentives for efficiency, quality, and avoidance of errors have changed. Third, prospective payment makes information provided to external agents less necessary. For example, one of the advantages of the diagnosis related groups (DRG) system is that it has greatly reduced the need for Medicare to become involved in the hospital's business. Cost reporting and creative accounting, certification of length of stay and the need to prepare excuses, and similar activities are now no longer necessary. All of this data—the two sets of books—are no longer needed, so the technical machinery to gather, aggregate, and launder or massage such hospital data is no longer necessary. There still remains a need to make sure that the output or volume measures, which are monitored by Medicare, are in the hospital's favor.

Finally, in contrast, there is now an increased need for accurate and useful internal data, for the hardware systems to generate and collect that data in a timely way, and for the software to analyze it in terms of its financial consequences. The result, as Scheffler has noted, is a burgeoning market in financial planning and resource allocation systems; the market in software to cope with (or at least justify one's actions in connection with) the DRG system approaches perfect competition.

There has been no corresponding change in the environment with regard to basic financial records—billing, payroll, and the like—although there has been a continuation of a long-running trend to substitute capital for labor in these functions. Information transfer within the process of care itself—medical records, orders for tests, and so forth—has not been subject to a massive change, although it has been growing. Finally, in an effort to control costs—a new motivation as far as many hospitals were concerned—there has been renewed interest in monitoring and controlling the process of care itself, and the people—largely physicians who are not hospital employees—who direct it.

Almost surely the increasing demand for technology for internal control offsets the falling demand for external justification, and so I must agree with Scheffler's conclusion—justified by the data on data processing expenditures—that such expenditures will continue to grow at a rapid clip. But how rapid, and what will determine the speed? I do not know how fast a "prodigious rate" is; the approximately 18 percent annual rate exhibited in Table 2–1 falls a little short of prodigiosity, in my opinion, especially since total hospital expenditures were also increasing at a double digit rate.

Moreover, and more importantly, there are some factors that could slow this rate down. I have no question that there is intensely strong industry demand for technology to control and monitor professional behavior in hospitals and to calculate the marginal cost and marginal revenue of alternative outputs. I also do not question that many hospitals, and especially not-for-profit ones, will buy virtually any such technology just to prove that they are doing something and to protect themselves from criticism should things go wrong. What I have a hard time convincing myself is that, either now or in the near future, *effective* and *productive* technology to perform these tasks will be available for sale. It is not true that information itself is useful and self-evident.

For professional behavior, I have yet to see the system that can effectively second guess or control the doctor, and really control his behavior if he is not in the mood to be controlled.

As far as accounting for revenue and costs is concerned, I am skeptical of the DRG cost figures that many of the software packages pump out. They allocate overhead costs, ignore economies and diseconomies of scope, make unsupported assumptions, and base costs on revenues—all sins in the economist's catechism. The figures for these software packages are nice and neat, and they can be used to justify actions; but do they work? I do not think we know yet, and I have to believe that a day of reckoning will come. Whether large hospitals have relatively higher expenditures on data processing than do small hospitals is in itself an interesting research question. Nursing homes, long-term care (LTC), and home care so far have not been major buyers of information technology. So I would be more comfortable predicting growth a little short of prodigious—perhaps 15 percent per year once the DRG changeover bulge works its ways through.

For physician services, let me also sound a somewhat pessimistic note. Physicians were always paid prospectively. The biggest change over the years has been the linking of insurance payment levels to other physician fees—the "reasonable and customary" approach. There followed what health care consultants felicitiously call "procinflation"—the explosion in the number of levels of differentiated services and procedures for which differentiated billing can and does occur. There are rumblings at the federal level to do something about this—to cut, to simplify, and to set prices. The largest growth in activity will occur outside the hospital. The solo physician—kindly GP or otherwise—is fast disappearing and being replaced by group practices large and small that ought to present a strong demand for information technology.

The next question looks not at the demand for information technology but its effects, past and future, on industry structure. In the past its effects have been minimal. Any cost reductions due to DP substitution were engulfed by the roaring inflation that characterized the hospital industry since the early sixties. The automated computerized medical record as a diagnostic aid (the subject of a number of ballyhooed demonstrations in the seventies) turned out, according to the oral tradition, to be a bust—it did not improve results because physicians did not use it much; and when they did, it did not affect outcomes much. In addition, there was no pressure to do much about costs when revenues rose when costs rose.

Will things be different in the late eighties and nineties? Will, in Scheffler's words, "information technology help to change the face of the health care industry"? Maybe, but only if it gets some help.

For one thing, providers will need to be offered incentives and knowledge on how to use data to make decisions—how to substitute the monitor screen for the seat of the pants. There is work going on here (literally, here at Penn), and new physicians are somewhat better trained in systematic medical decisionmaking—but it remains to be seen whether they will have the incentive to use that training.

Next, it may be that information technology could assist and encourage increasing debundling and reorganization in the medical care sector. Will the corporations formed to run the new magnetic resonance imager (Hillman and Schwartz 1986)—itself a product of computerization—find the information technology to transmit what it finds in a way consistent with (and perhaps even superior to) the same function organized in a more traditional way as a hospital department?

Scheffler mentions a number of systems that allow monitoring from home. Will these systems work? Can we computerize home care, especially for the increasing fraction of the population that is both elderly and affluent? Finally, can information technology aid and abet the fundamental revolution in medical culture—instead of asking why this patient should go home, asking why this patient should stay here? It will be interesting to see.

REFERENCE

Hillman, A.L., and J.S. Schwartz. 1986. "The Diffusion of Magnetic Resonance Imaging: Patterns of Siting and Ownership in an Era of Changing Incentives." *American Journal of Roentgenology* 146, no. 5 (May):963–69.

DISCUSSION OF CHAPTER 2
Kenneth E. Thorpe

In "Information Technology and the U.S. Health Care Industry: A New Direction," Richard Scheffler provides a useful overview of information technology in the health care sector. His work is especially noteworthy because it represents a pioneering effort to document and assess the growing role of information technologies in this industry.

According to Scheffler, the growth in health information technology has affected four aspects of the health care industry including medical training, patient care, patient education, and management. He observes that dramatic changes in hospital reimbursement methodologies, combined with the rapid diffusion of microcomputers, are largely responsible for the expanded use of information technologies in the health care industry.

The only omission in the chapter is that there is no discussion of the implications of the increased use of information technology on health and health care. Therefore, I will offer such a discussion.

The advent of the diagnosis related grouping (DRG) system used by Medicare is a revolutionary change in hospital finance. Prior to this system, hospitals submitted their bills to fiscal intermediaries when providing care to Medicare patients and were paid an amount deemed "reasonable and necessary." In contrast, under the DRG methodology, hospitals receive fixed prices set in advance depending on the patient's discharge diagnosis. Two critical changes have occurred in this reimbursement transition. First, payment levels for Medicare patients are now set before rather than after treatment. Second, the unit of payment changed from a per-diem to a discharge basis. The importance of this second change is that it has altered dramatically the information requirements of hospital administrators. Under the retrospective system, higher reported costs resulted in larger Medicare payments. Thus, it was not necessary to know the "true" marginal costs of treating individual patients. With the new fixed price payment system, a hospital administrator needs to know the resource costs of providing specific services. The requirement to have patient level cost data has led to changes in hospital cost accounting systems as well as changes in the information requirements of hospital administrators.

How hospital administrators and physicians use the newly generated patient level data has (at least) four important implications for health and health care. These following implications will be discussed below:

1. Increased efficiency
2. Restructuring the relationship between hospital administrators and physicians
3. Movement toward "product line" analysis and its implications for the scope of services provided
4. Confidentiality issues.

Administrators now have at their disposal an enormous volume of information regarding physicians and their patients. Detailed profiles of physician practice patterns, including their use of ancillary procedures and the length of time they keep patients in the hospital, can be created by the DRG system, which provides the incentive, and the new microcomputers and software technology, which provide the means. This information allows the administrator to review an individual physician's performance relative to other physicians. Of course, the actual impact of the new information technology on health and health care depends largely on how the information is used within the hospital.

One desirable use of the information is to increase hospital efficiency. Since hospital profits now occur when the fixed DRG payments exceed marginal treatment costs, there is an incentive to provide medical services of a given quality at least cost. Greater efficiency is achieved when hospital administrators are able to eliminate "unnecessary" hospital days and ancillary procedures and produce the same health outcomes. On the other hand, the mounting financial incentives for early discharge and reduced ancillary procedures may generate undesirable outcomes if the health status of the elderly is adversely affected. At this time, it is still too early to assess the impact of cost saving efforts by hospital administrators on health outcomes (Carter and Ginsburg 1985; Lohr et al. 1985).

The new information systems also have the potential to restructure the traditional relationship between administrator and physician. The advent of DRGs provides administrators an incentive to find methods of encouraging efficient practice patterns and discouraging costly ones. This incentive could change dramatically the traditional role of the hospital administrator vis-à-vis the physician. For example, detailed knowledge of physician behavior within the hospital could provide a device for administrators to challenge a physician's autonomy and practices. This would represent a substantial shift in the locus of power within the hospital away from the physician toward the administrator. At the very least, normative decisions by administrators regarding desirable physician practice patterns based on some measure of central tendency increases the likelihood of creating tremendous conflict between administrators and physicians (Stern and Epstein 1985).

Although the DRG payment system provides an incentive to reduce costs for all Medicare patients and services, it also provides incentives for administrators to commit resources to profitable services and to shed unprofitable ones. The DRG system has created a virtual gold rush for management consultants to streamline and optimize the distribution of cases within a hospital.[1] This "product line" analysis provides an incentive to use patient level data to specialize in services (e.g., obstetrics, surgery, burn care) where the Medicare payments exceed marginal treatment costs. Reducing the scope of services offered may be socially desirable if economies of scale are exploited, especially in areas that have too many beds. Yet, service reduction has the potential to negatively impact social welfare if local health care needs are no longer met. The potential reduction in the availability and scope of hospital services should be balanced against cost savings and streamlined operations.

The availability of patient level discharge data, treatment costs, and health outcomes has created a large demand by cost conscious third party payers and employers for access to this information. Such information would facilitate comparison shopping by examining treatment costs and health outcomes across hospitals. Patients could then be directed by third party payers or employers interested in reducing health care outlays to hospitals providing quality health care at relatively low costs. To some, access to this information is a critical component of creating competition within the health care industry.

The availability of patient level data may foster competition in the industry, but it may also violate traditional norms of confidentiality between physicians and their patients. This latter possibility has led some hospitals, physicians, and patients to oppose the demands by outside parties to disseminate patient level data outside the hospital. The battle over the public's right-to-know and the traditional relationship between physician and patient has recently escalated. In the center of this controversy is the type of information that Medicare's peer review organizations (PROs) may release.

Both hospitals and physicians have resisted the dissemination of "quality" of care data identifying individual patients, physicians, and hospitals. Some of the resistance may be traced to concern that the public would not have the sophistication or expertise to assess the data accurately.

Hospitals have been concerned about the potential impact the detailed cost and quality of care information would have on patient utilization patterns. The final disclosure rules, however, permit the PROs to release data identifying costs and quality of care information at the hospital, but not at the individual patient or physician level. Moreover, when hospital data are released, hospitals will have a thirty-day period to issue comments that must be included with the data. Thus, the battle over the "appropriate" distribution of medical care information has already begun and will certainly rage as a policy issue in the future.

The ultimate impact of information generated by hospital management information systems on society depends on how (and by whom) it is used. Clearly, the growing sophistication of these information systems will provide an opportunity to stem the growth in health care costs and promote efficiency in the delivery system. If such information is used to the detriment of other social goals—such as providing quality health care to the elderly—then its use should be monitored closely by government's physicians and their patients.

NOTE

1. Even a cursory examination of trade journals such as *Healthcare Financial Management* reveals the proliferation of management consulting and software available to "maximize" Medicare payments.

REFERENCES

Carter, Grace, and Paul B. Ginsburg. 1985. *The Medicare Case Mix Index Increase, Medical Practice Changes, Aging, and DRG Creep.* Santa Monica: The Rand Corporation.

Lohr, K.; R. Brook; G. Goldberg; M. Chassin; and T. Glennan. 1985. *Impact of Medicare Prospective Payment on the Quality of Medical Care. A Research Agenda.* Santa Monica: The Rand Corporation.

Stern, R.S., and A.M. Epstein. 1985. "Institutional Responses to Prospective Payments Based on Diagnosis-related Groups. Implications for Cost, Quality, and Access." *New England Journal of Medicine* 139:621–27.

3 THE IMPACT OF TECHNOLOGY ON THE INSURANCE INDUSTRY

David N. Young

Today many businesses, both industrial and service, are going through a process of transition. The best publicized examples are auto, steel, and banking; insurance may also be added to this list. How the insurance business came to be in a period of transition requires some explanation.

It may be helpful to divide the insurance business into two broad categories according to the kinds of protection they provide. The first area is the protection of human life values. The generic products of this area include life insurance, annuities, and accident and health coverages. The second broad category is the protection of assets and asset values; it is generally defined as the property and casualty business.

The insurance business can also be divided on the basis of who buys the product. Once more, there are two broad categories: The first group is composed of individuals who buy coverage for their own (or family) protection or for the protection of their assets (home and autos). The second buyer is the corporate purchaser who needs to protect assets or help employees protect themselves through the medium of group life and health products and retirement income funding. The broad category of corporate buyer can be segmented into two markets, the large corporate buyer and the small corporate buyer. The importance of this will emerge in the following discussion.

Insurance is a big business, and it is an important part of each of our daily lives. The need for insurance protection by both individuals and corporations is well documented. Because the insurance business is so vital to our individual needs and such an integral part of our commercial fabric, public policy, developed in the late nineteenth and early twentieth centuries, required that the business be regulated.

Unlike most of the other regulated businesses, the regulation of insurance companies was left solely to the states. However, as a result of the Employee Retirement Income Security Act (ERISA), which was passed into law in 1974, some elements of the employee benefits insurance market have come under federal regulation.

Public utilities have been regulated locally, within state boundaries or much smaller geographic areas within the state. Their service, however, was delivered only to a very local population. Banks, of course, have been regulated both at the federal and the state level, depending upon the source of their charter.

The insurance industry developed under a unique state-by-state process of regulation, even though many of the insurance companies regulated are involved in a commercial venture that is truly nationwide. Over the years, and particularly during the Reagan administration, many arguments for and against regulation have been voiced. Critics argue that regulation provides merely an umbrella of protection for the regulated industry. There is some truth to this allegation since one of the functions of state insurance regulators is to try to assure the solvency of insurance companies authorized to do business in their state.

Once an insurance company receives a charter from a particular state, it is able to enter into the business of insurance in as many states as it wishes, providing it meets the requirements of each and every state to which it applies. The charter it receives enables it to conduct the business of insurance. Anyone without a charter could not enter into the insurance business.

Insurance is a financial arrangement requiring capital. The basic function of insurance is to provide a risk transfer mechanism. The buyer agrees to pay a premium in exchange for the insurance company's guarantee of protection against specified losses listed in the policy. Technology plays no role in the risk transfer function.

Management and administration of the insurance business involves knowing what to underwrite and what not to underwrite, producing and distributing the product, collecting premiums, investing funds, paying claims, keeping records, collecting data, creating information to manage the business. It is these areas of service and support that provide the opportunity for creative use of technology.

The two functions—risk transfer, and service and support—are inextricably intertwined. For instance, one could have a massive amount of capital with which to absorb risk, but without a support mechanism to provide the services, there would be no insurance product. Similarly, without risk capital, but with the most sophisticated support and service mechanisms, one could not participate fully in the insurance or risk transfer business. If the two parts of the business (risk transfer and service) were separated, some interesting things could happen. This is exactly what occurred in the larger case market for both property and casualty and employee benefits or group insurance.

The property and casualty business, as a result of the risk transfer involved, developed an "underwriting mentality" and over time became underwriting "driven." Insurance companies went to great expense and devoted considerable time in attempting to select the best risks in order to minimize losses. The service side of the business, with the exception of engineering and loss control, received little attention. Engineering and loss control are important to insurers because they offer an opportunity to limit the potential for loss, thereby improving the quality of the risk. The insurance contract provided not only the risk transfer protection but also all the services bundled together.

There was a similar situation in the large case group insurance market. Originally almost all large corporate health insurance plans were insured. Exceptions were rare. Under the insured approach, the insurance company provided both the risk protection and almost all of the services incidental to the insurance contracts, primarily claim settlement. This was a pretty comfortable arrangement for many years; changes, however, began to take place quickly, and the pressures for change have not yet subsided.

Changes are taking place in the insurance business for many reasons. An early cause for change was the growing conviction among risk managers for large corporations that they could absorb significant risk without the use of insurance since much of their risk was predictable.

Regulation is also a cause for change. The group health marketplace provides an excellent example. Many states mandate benefits that must be included in insurance contracts issued within their jurisdiction. Often these mandated benefits are expensive, and employers can escape the expense of these mandated benefits by self-insuring.

Ironically, the states that mandate benefits to "protect" their residents (voters) end up creating incentives for employers to self-insure. When employers self-insure, the regulators lose the opportunity to provide "consumer protection" for employees since the plans are no longer insured and thus subject to their regulation. Additionally, employees covered under self-insured plans no longer have the insurance guarantee. This can be important in the event of bankruptcy or employer default.

Tax policy can also provide an impetus for change. Insurance premiums are taxed by the states; the tax is generally about 2 percent but can vary from state to state. If an employer chooses to self-insure, he escapes the tax liability. Thus the state provides an incentive to employers to self-insure to escape taxation.

Buyers believe that insurers took excessive pricing actions after periods of high losses (sometimes caused by excessive inflation) or, in the case of the property and casualty business, during "hard" markets. This situation, too, created pressure for change.

The high levels of inflation and high interest rates, which began in 1973 and are still a problem in the mid-1980s, are significant factors for change. Inflation has had a particularly strong impact on the insurance industry. In the property and casualty business, inflation builds up the cost and value of assets and the cost of replacing these assets. Thus the cost of insurance to cover these risks increases. Risk managers for large corporations often had risks that were geographically dispersed (both plants and people). Also, for some coverages (such as workers compensation) they had relatively predictable loss experience, given their size. These risk managers felt comfortable with accepting more and more of the risk by using significantly higher deductibles. Risk managers still continued to buy excess or "catastrophe" coverage, but premiums paid to insurance companies decreased significantly. Some coverages became totally self-insured by large corporations (workers compensation), where legally permissible.

Since insurance companies viewed some of the services they provided as an integral part of the insurance contract, they were not initially interested in providing these services with either a total or a significant elimination of the risk transfer. This opened the door for others to provide these services. Many corporations valued the engineering and loss control advice that had a favorable impact on their loss experience and thus their costs. Some of the major brokers moved into this void and began to offer their own services in these areas. This was the beginning of the unbundling of the insurance contract in the property and casualty large case market.

Later on, the same phenomenon occurred in the large case group insurance market. Originally almost all large corporate health insurance plans were insured. However, in the late sixties and early seventies, as inflation and resulting double digit interest rates became commonplace, corporate financial officers looked wistfully at the large reserve funds accumulated for incurred but unreported claim liabilities under their corporate employee health plan. As the cost of money escalated, inflation drove up the dollar value of these loss reserves that were an asset of the insurance companies.

Even though interest was credited on these reserves by insurers it was less than the cost of money. Ultimately, cracks began to appear in the solid wall of the insurance industry. Arrangements were slowly made to return these loss reserves to the buyer under a variety of arrangements. Many large corporations finally dropped all pretense of insurance and converted their plans to self-insurance, while often retaining the insurance company as the administrator.

Much like the property and casualty arrangements described earlier, the group insurance plan became first financially unbundled (from an insured arrangement to an uninsured arrangement) and then unbundled with regard to the services that were necessary to support the plan. Corporate benefit managers began to look for suppliers who might improve upon services previously provided by the insurer. Under the bundled concept, insurers did not always provide the highest level of service. There was not pressure to do so, since specific services were bundled together and not subject to individual negotiations and pricing. The buyer bought the entire package, risk transfer and the supporting services. Again, many of the major insurance brokerage and benefit consulting firms began to offer their clients those services that previously had been provided under the umbrella of the insurance contract.

Eventually, the trend to accept more risk, and buy less insurance, spread and moved down to ever smaller corporate buyers. The percentage of risk that the smaller corporations retained was less than the larger corporations, but the concept is the same. Less insurance premium was paid to the insurance companies and more services to support corporate purchasers were being provided by non-insurance company vendors.

It has been well documented that the commercial property and casualty business has been engaged in a competitive rate war for the past five years. It has been truly a buyers' market. Recent reports indicate that 1984 will be the first year of an overall operating loss for the commercial property and casualty companies since 1906, the year of the San Francisco earthquake and resulting fire. Now, however, the market is hardening and prices are rising. The expectation by some in the commercial property and casualty business is that as prices increase, more buyers will balk and they will increase deductibles and turn more and more to self-insurance or other alternatives such as offshore captives. An offshore captive is an insurance company, usually owned by its corporate sponsor, and established outside the continental limits of the United States in an area with very favorable laws or regulations concerning establishment of insurance companies and/or taxation of income.

Inflation, meanwhile, was also having an impact on that most stable of insurance businesses, individual life insurance. For years, some financial planners had been advising their clients to buy term insurance instead of ordinary life insurance and invest the difference in some other type of investment vehicle. Little by little they convinced people that this advice was sound.

The high interest rates of the 1970s probably did more to change consumer buying practice than anything else, however. Financial planners were able to eliminate even the risk of equities for conservative investors by using money market funds that were providing returns in double digits. This certainly was an improvement over the interest accumulation on cash values under an ordinary life contract.

Some smaller insurance companies, with little inforce business, saw these high interest returns as an opportunity and created universal life insurance. Universal life was a clear improvement over ordinary life because the insured's fund was immediately credited with the higher interest earnings earned by his premium dollars. This innovative new product proved to be immensely popular with the public, and the early proponents of universal life experienced significant growth. The larger, more mature life insurance companies were slow to introduce this revolutionary new product because they accurately foresaw that it would result in cannibalization of their inforce business. High margin products would be replaced by universal life, with reduced profit margins. When the IRS confirmed the tax-free buildup within a universal life policy, however, the large companies moved to protect their asset base and responded to growing market demands.

Changes have also taken place in the personal automobile and homeowner insurance lines. These changes were caused not so much by inflation or by limitation of risk transfer, but by different methods of distribution that created apparent efficiencies.

Most of the insurance industry relies upon independent agents and brokers as their sales arms. Agents typically represent several insurance companies, and through this multiplicity of carriers they are able to meet customers' needs.

Not all companies, however, use the independent insurance agent network. Some of these so-called "direct writers" developed a "captive" sales force in which their agents produced business only for them. State Farm and Allstate are primary examples.

Still other insurance companies decided to market their products directly by mail, advertising, and telemarketing without any agent involvement. GEICO used this approach.

Differentiated distribution systems appear to be more cost effective than the distribution system utilizing independent insurance agents. Using "controlled" distribution systems apparently enables these insurance companies to have a more positive impact on their underwriting results. Some of these companies, particularly State Farm, moved more quickly into automation, and this also had a favorable impact upon their expense level. In time, the market share of these companies began to increase, at the expense of those companies relying on the independent insurance agents.

Armed with this success, these direct writers who had previously limited their operation to personal lines coverages (auto, homeowners, life) have now moved into the small case commercial property and casualty market. They are becoming a significant factor in this market, which previously had been almost totally dominated by insurance companies utilizing independent agents.

Most segments of the insurance industry face significant challenges. Changes have to be made to survive in the current environment. Those who do not wish to change, or who cannot, will pay the ultimate market price—extinction.

Before I move on to examining the role that technology will play in restructuring the insurance and service business of the future, let me remind the reader that technology has an impact on the manner in which the service business is conducted, the scope and quality of services provided, the way products are distributed, and how money is transferred. It does not, however, have an impact on the actual risk transfer or capital intensive part of insurance.

One of the problems faced by major portions of the insurance industry is high expenses. This problem surfaces when services are unbundled from the risk transfer. It is also a factor in the bundled environment where the independent agency companies compete against those using direct or controlled distribution systems.

Here is an interesting example taken from the small commercial and personal auto/homeowners' markets. Various efforts at automation have been undertaken by the insurance industry to modernize the independent agent's office. Before automation, an agent would underwrite a risk and, being familiar with the insurance companies he represented, would submit the risk to the insurance company that he felt would be most appropriate for his customer. When the local branch office of the insurance company received the information from the agent, it underwrote the risk again.

If the risk was accepted, the policy was issued by the insurance company and delivered to the agent. Unfortunately, this often took a long time. The policy frequently contained numerous and significant errors, in which case it had to be rewritten by the branch office.

With automation, the agent submits his risk electronically after he has underwritten it. The computer rates the risk correctly, issues the policy correctly, and almost instantly bills his client, adjusts his accounts receivable and payable, and updates both his files and the insurance company files. This new process saves considerable time and expense in his office; it also reduces expenses in both the branch office and the head office of the insurance company.

In actual practice, most agents who have automated do not reduce staff (the staff may be their wife, son, daughter-in-law, or next-door neighbor) but are able to double and even triple their volume without adding staff. Since the insurance market is not sufficiently large for all agents to double or triple their volume, the spread of technology will inevitably cause some reduction in the number of agents.

The insurance companies have learned some interesting lessons from their automation effort. Although most of the agency automation systems allow for multiple company interfaces, in fact, the insurance company sponsoring the automation experiences an increase in volume. Much of this increase is the result of doing business electronically, but part of the increase is a result of the cost-sharing aspect of automation. The agent can pay for part of the cost of automation by increasing the amount of insurance placed with the sponsoring insurance company.

All of this automation would eventually enable the insurance industry to make significant staff (and, therefore, expense) reductions. The underwriting staff in both the branch office and home office will be reduced. Also, since much of the data necessary for both the rating bureaus and the insurance company will be automated, the clerical staff may be reduced. Fewer middle managers need to be involved in the process of converting data to information, a function that a computer performs so well.

The potential for technology to create opportunities for expense reduction is only one facet of the unfolding scenario. Right now it takes years to train a property and casualty insurance underwriter. Much of the training comes as a result of experience gained by evaluating numerous risks. However, through the use of expert systems, based on artificial intelligence technology, a novice underwriter could gain the knowledge of the most experienced underwriter. Further, the availability of computerized data bases would enable the novice actually to outperform his more experienced associate working without a decision support mechanism. With this capability underwriters will make better decisions and apply more equitable and accurate rating, which should improve profitability.

In the large case group health market, change is occurring at an accelerated rate. The large insurers have significant market shares on a national basis. They have automated much of the claim settlement activity, which represents the majority of their expense charges.

With the unbundling of services, however, new competitors have gained entry into this business. Besides some of the national brokers, new entrants—generically called third party administrators (TPAs)—have been created by entrepreneurs. These new firms offer a variety of services, the most important of which is claim service.

These TPAs are local and therefore very close to their customers. They are able to deliver an electronic claim settlement service promptly, accurately, flexibly, and—most importantly—for less cost than most of the insurers. They are able to do this because they concentrate on providing only claim service, not staffing to provide the broad array of services that some insurers offer. The unbundling of the insurance risk from the service function and the ability of the TPA to choose selectively both customers and services to offer has created competitive problems for the insurance industry. At the present time, the market share of the TPAs is growing more rapidly than either the commercial carriers or Blue Cross/Blue Shield.

Interestingly, some of the larger TPAs are growing into national concerns. One of the largest, Galbraith and Greene, is owned by a major insurance broker, Fred S. James, which is in turn owned by Transamerica, which also owns Occidental Life, a major life insurance company. Another large third party claim administrator is owned by Dun & Bradstreet and provides a variety of services, including claim service for many smaller insurance companies. It appears that TPAs are being integrated into the financial services marketplace.

The price of hardware continues to move in the right direction for these TPAs, as well as for the smaller local or regional insurance companies.

Also, the software to run the smaller and lower cost hardware is becoming more readily available, less expensive, and more user friendly. In essence, one of the barriers to enter the service business related to employee benefits has been reduced, if not eliminated.

In the large case property and casualty market, insurers are now trying to compete for service business by automating much of the information needed by corporations to manage the risk effectively. Now they have to compete not only against the large brokers but also against new, specialized firms that provide necessary data on losses and other specialized and personalized services. Much of the insurer's motivation for this commitment to service is to help retain whatever insurance coverage is available and to maintain relationships with customers.

Much of the insurance industry has an expense problem, and the automation effort must be directed toward the reduction of the number of workers required to support a given volume of business. This will be extremely helpful for several reasons. Lower expenses will improve the competitiveness of the insurance product and *possibly* reduce the tendency toward self-insurance. In addition, more of each dollar of revenue will be going to support risk transfer and should, over time, improve the company surplus position.

Surplus is critical to the insurance business since it enables carriers to write more business. With improved expense control, part of the savings could be used to reduce price, and part of the savings could be used to increase surplus. The latter is important because there is evidence that capacity in the commercial property and casualty field may be squeezed by the end of the decade.

The reduction in the number of employees of insurance companies will be matched by the reduction in the number of agents. Surviving agents will be highly automated and thus will be able to handle a substantially greater volume of business without staff additions.

The agent's efficiency will increase significantly in a variety of ways, and this will lead to greater efficiencies in the companies the agent represents. For instance, successful agents currently spend considerable time out of the office meeting with clients and prospects. If the agent needs to quote coverages, he must either gather the necessary information and go back to his office to prepare a quote or telephone his office and have the office prepare a quote and call him back.

The agent of the future will be armed with a portable computer that will enable him to quote and bind coverages on the spot. Some of these briefcase computers are currently in use in the individual life insurance business, but they are crude compared to what the future holds in store.

Think of the productivity gains for the agent and for the insurance industry. The data capture and entry that is done by the agent or agency is transmitted electronically to the insurance company and saves the company the expense of the data input.

The spread of automation will also result in reduction in the number of companies that an independent agent will represent. This will be good for both parties, the agent and the carriers. Experience to date with agency automation has confirmed this trend. Agents will find it too expensive to deal with many companies, and the companies have already concluded that it is not cost effective to try and wire up agents from whom they receive relatively little business. This will put pressure on insurance companies to write more and more of an individual agent's business.

Use of automation and telecommunication networks will enable insurance companies to disperse much of the work activity and decisionmaking so that it is accomplished closer to the customer. In the commercial property and casualty business the underwriting function will be materially aided by the use of expert systems and sophisticated data bases for decision support. This will be accomplished locally. Powerful personal computers linked to centrally located mainframes will enable many users to take advantage of the power of the mainframe but still allow a central control of data.

This move closer to the customer will help the insurance business become more market oriented rather than underwriting or product oriented. Teleconferencing and video conferencing will be used to communicate policy decisions and to allow a "face to face" discussion and resolution of business problems. This technology will also enhance the dispersion of function and decisionmaking to local offices. Furthermore, employee training and education will be greatly facilitated by teleconferencing and video conferencing.

Right now, Aetna Life and Casualty Company uses teleconferencing facilities utilizing satellite technology connecting Hartford with their offices in Chicago, Washington, and San Francisco. In addition to this teleconferencing facility, Aetna uses land lines to connect four different offices in and around Hartford. The latter arrangement saves considerable time and expense in commuting between the offices for meetings, and the former allows the company to communicate effectively with both people and customers in the distant locations. The company has found that the "culture" has not changed as rapidly as the technology; thus, it is still too "remote" for sales presentations where the buyers and the sellers are unknown to each other.

The electronic transfer of funds (EFT) will expand significantly. Aetna's uninsured group health business now uses wire transfers almost exclusively to obtain reimbursement from the policyholder for funds that have been paid on behalf of their employees. That is just the tip of the iceberg. Providers of services (doctors, dentists, hospitals) are being paid on a bulk basis, but not yet with EFT. In the future, Aetna will make payments not only to providers but also to individual employees by EFT. Commissions or other payments that are payable to agents and brokers will also be transferred and deposited electronically.

All of this will reduce expenses, since paper (checks, drafts) will be eliminated and reconciliation will be accomplished electronically. There will be additional savings generated by a reduction in mail volume.

In the large case market, particularly group health and workers compensation, the customer's computers will be linked electronically to their insurer's computers. In this way the insurer's data base will be available for data manipulation and report generation by the customer on his own premises. There will be some security problems, of course, but no doubt they will be solved.

One intriguing example of the opportunity afforded by the new technology is in the area of flexible benefits or "cafeteria" plans. These plans allow employees to choose from among a variety of plan options and thus build a package that more closely meets their personal needs. One of the reasons for the growing popularity of these plans with employers is the changing demographic composition of the work force. Flexible benefit plans can deliver a variety of insurance, savings, day care, legal, and other benefit plans through the group delivery mechanism at lower distribution costs than the individual products traditionally sold by agents.

Flexible benefit plans, however, create complexity because of the many benefit variables; they also create additional expense because of the complex administration they require. Automation can provide a value added service to assist employers in resolving these problems. Insurance companies can market these flexible benefit administration packages to employers and thus create another link with their customers. It is likely that in the future an interactive videotex system on the employer premises can be used to guide employees through the option selection process.

In summary, the technological revolution that is currently underway will substantially restructure the insurance industry. This restructuring is absolutely necessary because expense reduction is critical to the industry. Expenses are high now because of the "protection" of regulation and the bundling together of services and risk transfer under the umbrella of the insurance contract. When the risk transfer was tied so closely to the services, expenses were much less of a problem—there was no other game in town.

The insurance industry will grow significantly larger in terms of premiums and fees for services. The variety of services offered will expand dramatically to meet customer needs. There will be fewer companies. The insurance agency force will also decrease. Insurance companies will become much better marketers; as a result, they will compete aggressively to win back much of the insurance service business that they have lost over the years. This service business, apart from the risk transfer, will enable insurers to stay close to their customers.

It is impossible to discuss how technology affects the insurance industry structure without addressing the human issue. In order for the industry to take advantage of the promise and potential of the technology, it will be necessary to make changes in corporate cultures. Employees will have to be educated and trained to be comfortable with the new technology. This process will be easy for eager new recruits into the industry who are comfortable with this technology. It will be more difficult for older employees at all levels of the organization—including the most senior levels. Technology *will* provide the answers to the business problems. The unanswered question is whether managements can prepare themselves, and their employees, for the change.

By the year 2000, the business of insurance will be radically transformed. The principle of risk transfer will remain unchanged, but the delivery of products and services—and the scope of these services—will be far different from what we know today.

DISCUSSION OF CHAPTER 3
Howard Kunreuther

David Young has presented an excellent summary of the recent changes in the insurance industry and the role that technology is likely to play in marketing the insurance product. Young has clearly outlined the importance of firms moving from an "underwriting driven" mode, where only the good risks are taken, to a more service-oriented mode, where different risk management functions are offered to corporations. As Young points out, technology has aided this process by enabling insurance agents and brokers to offer a spectrum of services that suit the corporation's needs. Because technology can cut costs, insurance firms may be able to compete with other specialized organizations and banks for this business.

My comments will extend Young's remarks by addressing four questions:

1. What is the effect of technology on the different interested parties who are involved with insurance?
2. What is the effect of technology on competitive strategy for the insurance industry?
3. What are the welfare implications of new technology on the different interested parties?
4. What differences exist between the insurance industry and the airline industry in the context of competitive strategy?

THE EFFECT OF TECHNOLOGY ON DIFFERENT INTERESTED PARTIES

Consider the following hypothetical scenario. The Alpha Insurance Company has taken advantage of computerized technology to market special services through one of its independent agents (the Beta Agency) to one of its customers (Kappa Industries). Initially, Alpha offers packages for analyzing its risks (i.e., property losses, product failure, and the nature of its portfolio). It suggests where Kappa can self-insure and where it may need special coverage. It offers what is called a "cafeteria plan," which provides special features such as the ability to change premiums on a monthly basis so that there is less float than under normal plans, the rapid settlement of claims to reduce float, and special teleconferencing services for personal consultation between Kappa Industries and executives at Alpha Insurance.

These services appeal to Kappa and the company because they meet their own needs. When a rival insurer, Omega Insurance Company, offers another set of computerized services, it is difficult for Kappa to evaluate the rival's potential benefits since they are not comparable to their current plan. In addition, Kappa knows there would be a large set-up cost associated with investing in new computer software should they decide to switch insurers. They are reluctant even to consider this possibility.

Alpha also provides the Beta Agency with specialized computer packages for almost instantaneously accessing rate data and alternative plans. In return, Alpha requires that Beta represent only them when offering risk management services to different corporations. The result of this arrangement is that Alpha has a degree of monopoly power with its two other stakeholders, Beta and Kappa.

THE EFFECT OF TECHNOLOGY ON COMPETITIVE STRATEGY

Elements of the above scenario are consistent with ideas that McFarlan (1984) recently offered demonstrating how information technology affects competition. For example, as part of their competitive strategy, firms build barriers to entry. Thus, special features of Alpha's package make it difficult for rival firms like Omega to compete in the computerized insurance services market.

It can be difficult for firms seeking commercial insurance to obtain comparative data on such items as premiums. Theoretically, computer technology should enable one to make these comparisons but there is no incentive for insurers to share data with others. The Insurance Services Office (ISO) does publish premiums for standard coverage such as automobile and homeowners coverage. When it comes to commercial insurance, however, variations are enormous between types of coverage; there is no standard premium that would have any meaning for industrial firms.

It is desirable, however, for insurers to share data on claims with each other for relatively low probability catastrophic risks. This may help firms to set more meaningful statistical rates given the limited amount of data any one firm has on a particular risk. Sharing data may also help increase the capacity for coverage, as in the case of nuclear power plants, if the variance on losses is reduced by having added information.

Another way to improve the rate making process was noted by Young when he suggested that expert systems may train underwriters to make better decisions by using the knowledge of the most experienced underwriter in the firm. One may be able to go one step further by trying to model the behavior of an expert underwriter. Specifically, one could identify factors influencing his decision and, through statistical regression, determine what weight the underwriter places on each variable. For example, with respect to automobile insurance the rate set by an underwriter (the dependent variable) may be influenced by factors such as age, years of driving, location of car, and miles driven (the independent variables). The regression will determine how important each one of these factors is to the underwriter based on the decisions he has made.

A relevant question from an expert systems perspective is whether the regression does better in terms of performance (e.g., using measures such as the premium/loss ratio for different risk classes). If the answer is "yes," then the rule may serve as a guide for making decisions. For example, the underwriter may want to use the rule as an initial guide for setting rates but still use his own judgment for setting the final rates.

The experience with other decisionmakers, such as stockbrokers making portfolio decisions, admission officers determining which students to accept in college and graduate schools, and medical doctors diagnosing disease, suggests that linear rules perform better than the decisionmaker in many situations (Dawes 1979). Cases that are unusual may require special attention by the decisionmaker and the use of the rule may enable the underwriter, for example, to concentrate his efforts on the unusual rather than the routine.

WELFARE IMPLICATIONS OF NEW TECHNOLOGY

With respect to industrial firms, I agree with Young that in the short run they will have more options from which to choose. The long-run outlook appears somewhat more uncertain because of the difficulty firms will have in switching services.

Larger insurers will benefit because they can afford to invest in sophisticated new technology because of the volume of their business. Companies like Aetna should do well. Small firms like Alpha may not.

There is likely to be an acceleration toward the direct writer system. Agents or brokers who have a large business will adopt new technology because it is cost effective for them to do so and to commit themselves to one insurance firm. Small agents will very likely find it necessary to join forces and utilize some third party to provide them with computer services in much the same way as small banks that have created interbank networks.

AIRLINE–INSURANCE COMPARISON

There are some similarities and some differences between the way computer technologies have affected the airline and the insurance industries. Both groups want to differentiate their products in order to have some degree of monopoly power. The structure of the two industries is similar; the travel agent serves in his capacity as a middleman between the airline company and customer in much the same way as the insurance agent or broker does for the insurance company and its customers.

The information sharing function is the principal difference between the two systems. For the airlines there is an interconnection between all carriers through the airline reservation system. The official airline guide displays a flight on a personal computer if you give it departure time, desired arrival time, and cities. The computerized system does not supply prices because the number of fare changes in one day may be as high as 25,000. The differentiation between airlines is through promotions and vertical integration with hotel and rent-a-car companies.

It is difficult to get comparative insurance rates without many phone calls, because companies specialize with agents. Since the type of coverage and services provided will differ between insurers, it will be hard to differentiate between programs and policies purely on the basis of price, as one can do with airfares.

In conclusion, the emergence of computer technology opens new opportunities for new product lines. Specifically, banks are now demanding insurance policies to protect themselves from malfunctioning computer systems and computer crime. Insurance is in the positive position where it follows Says Law: The supply of new technology creates its own demand for insurance protection.

REFERENCES

Dawes, R. 1979. "The Robust Beauty of Improper Linear Models in Decision Making." *American Psychologist* 34:571–82.

McFarlan, F. Warren. 1984. "Information Technology Changes the Way You Compete." *Harvard Business Review* 62 (May/June):98–103.

4 TECHNOLOGY AND FINANCIAL SERVICES: REGULATORY PROBLEMS IN A DEREGULATED ENVIRONMENT

Almarin Phillips
Mitchell Berlin

Giant steps have been taken toward the deregulation of deposit financial institutions in the past several years. Except for the continuing prohibition of interest payments on corporate demand deposits, regulations governing rate maxima on various classes of deposits have been removed or drastically relaxed. The asset and liability powers of thrift institutions have been enlarged, making these organizations effective substitutes for commercial bank services for many bank customers. Technically, the ancient Glass-Steagall Act remains to separate commercial and investment banking, but there has in fact been considerable intermingling.[1] Similarly, McFadden Act and Douglas Amendment restrictions on interstate branching and bank subsidiaries have been loosened by state regulatory actions and through the use of loopholes found in federal laws.[2] Worldwide financial markets have opened. Funds flow across national boundaries—sometimes lawfully and sometimes not—taxing the ability of national regulators to insulate domestic markets from forces emanating in other countries.[3]

In the United States, the deregulation of financial institutions has not been without its difficulties. Some institutions have ignored or resisted fundamental market and regulatory changes. In so doing, they have exposed themselves to the potential and, in some cases, the actuality of extinction. At the opposite end of the spectrum, deregulation seems to have encouraged other institutions to engage in practices subsequently revealed to be gross mismanagement and fraud. Further, the course of deregulation has had differential effects depending on the size and functional types of financial institutions.[4]

The problems of deregulation are many. We will discuss two of the major ones. First, we consider monetary policy in the context of deregulation and new market phenomena. The very concept of money is less sharp than it was when modern central banking was developed. There are more types of institutions and more market instruments available as substitutes for commercial banks and their deposit liabilities. The intermediation process itself has changed so that the fluctuations in the velocity of popularly defined money aggregates may offset policy directed changes in the sizes of those aggregates.

Second, we examine issues relating to the "safety and soundness" of the emerging system. Increased inter- and intraindustry competition, differential regulatory effects, and, perhaps, more latitude for mismanagement and deceptive and fraudulent practices have led some to question whether the deposit insurance innovation of the 1930s is now sufficient to prevent panics, bank runs, and other more or less general liquidity crises. Related to this is the possibility of defaults arising from breakdowns in the highly complex technological delivery system.

THE BACKGROUND

Technology, market forces, and regulation have interacted in complicated ways in financial markets. Market innovations employing the abundance of new techniques in computing and information technologies have occurred at a rapid pace. Regulatory change has been slow, however. The more aggressive and innovative of the financial institutions have been restrained in important ways by regulators and by legal actions brought by firms in their own and in other financial sectors. Indeed, academics and a series of study commissions have for more than two decades virtually unanimously urged sweeping regulatory reform; these repeated recommendations were largely ignored until market conditions years later forced at least partial implementation.[5]

Alfred Marshall (1897) summarized well the diminishing relevance of old regulations and old market regimes when technology created new market opportunities. "When one person is willing to sell a thing at a price which another is willing to pay for it," Marshall penned, "the two manage to come together in spite of prohibitions of King or Parliament or of the officials of a Trust or Trade Union." So it has been in financial markets. When combinations of quantitative monetary controls and interest rate regulations made it impossible for banks to supply credit needs through traditional channels, new market techniques and new markets arose. On the one hand, suppliers of funds found non-bank financial intermediaries willing to pay rates in excess of those imposed by the regulations and, on the other hand, those demanding funds found non-bank intermediaries that could—at a price—meet their needs. While the new markets may have been regarded initially as aberrations—as temporary black markets—that turned out not to be the case. The black markets of one year became the legitimate markets of the next.

The financial history of the last decade is one of Marshall's dictum writ large. Those willing to pay for financial services—pay a *market* rate—have found others willing to sell such services—at a *market* rate—despite regulatory prohibitions on the offering of services and on the payment of market rates by the older institutions. Actually the process began long before 1970, but it was not recognized widely for what it was. Gurley and Shaw (1956) pointed out that growth in the liabilities of non-bank financial intermediaries permits the economy to function with less of the traditionally defined "money." Tobin (1963) made somewhat similar observations. It was not generally appreciated, however, that other markets less affected by reserve requirements and less affected by rate regulations would emerge to fulfill the market needs that banks and the other deposit institutions could not. Furthermore, few saw the prohibition of interest on demand deposits as a regulation that would fundamentally alter the ways in which money and moneylike balances are attracted, managed, and used and that would, indeed, even require reconsideration of the practical definition of money.

For context, however, a number of pre-1970 facts should be kept in mind. First, the growth in commercial bank time deposits, savings and loan deposits, mutual savings bank deposits, and credit union shares after 1950 was several times the rate of growth in bank demand deposits. Second, mutual fund net assets grew from around $2 billion in 1950 to over $50 billion in 1970. Third, in the same period, commercial and finance paper outstandings rose from virtually none to over $33 billion, and a market for this paper appeared.

Fourth, a small Eurodollar market developed, with dollar-denominated foreign deposits escaping burdensome domestic reserve and interest rate regulations. In large measure these deposits were holdings of a growing number of foreign branches of U.S. banks. Fifth, domestic negotiable certificates of deposit in denominations of $100,000 or more were introduced in 1964—and in short time became subject to both time deposit reserve requirements and Regulation Q interest rate regulations. Sixth, an organized Federal Funds market developed. Seventh, bank customers became increasingly sensitive to changes and differences in interest rates. Businesses developed sophisticated cash and funds management practices and, as evidenced by the 1965–66 and 1969–70 "crunches" and disintermediation, a growing number of individuals also moved funds as interest rate differentials appeared. This meant, among other things, that the flow of funds to the thrifts was jeopardized when higher or even equivalent rates appeared elsewhere. Eighth, banks resorted to extensive branching and multibank and one-bank holding company organizations to attract funds and to diversify. Finally, and harbingering the changes of the next decade, computerized internal and clearing operations among financial institutions and their customers and by their customers were in place by 1970.

After the late 1960s, the new mix of technology, regulations, and market forces created innovations in financial services at an accelerated pace. When inflationary forces heightened and nominal interest rates rose, policy efforts to restrict growth in the conventional monetary aggregates induced increased use of intermediation channels other than bank loans and bank deposits. The enormous growth of assets other than bank demand deposits and the accompanying rise in turnover rates are shown in Table 4–1.

NOW accounts were introduced by Massachusetts mutual savings banks, with commercial banks contracting to serve as clearing agents. Here were found interest bearing checking accounts for small, household depositors. Share draft accounts at other thrift institutions provide a similar service. Money market mutual funds were started in 1972 for institutional accounts but quickly were oriented toward services for individuals and nonfinancial businesses as well. Banks themselves marketed small and large denomination certificates of deposit. Many of these were of short maturity, and the large denomination certificates were negotiable. Thus, both large and small certificates were to a degree—and to certain customers—partial substitutes for noninterest bearing bank demand deposits. It was only in 1980 that regulations allowed commercial banks to offer money market deposit accounts in competition with money market mutual funds. The same year witnessed the start of the effective phasing out of other aspects of Regulation Q.

Table 4–1. GNP, Selected Money, and Asset Aggregates and Turnover Rates, 1968 and 1984.

	1968	1984
Gross national product (billions)	$873.4	$3662.8
M1-A. Currency plus all checkable deposits (average for year)	192.3	543.3
M1-B. Currency plus bank demand deposits (average for year)	192.2	400.1
Income velocity of M1-A	4.54	6.74
Income velocity of M1-B	4.54	9.15
Commercial paper (December, billions)	$22.5	$161.8
Banker's acceptances (December, billions)	2.2	41.3
Money market mutual funds (December, billions)	—	230.2
Overnight repos and Eurodollars (December, billions)	—	57.5
Large denomination time deposits (December, billions)	37.5	416.2
Small denomination time deposits (December, billions)	100.5	885.6
Money market deposits (December, billions)	—	415.1
Checkable deposits other than commercial bank demand deposits (December, billions)	0.1	153.3
Turnover of demand deposits, major New York banks (December)	136.8	1910.8

Sources: Board of Governors of the Federal Reserve System; Council of Economic Advisors.

Underlying the changes shown in Table 4–1 are radical reductions in the transactions costs involved in asset switching. New markets for new instruments and improved efficiencies in markets for old instruments were facilitated by the developments in computing and information technologies. Market information became more complete, more broadly available, more timely, and less costly. The costs involved in transacting and in clearing balances fell by orders of magnitude.

This reduction in transaction costs for asset transfers and account clearing has affected the nature and efficiency of the payments system. Suppose that just a few years ago someone decided to buy a TV set but, despite having other assets, the person had inadequate cash and/or checking account balance. A down payment might have been made so the merchant would hold the set. Then, a loan from a bank might be arranged, some securities might be sold (at fixed commission rates), or funds might be withdrawn from a savings account. With time delays and other transactions costs, an adequate *collected* balance would ultimately appear in a checking account and payment for the TV set could be made. The merchant, in turn, would deposit the check to his account and, when that became a *collected* balance, he could use the proceeds to replenish inventory, pay wages, and so forth.

The process is now very different. The purchaser of the TV set, we assume, has a plastic card issued by some host institution—not necessarily a bank. The card, by the nature of the information contained thereon, in the hardware and software of the system to which it affords access, and the contract between the cardholder and the issuer, indicates the assets to be exchanged for the TV set. The assets might be in an account with a securities or commodities dealer, a cash reserve in a life insurance policy, shares in a money market mutual fund, or any of a number of account types at deposit financial institutions. Payment might also be made through activation of a line of credit, with an increase in the payer's holdings of which have been reduced (or the same nominal value of liabilities increased). The merchant, in turn, can transfer virtually instantaneously the funds he has received to increase holdings of any assets (or reductions in any liabilities). The average size of a particular transactions balance—say, a checking account balance—maintained by the buyer of the TV set is largely irrelevant to her ability to buy a TV set or other things. Further, there need be no correspondence between the type of asset she uses to buy the TV set and the type of asset the merchant acquires as a result of the transaction. Neither of their checking account balances at any point in time is critical in determining the aggregate of their expenditures and receipts. And neither needs to have such a balance at any time other than the instant the payment is made, if at all. On average, each can keep close to a "zero balance" bank account.

This new mode of transacting would not occur, of course, if the cost of exchanging assets were high. And they were high in the past. As a consequence, substantial positive balances were held in noninterest bearing checking accounts to minimize those costs.[6] In the future, as transaction costs fall further in response to new information processing technologies, the period of time over which an individual or business will wish to hold such balances is bound to decrease further. Households and businesses will wish to hold only those assets for which there are no preferred alternatives—given transactions costs, interest rates, and other items affecting the attractiveness of the assets. The old type of deposit financial institution liabilities—that is, noninterest bearing demand deposits, and various below-market yielding savings instruments—are likely to be among this preferred group of assets.

TECHNOLOGY AND QUANTITATIVE CONTROLS: THE PROBLEM AND A PARTIAL SOLUTION

The overall effect of lowered transactions costs is surely to limit the efficacy of historic quantitative control of the monetary aggregate. Thus, whether one were to pursue a "Chicago School" policy, opting for a fixed rule with respect to the growth of a monetary aggregate, or a policy based on neo-Keynesian views, with discretionary control of such an aggregate and emphasis on interest rates, it is arguable that neither will work very well. The problem is that when the authority elects to control a monetary aggregate—really, any arbitrary aggregate—technology makes it possible for a new market to arise in which there is trading for a new, moneylike instrument. That is just what was happening as CDs, NOW accounts, commercial paper, Eurodollars, repos, money market funds, and other new instruments and markets came into existence.

As these new instruments are used as money, they are sold and purchased ever more frequently. Consequently, the turnover rate or velocity of a money aggregate (with a fixed definition) rises. And, depending critically on how money is defined, the increases in velocity are not trivial. The income velocity of what we define as M1-A (currency plus all checkable deposits) increased from 4.54 to 6.74 per year between 1968 and 1984; that for what we call M1-B (currency plus demand deposits at commercial banks) more than doubled, going from 4.54 to 9.15 per year.

Looked at as the turnover rate of demand deposits—the use of these deposits for final purchases of goods and services, intermediate goods and services, factor payments and exchanges of real assets, financial instruments and currencies—the effects are much more dramatic. For major New York City banks, the demand deposit annual turnover rate increased from 136.8 to 1510.0 between 1968 and 1984. This rate had been about 50 in 1960 and reached over 2,100 in late 1984.

It is possible to sketch an appreciative or descriptive theory of this process. Thus, consider the following (incomplete) system of identities and equations depicting the macroeconomy:

(1) $i = i(\overline{M}, Y, \dot{P}, N, ...)$

(2) $N = N(\overline{M}, Y, \dot{P}, i, ...)$

(3) $Y = C + I = MV$

(4) $C = C(Y, i, \dot{P}, ...)$

(5) $I = I(dy/dt, i, \dot{P}, ...)$

(6) ∴.

In this system, i represents the level of market-determined interest rates, $\overline{M}$ is a monetary aggregate comprised of the deposit liabilities subject to direct control by the central bank, Y is the national product, and $\dot{P}$ reflects inflationary expectations. We use N to depict an aggregate (of possibly changing composition) of non-$\overline{M}$ deposit and non-deposit liabilities of banks and non-bank financial institutions. The other variables take their normal macroeconomic definitions. A number of variables, identities, and equations not specified here would complete the system. Each variable and equation refers to a point in time, in an essentially dynamic model.

Now suppose that the central bank elects to restrict the growth of $\overline{M}$, due perhaps to its perception of $\dot{P}$. Following conventional theory, this policy action has the (partial) effect of increasing i, in equation (1). From equation (2), the policy action will cause an increase in N. The latter effect arises in part for reasons suggested by the old "availability doctrine."[7] That is, since borrowers are constrained by the monetary policy action from loans the effect of which is to increase $\overline{M}$, they turn instead to borrowings, the effect of which is to increase N, non-$\overline{M}$ deposit, and non-deposit liabilities.[8]

If interest rate regulations prevent market-determined increases in the rate paid on $\overline{M}$ deposit balances, another effect comes into play. The increase in i causes businesses and households to demand smaller $\overline{M}$ balances and larger N balances. Thus, there is an increased demand for the N liabilities at the same time the unavailability of $\overline{M}$-based loans increases the supply of N liabilities.

The equilibrium or convergence properties of this process are not clear. Tobin (1963) notes that the increase in i from equation (1), plus the added effects of increases in (i) due to increases in the outstandings of the N liabilities, ought to dampen aggregate demand through equation (4) and (5). The increase in i should eventually bring about some sort of $N/\overline{M}$ equilibrium relationship. At the same time, however, the impact of new technologies may more than offset any static equilibrating forces. "Learning" occurs on both the supply and demand side of the market for *new* N-type instruments. Transactions costs fall as learning progresses, or trading volumes rise, and as the use of the new instruments spreads. The markets for the N-type instruments become more efficient. If in addition there are exogenous or endogenous supply side factors making $\dot{P}$ insensitive to policy tolls working on the demand side, N may continue to grow irrespective of the restraints on $\overline{M}$.

The situation is such that, with only slight exaggeration, a decision by the monetary authority to "push down one button" to restrict the growth of one monetary aggregate causes another "button"—unrecognized and unpredictable—to pop up to take the role of the first. This may be so pronounced a response mechanism that MV is not perceptably affected. That is, the elasticity of V with respect to M could be as large (absolutely) as -1.0. Technology and the market may interact so that a particular monetary policy, once used effectively, subsequently becomes ineffective.[9]

A delineation of the sufficient conditions for reestablishing a stable relationship between some $\overline{M}$ aggregate and other macroeconomic variables is well beyond our capabilities. We do recommend two necessary steps to reestablishing the efficacy of central bank quantitative control techniques. The first of these is the further deregulation of interest rates and deposits. Because of developments in technology and market sophistication, non-deposit institutions can fashion payments, savings, and investment instruments of virtually limitless varieties. What are now money market funds with fairly high initial deposits and minimum payment orders can easily be changed to increase or decrease either or both of these conditions. They can be changed to term contracts without immediate and third party redemption privileges. They can be used as the vehicle for credit or debit card use in selected or in general application. They are already available as funds shifting devices, providing holders the option of moving holdings across various maturities, between taxable and nontaxable investments, among different types of fund assets, and from one institution to another (e.g., from a bank deposit to a fund, and vice versa).

Interest bearing instruments with varying negotiability, redeemability, maturity, risk, and tax features are attractive to business and household holders or any users of funds. The deposit structures of the present deposit institutions need to be freed of arbitrary rate regulations. This recommendation applies to those deposit structures that separate the old demand deposits from NOW and other types of transaction accounts as well as those that distinguish between individuals and nonprofit organizations and all other depositors. Regulations should be rescinded so that institutions could offer whatever type of "deposit" contract they wish to whomever they wish. For example, what are now regulated "penalties for withdrawal" would be, if they appeared at all, no more than contract terms arranged by particular buyers and sellers on particular accounts.

There has long been recognition of the "blurring" between demand deposits and other deposits of banks. We urge that there be a specific policy redirection for the law and companion regulations to drop such distinctions. With automatic transfer accounts, cash management accounts, and the rapid and nearly costless transfers to, from, and among what are now noninterest bearing demand deposits and other liabilities of banks and non-banks, the only consequence of retaining the demand deposit classification will be to have the measured turnover rate of demand deposits approach infinity as a limit. As we pointed out earlier in our discussion of the new technological mode of transacting, the days when individuals and businesses will hold for any appreciable period a bank balance at zero interest (or with other unattractive terms) in return for the ability to make transactions are largely past.

The elimination of deposit interest rate regulation would not mean that every type of account would bear the same market rate. Rather, it would mean that market rates would appear that explicitly account for the varying contractual terms. Rate regulations, among other distorting effects, have tended to cause "packaged" pricing, often including apparent "free" transacting. Transactions are not costless. Without regulations, the market rates paid on various deposits will tend to reflect the value of the features of the account as determined by the preferences of buyers and costs and sellers, with at least the freedom for explicit pricing to cover transactions costs.

There is a second necessary step to reestablish the viability of central bank's quantitative control techniques. There must be a change in the availability and conditions for deposit (reserve) accounts at the central bank. We recommend that all mandated reserve requirements be abolished and that the central bank be required to pay interest on balances kept with that bank. Any financial institution desiring such balances would be permitted to have a reserve account. Such a policy change would have major implications for the historic institutional separation of commercial banks—whose liabilities we have thought were uniquely "money"—and the non-bank intermediaries. Yet functionally the change is quite in the tradition of central banking. The rationale for reserves at the central bank is their use in controlling the creation of money.

Reserve requirements in their present noninterest bearing form are universally recognized as being the equivalent of a tax. As such, they impose burdens on all institutions to which they apply. Mandatory reserve requirements, like interest rate maxima, spawn new means for avoiding them and are, over time, self-defeating in the present technological and market environment. Further, because of the taxlike effect, they invite other institutions not subject to reserve requirements to provide the same service on a tax-free basis. In theory, one might try the converse and mandate reserve requirements for every provider of deposit-like services. This is not a practical solution however. Given the manifold technological opportunities available for providing such deposit-like services, it would be impossible to find, impose, and enforce reserve requirements on them all.

Interest payments aside, accounts at the central bank are attractive to institutions because of their use in interbank, interregional, and international clearing. This use of such accounts would continue so long as central bank pricing for and the quality of such services do not bring forth alternative clearing organizations. Many institutions with clearing requirements would, we suspect, find it more efficient to clear through balances at other banks. The latter, however, would form a nexus of institutions that, in turn, would keep balance at the central bank. An efficient hierarchical network of clearing arrangements would be encouraged.

With these arrangements, the central bank would have improved interest rate and quantitative controls. By raising the rates paid on reserve balance, the central bank would induce individual institutions to act to increase those balances. Other assets would tend to be sold, lowering their prices and raising the yields on them and, of course, other market rates of interest. The reverse would occur were the central bank to lower the rate paid on reserve balances.

While the market effects described would occur in response to variations in the central bank's actions with respect to the interest rate on reserve balances, the overall quantity of these balances would be unaffected. In the absence of the central bank's acting to change the supply of central bank credit (through open market operations, discounting and other lending, and ignoring changes in float, the gold stock, special drawing rights, Treasury balances, and currency in circulation), the total of these balances is fixed. They can be increased or decreased by the central bank, but not by changes in the portfolio preferences of the individual financial institutions concerning their holdings of central bank balances. As is true now, what one institution gains (loses) in reserves by such transactions is offset by losses (gains) in the reserves of others.

With the suggested scheme, institutions holding reserve balances would be doing so voluntarily. The taxlike effects of reserve requirements would thus be avoided. Further, individual institutions could use central bank balances for liquidity reserves and "secondary reserve" purposes. Central bank open market operations would work much as they do now, and with the same or improved consequences. Total reserve balances would rise with open market purchases and decline with open market sales. The "loosening" or "tightening" of money would spread over the entire set of money and funds markets, more perfectly, perhaps, than is now the case. The market would serve to reestablish reasonable stability in the relationship between "base money" and policy-related economic aggregates—GNP and the price level.

SAFETY AND SOUNDNESS: THE PROBLEM AND DIRECTIONS FOR SOLUTIONS

After three decades of slow change, financial markets have been experiencing radical change. Yet all this while, the regulatory system governing "safety and soundness" has been remarkably static. The basic elements of the arrangement started with the Banking Act of 1933 and may be summarized as follows:

Deposit Insurance System

The Banking Act set up a deposit insurance system for commercial banks and mutual savings banks in which insured institutions pay a fixed rate independent of the composition of their balance sheets. A similar arrangement for savings and loan associations was created in 1934. Although deposits are by law insured up to some fixed amount (now $100,000), the disposal of the marketable assets and liabilities of failed institutions through "purchase and assumption" has led to effective 100 percent insurance for all deposits—at least until the 1980s.

Limits on Assets and Liabilities

Direct regulation of the permissible assets and liabilities for particular institutions was mandated. Each of the specialized institutions—commercial banks, mutual savings banks, and savings and loan associations—are restricted with respect to the set of financial assets and services they can offer. Institutions are further subject to detailed balance sheet regulations—maximum allowable loans to particular customers, maximum percentages of a particular class of assets, reserve provisions, and so forth.

Monitoring of Banks

In the case of the banking system, the Act required the monitoring of balance sheets through quarterly reporting and periodic examination by the regulatory agencies. When examiners uncover problems, banks are subject to direct intervention by regulatory authorities with substantial enforcement powers.

Disentangling the effects of safety and soundness regulation, the use of macroeconomic tools, and the general economic environment on the solvency of insured institutions is a difficult task. Nonetheless, the effectiveness of the regulatory system can be assessed in part by the fact that it has been generally successful. The periodic banking crises that were a familiar feature of the American scene up to the Great Depression were not a problem for over fifty years. Compared to the period prior to 1933, bank failures have been infrequent and localized events. However, in the last decade a number of problems have arisen that have shaken the regulatory system. Public debate over regulatory reform has now reached the stage where suggestions by academics and regulators have been fashioned into concrete proposals centering on these problem areas.[10]

There seem to be three perceptions underlying the current reform proposals. First, people feel that the riskiness of the banking environment has increased. The interactions among technological developments, financial innovation, macroeconomic instability, and de facto and de jure regulatory changes have given rise to this perception. The substantial increase in the number and size of problem and failed banks, and the succession of major financial strains of the last decade, are both well documented.

Second, people think that in the current regulatory environment, banks have an inherent bias toward excessive risk taking. The joining of de facto 100 percent deposit insurance, insurance premia that are not risk-related, and the small capital commitments by bank equity owners results in there being no economic group with a substantial interest in controlling risk. As banks get into trouble, moving closer to a position of zero net worth, the incentives for excessive risk-taking increase. In an environment with greater market opportunities and market pressures for risk taking, this bias becomes more pronounced.

Third, many think that the current regime of examination and direct balance sheet control is costly and inefficient; it is thought that increased reliance on market and marketlike mechanisms is likely to achieve better results at a lower regulatory cost.

Before considering the proposals in detail, the basic premises behind the public debate require examination. There is no doubt that the financial system and the regulators are dealing with strains arising in part from de facto and de jure deregulation. Formerly insulated institutions face competition from unfamiliar opponents and, as institutions move across traditional product and geographic market barriers, there have been significant increases in the number of troubled and failed banks. The failures can be viewed as a competitive shakeout—perhaps analogous to the shakeout occurring in the 1930s, when an excessively large population of banks was pruned of many competitors. The question is whether further deregulation of geographic and product line restrictions will lead to a secular increase in instability that threatens even efficient institutions.

Deregulation has a double edged blade. Debate has focused excessively on the risk-increasing aspects without sufficient attention to the risk-reducing features. In fact, there are a number of reasons to believe that further deregulation will *enhance* the ability of financial institutions to regulate risk and will *reduce* the social costs of risk taking. An obvious but underemphasized effect of deregulating product line and geographic restrictions is the creation of new opportunities for diversification of both the asset and liability sides. To the extent that regional shocks and product line risks are independent, greater opportunities for interstate branching and product line extension can reduce risks. The current rash of problem banks in the farming states, for example, can be viewed as the natural result of compelling institutions to maintain an undiversified portfolio.

The same can be said for expanded commercial bank powers in underwriting and brokerage activities—and there are reasons to believe that the risks of these activities have been overstated.[11] The *covariance* of the returns of traditional commercial lending and brokerage activities will be crucial determinants of the riskiness of a portfolio composed of both. Recent evidence indicates that potential gains from diversification exists.[12]

Further, the pace of financial innovations means that institutions have to offer new financial services to avoid losing traditional customers. The rhythm of innovation itself creates a source of risk that can be minimized only by allowing institutions to respond. For example, while commercial paper offerings had traditionally required the backing of a bank line of credit, this is no longer the case. The deepening of commercial paper markets in the last two decades and the consequent increased liquidity of such assets has broken this link. Unless commercial banks are permitted to underwrite commercial paper, a traditional and important part of their clientele will be lost. This is an especially telling illustration since a bank's potential risks from a line of credit supporting commercial paper offerings and from direct underwriting of the same offering are essentially the same.

The age in which a banker could assume a stable liability base in the form of "core" deposits and a stable group of loan customers with a restricted set of financing alternatives no longer exists. A measure of stability can be achieved, however, if institutions are able to offer a spectrum of assets, liabilities, and fee-based services and, to some extent, to internalize the flows that now cross legally defined institutional boundaries.

While increased geographic and sectoral competition have been viewed as factors increasing the risk to particular institutions, one can also expect a reduction in the social and financial costs of risk taking. The lowering of regulatory entry barriers should reduce the social costs of individual bank failure. An increase in the number of potential entrants in any and all of a particular bank's markets reduces the costs of closing the institution. Transferring the failed bank's assets is facilitated by the proliferation of potential purchasers. Moreover, the regulatory agencies can intervene and close banks more rapidly, thereby reducing the risk of payout by the insurance system. The existence of more, and more powerful, "nearby" competitors permits regulators to intervene on the basis of "economic" rather than "book" value. Such intervention, in itself, changes the equity holders' risk-return trade-off and enhances the disciplinary role of equity.

The view that 100 percent de facto deposit insurance ensures that no agents have an interest in limiting risk taking by banks may be an overstatement. The exclusive focus upon insured depositors and equity holders ignores the potential disciplinary role of loan customers. Although one-time loan applicants cannot be expected to take great interest in the riskiness of their lender's portfolio, those customers with long-term, repeat relationships and established lines of credit do form a group with continuing interests in the viability of the bank. Refusals to extend credit and noncompetitive loan terms arising from a bank's inefficient or excessively risky operation will drive these customers away. This behavior may be a source of discipline on bank management risk practices regardless of the de facto full insurance.

The difficulty of transferring the loan relationship in a purchase and assumption means that there is a "partially insured" bank customer. Further, with product line deregulation, the customers of a bank will have dealings across a larger range of products—consumer finance, insurance, mutual funds, and the like. This will tend to create classes of "partially insured" customers for whom the failure of a bank will be costly.

Despite these risk-reducing aspects of deregulation, reform proposals have been presented by most of the institutional and regulatory actors. The proposals with the greatest support are:

1. Developing a system of risk-related insurance premia
2. Replacing 100 percent de facto insurance with one of only partial insurance
3. Replacing the periodic and discretionary imposition of minimum capital requirements with a strict minimum
4. Replacing the secrecy of the current bank examination process with increased public disclosure.

These proposals have been subjected to extensive academic debate; the theoretical grounding for each is surprisingly slim. There are three types of shortcomings. First, the proposed changes have ambiguous effects on risk taking and the stability of the financial system. Second, practical implementation will be difficult and the regulatory burden will not necessarily decrease. Finally, the ability to mandate taxlike insurance premia on the risk taking of a restricted subset of financial institutions may be frustrated by the existence of unregulated institutions and activities.

Risk-related Premia

The rationale behind replacing fixed rate premia with risk-related premia is straightforward.[13] Charging banks premia that vary directly with the riskiness of their activities will, in principle, induce a more efficient portfolio choice. An optimally calibrated system of risk premia will induce banks to impute full social cost considerations in their portfolio decisions.

The first and perhaps overwhelming problem with such a scheme is the difficulty of accurately gauging risk ex ante. Any attempt to measure ex ante asset and interest rate risk accurately would, at the minimum, require a substantial increase in the monitoring of bank portfolios. While measurement of these sources of risk is by itself difficult, the problem is complicated by two other considerations. First, these risks are not independent. Santomero (1983) has shown, for instance, that variable rate loans, which reduce the average maturity of the bank's assets and in turn reduce interest rate risk, have the effect of increasing default risk. Proper measurement would require analysis of the covariance between risks. Second, the existence of externalities implies that the social costs of risk taking must be measured. Informational externalities affecting depositor behavior and contagion effects are important features of the banking system. In a model that abstracts from the problem of measuring externalities, Pyle (1983) has shown that even small measurement errors lead to large miscalculations of actuarially correct insurance premia.

The inevitability of mismeasurement raises problems independent of the questionable effects on resource allocation. In addition to monitoring costs, one can expect an increase in bargaining costs as banks appeal bad ratings. The monitoring apparatus will have to be supplemented by an appeals process that increases the regulatory burden. Furthermore, the fluidity of the modern financial system will lead to attempts at "tax evasion." Activities with overpriced risks will tend to be shifted toward unregulated sectors of financial markets. Indeed, this may be true of any system that levies premia on particular institutions that reflect full social costs of failure.

Recognizing that any serious attempt to measure risk accurately is impossible, the FDIC (1983) has proposed an arbitrary premium structure that independently weighs two elements. These are the bank's loan loss history and a measure of the duration of the bank's balance sheet. The former may have undesirable incentive effects that compromise a potentially useful direction for regulatory practice. While banks probably have some incentive purposely to take on excessively risky loans, the important systemic problems arise from *many* banks taking on similar loans that only *subsequent* events prove to have been a mistake. The recent experience with energy loans is a prime example.

The Quarterly Call Reports, which will be the source of the bank's loan loss history, have become an increasingly important source of information allowing the regulatory agencies to diagnose developing problems at an early stage. The reduced cost and increasing sophistication of information systems have made this possible. By tying insurance premia to loan losses, regulators will create undesirable incentives for banks to withhold information for as long as possible. The relative infrequency of on-site examinations create ample opportunities for banks to withhold information. Variable rate premia based on loan losses will compromise the regulator's ability to recognize systemic problems in a timely way. Perhaps a more desirable direction would be the design of penalties for inaccurately transmitted information. On-site examinations would be used to assess the truthfulness of the information in the Call Reports.

The fascination with the use of pricing schemes to tax ex ante risk taking may be misplaced. A number of writers have noted that the deposit insurance system differs in a fundamental way from private insurance schemes.[14] The regulator's ability to close down failed institutions implies that, at least theoretically, depositor losses from bank failure can be driven to zero if banks are closed before they reach zero net worth. For the most part this has remained only a theoretical possibility because substantial political pressures have led to very conservative closure policies. These political pressures are largely the result of the social costs of closing institutions that are, in turn, the result of substantial entry barriers. The continued lowering of entry barriers through geographic and product line deregulation would reduce the welfare and financial loss associated with the closing of failed institutions and should increase the political attractiveness of doing so.

Partial Coverage

The FDIC has proposed that the insurance agencies precommit themselves to a maximum percentage payout to uninsured depositors. The reasoning is that such depositors would then have an incentive to monitor bank risk because of the threat of loss. While it is plausible that this would lead to enhanced market discipline, the net effect of such a program may be greater instability. Before any such program is implemented, a number of issues must be considered.

The first problem is that increased monitoring of the bank's portfolio is only one possible response to partial insurance. Since information collection is costly and, on the contrary, movement in response to even questionable information is relatively costless, one wonders whether increased monitoring is a likely outcome. An equally likely outcome is a joint strategy of purchasing liabilities of shorter duration and moving funds at the first sign of trouble. Both effects, the shorter duration of the bank's liabilities and the increased speed of withdrawal in response to any sign of trouble are, in themselves, destabilizing.

This, of course, ignores the fact that banks, faced with the possibility of large-scale withdrawals in response to bad news, may have ex ante incentives to reduce excessive risk taking. Recent theoretical work, however, has shown that the deposit contract is uniquely subject to depositor runs.[15] Informational externalities lead to a gap between depositors' marginal private valuation of moving funds in response to bad information and the marginal social valuation of such movements. Rational behavior by depositors can lead to the socially inefficient liquidation of bank assets. The distance between the depositor's and society's valuation of moving funds will increase if interdependencies between banks lead to contagion effects that amplify the consequences of individual bank failures. There can be no presumption that rational behavior by uninsured depositors leads to a socially optimal outcome. In turn, there is no reason to assume that the banks' ex ante risk taking will be optimal under the threat of depositor runs.

Even assuming that depositors have an incentive to monitor the riskiness of their bank before depositing funds, another problem arises. Some have argued that higher deposit rates will be the primary mechanism through which the discipline will be imposed. Troubled banks will be forced to pay a risk premium to attract funds from partially insured depositors. The higher cost of funds in response to greater perceived risk appears to have the same effect as a variable rate insurance scheme—the market would impose penalties for excessive risk taking. Unlike the higher risk premia paid to the insurance agency, though, higher deposit rates may create incentives for *greater* risktaking. In a slightly different context, Stiglitz and Weiss (1981) have shown that higher rates can lead to riskier portfolio choices, because borrowers face strictly limited downside financial risks in the event of default. This implies that the requirement of higher deposit rates is limited as a strategy for controlling risk. Beyond some maximum deposit rate, further increases reduce the depositor's welfare. Therefore, even with ex ante monitoring, the strategy of holding shorter duration liabilities and running in response to bad news will supplement that of demanding higher rates.

Increased Capital Requirements

Increased capital requirements are proposed as a means of increasing the bank's downside costs of excessive risk taking. It is argued that equity owners, faced with a larger cost of bank failure, will be motivated to control risk taking by bank managers. Further, forcing banks to increase access to capital markets will induce less risk taking in order to minimize the cost of capital. Finally, larger capital requirements are proposed as a means of reducing payouts by the insurance agencies. Losses will be charged to equity before the insurance fund.

Koehn and Santomero (1980) have analyzed a particularly troublesome problem with this proposal. If the minimum capital requirement is binding, banks will *increase* portfolio risk to increase the expected return on capital. Therefore, the effect of larger capital requirements is ambiguous—the less risk adverse the bank, the more likely an increase in capital requirements will *increase* the probability of failure. To ensure an unambiguous reduction in the systemwide probability of bank failure, capital requirements would have to be set on a firm-by-firm basis, with corresponding increases in the regulatory burden.

Santomero and Watson (1977) have raised additional concerns in a general equilibrium framework. Using a model in which higher capital requirements are assumed to reduce the probability of bank failure, they show that the social costs of diverting excess capital toward the banking system may reduce the rate of physical capital formation by raising the cost of borrowing. Although these results are not conclusive, an important point emerges. Determining an optimal capital standard for the banking system on partial equilibrium grounds is suspect.

There is a connection between the earlier discussion of partial insurance schemes and minimum capital standards that should be mentioned. Limitations on the depositor's ability to impute a risk premium in deposit rates without inducing more risk taking by banks may be counteracted by greater bank capital. A more highly capitalized bank can offer higher rates without reducing depositor welfare, because capital serves as collateral, increasing losses for bank equity if there is a default.

Public Disclosure

There has been little theoretical work examining the likely effects of greater public disclosure of the regulator's information about banks. Commentators have been content to note that partial insurance schemes that exploit market discipline should be supplemented by the provision of more public information. The essential notion is that market discipline will be more rational when rumor is displaced by "fact."

Although this approach merits further consideration, a basic problem remains: Information asymmetries will exist, even with more public disclosure. We have argued that these asymmetries are a fundamental constraint on the regulator's ability to design optimal insurance premia. Similarly, the information available to depositors will, of necessity, be very imperfect. The problems with partial insurance schemes still exist even when public disclosure improves the quality of the information available to depositors.

CONCLUSIONS

Our look at the effects of deregulation on continuing regulatory needs for deposit financial institutions has produced one clear conclusion. Despite an apparent consensus that both monetary policy and deposit insurance have important continuing roles, neither is likely to work well without basic changes. Indeed, we go further; in plausible circumstances the continued use of either or both may add to rather than reduce system-wide instabilities.

We are not so confident in our diagnoses that we are able to prescribe sure cures. We are confident enough to assert that the technologies now available to financial institutions and their customers have altered fundamentally the regulatory mechanisms that can be used effectively for implementing monetary policy and for assuring an optimal level of safety and soundness in the financial system.

NOTES

1. For a description and analysis of the process involved in this intermingling, see Phillips (1978). See Kaufman (1985) for an excellent discussion of the securities activities of commercial banks.
2. See Hawke (1985) for detail.
3. See Key (1985) for detail.
4. See Kane (1983) for an analysis of the situation in the thrift industries.
5. For comments on the difficulties inherent in regulatory reform, see Jacobs and Phillips (1983).
6. The underlying theory is well-known and basically the same as that pertaining to inventories of other assets. See Baumol (1952).
7. For a discussion of the availability doctrine, see Mayer (1968). An argument very close to that being made here appears in Smith (1956).
8. On this point, see Grantham, Velk and Fraas (1977), Kling (1981), Latane (1954), Minsky (1957), and Smith (1956).
9. This raises the specter of "Goodhart's Law," an assertion that the use of monetary controls has the effect of loosening existing relationships between money and the economic variables the central bank wishes to influence. See, in particular, Goodhart (1981) and Evans (1985).
10. See FDIC (1983) and FHLBB (1983).
11. For an evaluation of the relative risks of securities underwriting and commercial lending, see Giddy (1985) and Saunders (1985).
12. For evidence of diversification gains from the expansion of bank powers, see Heggestad (1975), Eisemann (1976), and Wall and Eisenbeis (1984).
13. For more extensive critical discussion of these reform proposals, see Goodman and Shaffer (1983) and Merrick and Saunders (1985).
14. See, for example, Horvitz (1983).
15. See Chari and Jagannathan (1984), Cone (1983), Diamond and Dybvig (1983), and Jacklin (1983).

REFERENCES

Baumol, W.J. 1952. "The Transactions Demand for Cash—An Inventory Theoretic Approach." *Quarterly Journal of Economics* 66 (November).
Chari, V., and R. Jagannathan. 1984. "Banking Panics, Information, and Rational Expectations Equilibrium." Banking Research Center, Northwestern University, Working Paper #112 (July).

Cone, K. 1983. "The Regulation of Depository Financial Institutions." Ph.D. dissertation, Stanford University.
Diamond, D., and P. Dybvig. 1983. "Bank Runs, Deposit Insurance, and Liquidity." *Journal of Political Economy* 91 (June).
Eisemann, P. 1976. "Diversification and the Cogeneric Bank Holding Company." *Journal of Bank Research* 7 (Spring).
Evans, P. 1985. "Money, Output and Goodhart's Law: The U.S. Experience." *Review of Economics and Statistics* 67 (February).
Federal Deposit Insurance Corporation. 1983. *Deposit Insurance in a Changing Environment* (April).
Federal Home Loan Bank Board. 1983. *Agenda for Reform* (March).
Giddy, I.H. 1985. "Is Equity Underwriting Risky for Commercial Banks." In *Deregulating Wall Street*, edited by I. Walter. New York: John Wiley & Sons.
Goodhart, C. 1981. "Problems in Monetary Management: The U.K. Experience." In *Inflation, Depression and Economic Policy in the West*, edited by A.S. Courarkis. Totowa, NJ: Barnes and Noble.
Goodman, L., and S. Shaffer. 1983. "The Economics of Deposit Insurance: A Critical Evaluation of Proposed Reforms." Federal Reserve Bank of New York, Research Paper #8308 (August).
Grantham, G.W.; T.J. Velk; and A.G. Fraas. 1977. "On the Microeconomics of the Supply of Money." *Oxford Economic Press* 29 (November).
Gurley, J.G., and E.B. Shaw. 1956. "Financial Intermediaries and the Saving-Investment Process." *Journal of Finance* 11 (May).
Hawke, J.D., Jr. 1985. "Public Policy Toward Bank Expansion." In *Handbook for Banking Strategy*, edited by R.C. Aspinwall and R.A. Eisenbeis. New York: John Wiley & Sons.
Heggestad, A. 1975. "Riskiness of Investments in Nonbank Activities by Bank Holding Companies." *Journal of Economics and Business* 27 (Spring).
Horvitz, P. 1983. "The Case Against Risk-Related Deposit Insurance Premiums." *Housing Finance Review* 2 (July).
Jacklin, C. 1983. "Information and the Choice Between Deposit and Equity Contracts." Graduate School of Business, Stanford University, Working Paper (November).
Jacobs, D.P., and A. Phillips. 1983. "Reflections on the Hunt Commission." In *Financial Services: The Changing Institutions and Government Policy*, edited by G.J. Benston. New York: Prentice-Hall, for the American Assembly.
Kane, E.J. 1983. "The Role of Government in the Thrift Industry's Net-Worth Crises." In *Financial Services: The Changing Institutions and Government Policy*, edited by G.J. Benston. New York: Prentice-Hall, for the American Assembly.
Kaufman, G.G. 1985. "The Securities Activities of Commercial Banks." In *Handbook for Banking Strategy*, edited by R.C. Aspinwall and R.A. Eisenbeis. New York: John Wiley & Sons.

Key, S.J. 1985. "The Internationalization of U.S. Banking." In *Handbook for Banking Strategy,* edited by R.C. Aspinwall and R.A. Eisenbeis. New York: John Wiley & Sons.

Kling, Arnold. 1981. "Financial Innovation and the Monetary Transmission Mechanism." *Research Papers in Banking and Financial Economics.* Washington, D.C.: Board of Governors of the Federal Reserve System.

Koehn, M., and A. Santomero. 1980. "Regulation of Bank Capital and Portfolio Risk." *Journal of Finance* 35 (March).

Latane, H.A. 1954. "Cash Balances and the Interest Rate—A Pragmatic Approach." *Review of Economics and Statistics* 36 (November).

Marshall, A. 1897. "The Old Generation of Economists and the New." *Quarterly Journal of Economics* 11 (January).

Mayer, T. 1968. *Monetary Policy in the United States.* New York: Random House.

Merrick, T., and A. Saunders. 1985. "Bank Regulation and Monetary Policy." *Journal of Money, Credit and Banking* 17, no. 4, part 2 (November): 691–717.

Minsky, H.P. 1957. "Central Banking and Money Market Changes." *Quarterly Journal of Economics* 71 (May).

Phillips, A. 1978. "The Metamorphosis of Markets: Commercial and Investment Banking." *Journal of Comparative Corporate Law and Securities Regulation* 1.

Pyle, D. 1983. "Pricing Deposit Insurance: The Effect of Mismeasurement." Federal Reserve Bank of San Francisco Working Paper (October).

Santomero, A. 1983. "Fixed Versus Variable Rate Loans." *Journal of Finance* 38 (December).

Santomero, A., and R. Watson. 1977. "Determining an Optimal Capital Standard for the Banking Industry." *Journal of Finance* 32 (September).

Saunders, A. 1985. "Bank Safety and Soundness, and the Risks of Corporate Securities Activities." In *Deregulating Wall Street,* edited by I. Walter. New York: John Wiley & Sons.

Smith, W.L. 1956. "On the Effectiveness of Monetary Policy." *American Economic Review* 46 (September).

Stiglitz, J., and A. Weiss. 1981. "Credit Rationing in Markets with Imperfect Information." *American Economic Review* 71 (June).

Tobin, J. 1963. "Commercial Banks as Creators of 'Money.' " In *Banking and Monetary Studies,* edited by D. Carson. Homewood, IL: Richard D. Irwin.

Wall, L., and R. Eisenbeis. 1984. "Bank Holding Company, Nonbanking Activities and Risk." In *Proceedings of a Conference on Bank Structure and Competition.* Federal Reserve Bank of Chicago.

DISCUSSION OF CHAPTER 4
Peter Linneman

Phillips and Berlin present a thorough and interesting introductory overview of the major regulatory problems that have developed as the result of financial markets that have been both de facto and legally deregulated in the past decade. Specifically, the authors evaluate the problems inherent in pursuit of the two traditional policy objectives of financial regulation in the current marketplace: the effective control of the money supply and the soundness of financial institutions. The authors conclude generally that the problems that have been spawned by increased technology and reduced financial transactions costs can be alleviated by further deregulation; there need be no new or major regulatory response.

One of Phillips and Berlin's more interesting observations is that technological advances combined with financial ingenuity caused new unregulated competitive markets to appear, particularly when regulatory constraints were very binding. The authors refer to these new markets as "black markets" (since these new markets were always legal, they are perhaps more accurately referred to as "gray markets") that have grown from aberrations to full-fledged markets. Regulations introduced fifty years ago in an attempt to solve the problems of that time may now be doing more harm than good. They persuasively argue that largely unregulated financial markets would perform better in terms of both policy objectives than markets upon which a number of patchwork regulations are imposed. They correctly argue that a process of patchwork reregulation would only strengthen the financial gray markets by encouraging funds to flow from regulated to unregulated markets.

I will comment only very briefly on the authors' analysis of the policy problems of controlling the money supply. They echo the concerns of others about the definition of the money supply, which becomes blurred and arbitrary as financial gray markets have developed more liquid and sophisticated investment instruments. This problem is heightened by increased interest rate and risk elasticities of investors that are the result of the greatly reduced transaction costs brought about by technological advances. However, I feel that the authors overstate the Fed's loss of control of the relevant money supply for policy.

The two real policy questions in this regard are the following: Are there reasonably stable relationships between measures of economic activity and alternative definitions of money?; and, Is there a relatively stable relationship between these definitions of money and the supply of reserves and currency? While I suspect less stable relationships exist in these regards now than a decade ago, I would be surprised to find that these relationships have disappeared. It is interesting to note that the reduced Fed control of the money supply seems to suggest that the Fed should follow a Friedmanlike rule that concentrates on a steady and predictable growth of what it can control—namely, the supply of reserves and currency. As effective policy control of the money supply diminishes, the Fed should simply concentrate on providing a stable, predictable environment for investors. This would be accomplished by a Friedman fixed monetary expansion approach to the supply of reserves and currency (so called "high powered" money) that would save investors from constant intermediation.

The authors also argue persuasively that if the Fed were to pay interest on voluntary (rather than required) reserve accounts, the Fed's traditional control of the money supply would increase. Eliminating the implicit tax on traditional depositories seems to be a far more manageable approach to restoring the deposits subject to Fed control than the approach put forward by popular proposals, such as the one requiring non-bank depositories to hold reserves at the Fed. The approach suggested by the authors would provide the Fed with an additional control variable (the reserve fund interest rate) and would avoid the regulatory difficulties involved in defining what non-bank depositories are.

The discussion of ways to improve the soundness of financial institutions is characterized by what I call a weakest link approach. Simply stated, the authors argue that although popular regulatory proposals (such as risk-related insurance premia, increased capital bases, partial deposit insurance, and reduced secrecy with respect to balance sheet monitoring) will tend to make the regulated institutions more immune to mismanagement, these proposals will increase the attractiveness of the unregulated and less monitored gray markets by increasing the cost of regulated institutions. This policy may well result in a decrease in general soundness because more deposits may actually be put into riskier assets. Since the assets of regulated and unregulated markets are interlinked, the consequences of the failure of one of these large unregulated funds would seriously impair the soundness and safety of the financial system. Thus, by driving more funds into relatively risky unregulated assets, these alleged safety increasing reforms would actually be placing greater emphasis and strain on the weakest link in the financial system.

While this argument is intuitively plausible, one wonders whether the cost increases associated with some of the popular reform proposals would be sufficiently large to trigger the degree of intermediation suggested by the authors. It is particularly questionable whether overall system risk would rise if one assumes that many of the deposits lost by regulatory depositories would move into similarly low risk assets such as money market funds and federal securities. However, the authors argue persuasively that each of the major popular proposals to improve the soundness of financial institutions will have few, if any, beneficial impacts.

In sum, Phillips and Berlin present provocative and enlightening discussions of the problems that exist in financial markets as the result of the deregulation that was forced by technological advances.

DISCUSSION OF CHAPTER 4
Robert P. Shay

Phillips and Berlin have written a wide-ranging analysis of regulatory problems in a deregulated environment. While I agree with their recommendations for freer banking markets, I have many differences in the analysis that underlies the advocacy of these recommendations.

To begin with, Phillips and Berlin fall into the conventional trap of blaming deregulation for problems that probably would not have arisen without the imposition of inflexible regulations continued for too long by inflexible legislators and regulators. Further, they place the blame for some of the deregulatory problems upon the regulated institutions that chose the path of slow extinction over fast extinction when threatened by deregulation. For example, they state:

> Some institutions have ignored or resisted fundamental market and regulatory changes. In so doing, they have exposed themselves to the potential and, in some cases, the actuality of extinction. At the opposite end of the spectrum, deregulation seems to have encouraged other institutions to engage in practices subsequently revealed to be gross mismanagement and fraud.

The first and second sentences constitute classic overstatement of fact and I would guess that they are aimed at thrift institutions. The third sentence attributes scandalous practices to deregulation that have little to do with deregulation in my opinion.

Yet, if it is the thrift industry that is the class of institution that takes the blame, it is a bum rap. The problems of New York's thrifts are the most severe in the nation. They had been asking the state legislature for new powers and tried to have usury ceilings lifted for over a decade before action was taken but they always came home with crumbs. No wonder they are in trouble today. Limited to fixed rate mortgages under usury limits and short-term liabilities, they were constrained and undiversified. Although extinction was certain, they chose to buy time by opposing the rapid removal of Regulation Q unless asset constraints were removed. New England's thrifts did better because they were given consumer lending powers while they pioneered the NOW account. So, who is to blame? It was the inflexibility of regulation—and not the actions of the regulated institution—that got blamed in my book.

I also disagree with the authors' view that deregulation encouraged gross mismanagement and fraud by some institutions. I do not see that Penn Square's collapse involving major commercial banks had much to do with deregulation, nor did the problems of First Pennsylvania, nor did the well-publicized ventures of the Butcher empire in Tennessee. Taking chances with brokered deposits is a more reasonable way to support the charge of gross mismanagement, but I would rather classify it as placing a bet to get out of trouble. Gross mismanagement is characteristic of actions under economic duress, and there is little evidence that deregulation itself is a cause of it.

TECHNOLOGY AND QUANTITATIVE CONTROL OF THE MONEY SUPPLY

Phillips and Berlin's discussion of emerging pressure on the regulatory system and the increasing velocity of money is most useful, as is their observation that the "black markets of one year become the legitimate markets of the next." I disagree, however, with their criticism of the concept of money.

It is not entirely clear that Phillips and Berlin believe that there is any identifiable concept called money, but I retain the notion that as long as settlement in the market is not barter, those accounts used for settlement can be called money. However, I support their recommendation that demand deposits should not be distinct from other deposit accounts by law or by regulations, and that demand deposits and other transaction accounts should pay market interest rates. However, the concept of money that includes transaction accounts used for settlement purposes remains valid. Prevailing practice should decide what accounts are transaction accounts.

I do not agree with the analysis of why, in a world with advanced technology, quantitative or indirect control of a monetary aggregate cannot work. I would support the abolition of reserve requirements, as suggested by the authors, but I am not sure that the payment of interest on reserve balances at the Fed would necessarily resolve the problems that technology poses for monetary control.

Phillips and Berlin assume that the payment of interest on reserve balances can attract enough reserves to control the aggregate amount of reserves and currency. To me this represents control of a monetary aggregate, but the difference between us is probably only semantics. To attract reserves the Fed would have to pay market rates for funds and thereby drive market rates higher. Banks could continue to operate on a net deficient reserve position as long as the Fed kept the discount window open, preferably at market rates.

Why, however, is there a need for the Fed to attract any reserve balances? The Fed could operate with open market purchases and sales and let the discount window serve the function of lender of last resort. Would the Fed then be controlling only currency in circulation? My guess is that Phillips and Berlin would answer that the Fed would control interest rates. If so, however, by what criteria would the Fed control either the level or the term structure of interest rates?

While Phillips and Berlin concede that their approach is only a partial resolution of the problem, I am not sure that it would be an improvement. The Fed loses some control over the payments system—that is, the settlement of balance through debits and credits to accounts at the Fed—when they are forced to charge market rates for clearing services. The interaction between the control of reserves and currency and the payments system has increased as technology makes it possible to transfer funds swiftly. The authors have shed considerable light on an emerging problem, but resort to controlling interest rates in the marketplace still seems to me to be a second best solution. I would favor the control of reserves and currency by the payment of interest on reserve balances provided that financial institutions were required to make settlements, through the Fed, directly or indirectly.

SAFETY AND SOUNDNESS

On the twin question of safety and soundness, I find myself in fundamental agreement with the authors. There are, indeed, reasons to believe that further deregulation will *enhance* the ability of institutions to regulate risk, and they have noted them effectively.

I also agree with their analysis of the problem of establishing rate premia related to risk, and I would also reject that method of solving the present dilemma. A combination of federal insurance coverage, as low as $25,000 or less (leaving the banks to obtain private insurance for the excess), would suit me now, together with regulatory control of capital requirements.

5 THE IMPACT OF INFORMATION TECHNOLOGY ON TRADE IN SERVICES

Geza Feketekuty
Kathryn Hauser

Late last year, the Chicago Mercantile Exchange and the Singapore stock exchange announced the establishment of an electronic hook-up between the two exchanges that will permit global trading around the clock, twenty-four hours a day.

U.S. judicial opinions are abstracted and entered into an electronic data base in Korea, kept on file in Mead Data Central's computers in the United States, and are accessible via electronic hook-up by lawyers in London, Paris, or Dubuque.

A worldwide network of computers and communication circuits enables Bechtel to coordinate the activities of engineers in India, project managers in San Francisco, and construction supervisors on site in Saudi Arabia.

Citibank's system enables corporate treasurers to monitor checking account balances in Citibank branches around the world.

These four examples illustrate how the introduction of new computer and communication technology has opened up new trade opportunities in services. It is now possible to trade almost any type of service that can be delivered electronically, including data processing, computer programming, video and audio entertainment, training and education, legal services, accounting, engineering, banking, insurance, research and development, publishing, advertising and public relations, and communication and information services. International trade in services is estimated to exceed $600 billion annually.

The dynamism and potential for trade in services is an extension of the role services play in the domestic economy. In the first section, we will give an overview of services in our economy and explain the rapid growth in demand for information services. Then, in the second section, we will explore five key developments in the application of information technology that account for new trade opportunities in the services field. These may be summarized in the following way:

- Advances in microelectronics have reduced the cost, increased the speed, and improved the reliability of data storage and communications, thereby making trade in information based services a viable economic activity.
- The use of communications technology has led to the creation of new products and services that increase the possibilities for international trade.
- The use of communications technology has given rise to new production processes requiring substantial service inputs, thereby increasing the demand for internationally traded services.
- The use of communications technology by multinational corporations has allowed services to be provided on a worldwide basis, leading to greater efficiencies and specialization in services trade.
- The emergence of international networks has created new possibilities for trade in services by creating a mechanism for pooling and sharing information.

We will conclude this paper with some thoughts on what can be done, in terms of trade policy, to assure that the new trading opportunities brought about by technological advances in communication and information are not restricted by trade barriers.

GROWTH OF SERVICES IN THE ECONOMY

Year after year, data released by the government shows the accelerated growth of service jobs in the economy. Since 1960, the percentage of nonagricultural employment engaged in service activities has grown from 62 to 72 percent. Not only has there been a fundamental shift away from manufacturing and into services, but the service sector continues to provide significant job opportunities. Over the past two decades, some 86 percent of job growth in the economy has been in the service-producing sector. During the 1970s, close to 90 percent of the 19 million new jobs created in the United States were white collar rather than blue collar. This trend continued through the recession of the early 1980s. Since December 1982, the bottom of the recession, 69 percent of the new jobs created in our economy are in service industries (CEA 1985).

At the end of 1983, over 53 million Americans were employed in service industries, excluding government. Of these 9.5 percent were in transport services; 10.1 percent in wholesale services; 10.4 percent in finance, insurance, and real estate; 30.8 in retail services; and 37.6 percent in a general category called services. From the point of view of trade in services, this latter category is most significant because it contains the business-related services of communications and information, data processing, accounting, law, advertising and public relations, equipment rental and leasing, and management consulting. In 1983 alone, over 240,000 jobs were created per month in these business-related services. All are highly dependent on applications of modern information technology and have thus been affected the most by changing technology (CEA 1985).

The employment boom generated by the introduction of information technology is not limited to service firms but extends to manufacturing firms as well. Firms primarily engaged in the production of goods use information technology extensively to provide in-house services, such as accounting, data processing, and financial management. In some cases, the services provided in-house have become so specialized that the parent company has created separate profit centers to take advantage of the expertise in particular service sectors. A good example of this is the McDonnell Douglas Corporation, which developed a data base for its internal research and development activities and now has a separate subsidiary that sells on-line data services to the general public throughout the world. McDonnell Douglas, a traditional manufacturing firm, thus is now also an international services business.

Services employment within manufacturing firms accounts for a large portion of the continuing growth in white collar employment in the United States. However, under the current data collection methodology, revenues generated by services operations within manufacturing firms are counted as part of the broad manufacturing category. Consequently, the data actually underestimates the full extent of services employment.

The traditional distinctions between manufacturing and services employment are blurred because information technology has dramatically altered the way manufacturing and services firms do business and the kinds of business they perform. RCA was recently reclassified as a services company, after having been counted in the past as a manufacturing company; and IBM is beginning to ask itself whether it is primarily a manufacturing company or an information services company. While seemingly unimportant, such categorization directly affects the type of data that is collected and our ability to quantify the true value of services in our economy.

Even without perfect data, the importance and dynamism of the U.S. service economy is clear. Modern communications technology has led to the growing use of knowledge and information as inputs into the production of goods, as well as the production of other services. On the goods side, less labor is used in the physical production of goods and more labor is used in the processing of information supporting the production of goods. As factories automate, they need fewer workers on the assembly lines, but more workers to program computers and to design the robots. Moreover, as goods produced are more technologically complex, a larger amount of resources must be devoted to research and development, planning and marketing.

Similarly on the services side, there has been a shift from blue collar employment, involved with the physical production of services, to white collar employment, involved with handling information. Information technology has made possible new types of services. There are numerous examples. Air reservation systems have facilitated international air travel. Computer monitoring systems enable transportation companies to trace individual shipments from point of origin to final destination. Computer and information handling systems allow retailers to store large amounts of information about potential customers and to direct marketing efforts to likely buyers.

The impact of information technology on trade in services is significant. It has made trade in many services possible, practical, and more efficient. Information technology has revolutionized the international banking industry, making it possible not only to collect and exchange massive amounts of financial data, but also to transfer money instantaneously and trade in foreign exchange. In large part, information technology is responsible for the growth of the Eurodollar market. Similar transformations have occurred in the insurance, data processing, and construction/engineering industries. In the following section we discuss five developments that help explain the significant impact of information technology on trade in services.

Information Technology Has Improved the Delivery of Information-based Services

With the advent of computer-to-computer communications technology, the traditional concepts of time and distance have less meaning. Satellite and fiber optic cable technology make it possible to transmit information instantaneously. It makes little difference where in the world the buyer and seller or user and provider of electronically coded information are located. Advances in communications technology and information storage and processing have made it possible to produce services in one place and to consume them somewhere else, and to produce services at one point in time (during working hours in Dallas) and to consume them at a later point in time (during working hours in Riyadh).

Before the advent of modern communications technology, most services had to be produced where they were consumed. The production of business services, for example, was highly dependent on timely information inputs and outputs, and this made geographic proximity necesssary. Most business services had to be performed where the manufacturing took place. With modern communications and data storage and processing, however, it is possible to receive and deliver information instantly over great distances, and this means that the two activities can be separated geographically.

Furthermore, technological advances have been so great in recent years that the cost of communications is declining in real terms. The cost for a typical international voice or telex message was $3 per minute in 1970; today the cost is only a few cents (Spero 1985). Beyond a certain point, the cost of transmission does not increase with greater distance. Communication technology has progressed to the point where 64 kilobits of information can be transmitted per second with complete reliability. In the very near future, computer-communication links are expected to operate at 1.5 megabits per second.

At the same time, the technical capacities of computer-to-computer communications have risen sharply. Increased computer power has made possible major advances in computer-aided design, information storage and retrieval, electronic banking, and hundreds of other computer-based services. Any service product that can be reduced to electronically coded bits of information can be delivered to any point in the world, with great reliability, at relatively little cost and with no time lag.

The operation of a construction/engineering firm provides an illustration of the way a firm can tie together its activities through the use of information technology. With modern information technology at its disposal, the San Francisco-based Bechtel company can determine the most efficient allocation of resources to gain economies of scale. Applications of information technology allow it to better manage equipment, people, and shipping schedules to minimize the idling of resources while waiting for missing inputs. The company can take advantage of differential labor costs by employing less expensive architects in India to draft construction plans, which become instantaneously available to supervisors in one corner of the world and project managers in another. Bechtel can use up-to-the-minute financial information to get the best financing rates from New York banks and insurance from a London company. It can then manage the construction of the project in the middle of Saudi Arabia by using Korean workers, Indian architects, American managers, and European materials. Computer communications makes it all possible.

Information Technology Facilitates the Creation of New Products and Services

As it has become cheaper, faster, and more efficient to store information and to transmit information electronically, both manufacturing and service industries have taken advantage of the economies of scale made possible by the centralized production and electronic distribution of services.

Modern information technology has made it possible for banks to take advantage of economies of scale by centralizing information resources in areas such as foreign currency trading or economic forecasting on a global scale. The collection of information from a wide variety of sources in one place allows banks to provide a broad range of financial information to their customers. Without information technology, this material might not have existed in the first place, might not have been available in a useable form, or might not have been cost efficient to provide to all consumers.

In other cases, it has become more efficient to distribute the production of specialized services, while centralizing access to the total pool of services. For example, data base vendors have distributed the development and maintenance of data bases covering various fields of knowledge among many different geographic locations, while offering users centralized access. Market-oriented specialization at home leads eventually to trade. Data processing centers that initially served a limited local market now service clients around the world on a twenty-four-hour basis, and utilization of large computer centers in the United States shifts from one continent to another as users in different time zones start their work day.

Information Technology Has Led to the Development of New Production Processes

The introduction of modern communications and information technology has revolutionized manufacturing processes. More automated forms of production require less input of physical labor and materials and more input of information and knowledge. The result has been a sharp increase in the demand for professional services by scientists, engineers, designers, computer programmers, and managers, relative to the demand for blue collar labor. The end product, be it a car, television set or computer, contains more information and knowledge inputs than was the case in the past.

The American automobile industry offers a prime illustration of the way in which modern technology has revolutionized production processes. GM plans to invest $5 billion in a highly integrated manufacturing and assembly complex to produce a new, innovative small car called the Saturn. The complex will be designed to take advantage of the latest information and data processing technologies. A big part of the design work will be done by Electronic Data Systems Corporation, the Texas computer company that GM acquired for $2.5 billion last year. Computer hardware and software are expected to make up 40 percent of Saturn's total cost (General Motors/Saturn 1985).

Information technology's role in manufacturing is not limited to the production process. It plays a key role in the marketing and delivery of products. Moreover, most technologically sophisticated products require a stream of supportive services over the lifetime of the product. Often, such products can be sold only "bundled" together with the necessary supportive services in a single package. International trade in services has thus become inextricably linked to trade in goods.

The concept of bundling is clearly illustrated by the sale of computers. Twenty years ago, roughly 80 percent of the price of a typical computer package was hardware and 20 percent was in associated software. Today, this ratio is reversed. Only 20 percent of the price for a typical computer package today is related to the computer hardware, while 80 percent of the price is accounted for by such elements as:

1. *Software* to make the computer work
2. *Engineering services* to demonstrate how to use the computer and integrate it into any existing communications/information structure
3. *Systems consultant services* to ensure that the software suits the customer's needs and is appropriate for the hardware
4. *Training services* to explain how to operate the hardware
5. *On-going information services* to alert the consumer to new developments in the technology of the hardware and software or better ways to make use of the technology
6. *Maintenance* services to ensure the continued operation of the computer.[1]

Similarly, sophisticated industrial machinery and robots cannot be sold without engineering support, software, maintenance, and other supportive services. In fact, their sales are dependent on the provision of these supportive services. Increased exports of technologically sophisticated products thus leads to increases in trade in services. Any barriers to trade in such equipment can limit trade in the attendant services. Likewise, barriers to trade in software, engineering, or maintenance services, or other restrictions or limitations on services trade, can restrict trade in technologically sophisticated goods.

All of the new production processes made possible by applications of information technology create new demands for international trade in services. With the growing importance of business services to modern manufacturing processes, a manufacturing company that wants to be globally competitive needs to have access to the best service inputs available, whether at home or abroad. (This development has sharply increased international trade in business services.) The more important business services have become for efficient production, the more trade in services has grown.

Multinationals and Services Trade: The Importance of Information Technology

The growth in the number of multinational corporations and the increase in the scope of their activities has prompted a sharp rise in demand for services that can be provided on a global basis. Multinational firms find it more efficient to purchase services such as insurance or accounting from companies that can deliver the service globally and assure uniform quality, rather than by contracting with numerous suppliers around the world. Service firms have thus been quick to follow American multinational manufacturing corporations into foreign markets to serve their global needs. Once such service firms establish themselves abroad in support of their American clients, they tend to expand the scope of their activities to foreign clients. Trade in services has therefore been a natural outgrowth of the establishment of U.S. manufacturing subsidiaries abroad.

Multinational corporations make significant use of information technology on a global basis. The Organization for Economic Cooperation and Development (OECD) conducted a survey of some 200 international manufacturing and service firms from ten countries in 1982–83, in an attempt to describe the use and effect of information technology (OECD 1983). According to the firms surveyed by the OECD, the following production functions are handled through the use of information technology:

1. *Production control*, illustrated by the growth in robotics and computer-assisted manufacturing
2. *Research*, in particular the coordination of functions among research divisions or improve information resources available to staff
3. *Design/engineering*, as seen with computer-aided design, for example
4. *Marketing*, especially for transmitting information about local conditions, enabling direct ordering and arrangements for credit
5. *Distribution*, including scheduling, routing, and producing required transport or export documentation
6. *Order processing*, to tie together interdependent production facilities and eliminate unnecessary duplication
7. *Maintenance*, such as to track after-sales defects and maintenance histories and provide useful information to product designers.

Equally significant applications have been efforts to improve the internal management processes of firms through greater centralization of certain managerial support functions. According to the survey, the most important applications are in the following areas:

1. *Financial reporting and consolidation,* in particular to standardize firms' internal financial reporting
2. *Financial management,* such as for the central management of currency exposure or monitoring of credit risks
3. *Data processing,* either centralization or decentralization of this function depending on the firm
4. *Administration/clerical work,* including filing, maintenance of personnel records, bookkeeping, and, increasingly, message transfer.

As a result of the application of information technology, ordinary business activities of multinational companies have changed considerably. Multinationals have used information technology to improve global management and establish the basis for world product mandating. IBM's worldwide communications network, for example, enables it to introduce design changes in all of its manufacturing facilities on the same day. Similar facilities enable RCA to produce integrated circuits in one country, picture tubes in a second country, and to assemble the television sets in a third country.

The concepts of global management and world product mandating are equally applicable to multinational services firms that make use of information technology. Firms such as Bechtel, Citibank, Arthur Anderson, Arthur D. Little, AIG, and American Express can coordinate global operations, efficiently allocate resources, and instantaneously transmit information to ensure their competitiveness. These firms are at the forefront of the growth in international trade in services.

Multinational companies use information technology to "trade" services internationally in two distinct ways. First, they use communication channels to export and import internal managerial services such as accounting, financial reporting, and legal services from parent to subsidiary, subsidiary to subsidiary, or subsidiary to parent. Second, many multinational companies use these same communication channels to sell services to outside purchasers located in other countries. Thus, Boeing Computer Services sells data processing services performed in the United States to clients located in many parts of the world.

Modern information technology has also improved the efficient delivery of many services provided by and for smaller businesses and increased the demand for information services by households. We want and are supplied with more information about our financial transactions, about transportation possibilities, and about what is going on. We are also buying more entertainment services through cable television and video cassettes.

Networking

Applications of information technology and the tremendous growth in trade in services that it has generated has given rise to new systems, known as value-added communication networks, linking users and providers of information. Through a system encompassing computers, communications circuits, and input/output terminals, individuals at widely scattered locations can put information into the network and take information out of the network. Networking has fundamentally affected the way in which the U.S. economy functions and, by extension, the way in which the international economy will function in the future. Indeed, networks are at the heart of the post-industrial revolution.

While the common purpose is to share information, networks take different forms. Certain networks are interactive; that is, they allow the party accessing the information to add to the data base or make changes in information already stored. Other networks operate as one-way information streams.

Networks operate on three levels. First, *private networks* link individuals with common interests, allowing them to swap ideas and share information. On an intrafirm basis, private networks are used for internal corporate communications and can tie together laboratories, automated manufacturing plants, warehouses, and decisionmakers around the world. Second, *limited participation networks* facilitate the sharing of information specific to a certain industry. Third, *public networks* make available information to anyone willing to pay the access charges.

Private Networks. A number of multinational firms maintain private communications networks for internal corporate communications purposes to supplement public communications systems, such as international telephone service. Among the reasons for maintaining private networks are:

1. *Price*, particularly if the volume of transactions surpasses a certain level, economies of scale can be achieved
2. *Availability of service*, often an important factor for those firms doing business in parts of the world where communications facilities are substandard
3. *Control over system* to ensure faster response time or greater security than would be available through an industry or public network
4. *New business potential* of offering direct access to information and related information services not otherwise available to the general public.

Aside from internal communications functions, networks can serve a number of other purposes. One of these is credit authorizations. Companies that provide credit card services rely heavily on private networks to authorize purchases to prevent the use of lost or stolen cards and to prevent users from exceeding their credit limits. In addition, these companies use information technology to monitor their currency reserves, since they can have substantial cash flow problems. Future applications of information technology by such companies as VISA and MasterCard include billing and, possibly, the sale of economic information that they, like some banks, are already collecting for internal financial management.

Limited Participation Networks. Where it is economical to pool resources and cut costs of generating information of common interest to an industry, firms have grouped together on a global basis to develop industrywide networks. Access is restricted to members of the network, in many cases companies of the particular industry. Limited participation networks are widely used by firms involved in such technical services as oil exploration, where the cost of producing a data base on a company-by-company basis is extremely high. The largest users of this type of network are the airline and banking industries, both of which depend on large amounts of up-to-the-minute information in order to provide efficient, effective service.

Beginning in the late 1940s, the commercial airline industry began making extensive use of information technology to coordinate flight information. In 1947, a small group of airlines formed the Societe Internationale de Telecommunications Aeronautique (SITA), an association based in Paris that now has over 240 members. Through the SITA network, members share information about such diverse matters as seat assignment, identification of special dietary needs, credit card authorization, departure control, and meteorological information. In the future, SITA plans to expand the use of information technology to include cargo and baggage handling, flight planning, air-to-ground communications, and fare quotation services.[2]

The need for rapid and accurate information is crucial for the banking industry, as well. Information is vital to the ability of banks engaged in international business to respond quickly to changing market conditions. Yet, it is difficult for one bank, on its own, to acquire all of the international financial information it needs. There was thus a strong incentive for banks to join together in 1973 to form the London-based Society for Worldwide Interbank Financial Telecommunications (SWIFT). Initial membership included 239 banks from fifteen countries. By 1979, 513 banks participated in the network, and by 1983, SWIFT had grown to 1,017 banks in forty-four countries. Over the same period, the number of daily messages carried by the system grew from 150,000 to 350,000. Working together, banks belonging to the SWIFT network have increased their information resources and reduced the cost of individual international financial transactions.[3].

Public Networks. Public data networks have proliferated at an astounding rate in recent years. Current estimates are that there are 2,400 on-line data bases in existence today, with hundreds more being added each month. At a cost between $5 and $75 an hour, an individual can connect his personal computer to telephone lines and access these data bases from any country with adequate communication facilities (Seligman 1985).

The traditional customers for on-line data bases were research librarians. Today, the major users are professional and business executives who will actually use the information in the course of their daily work. The amount of information available to them is astounding: everything from the latest medical research on parasitic diseases, commodity futures quotations, biographies of nineteenth Century French female poets, and an individual's checking account balance.

The largest data base is Dialog Information Services, a subsidiary of Lockheed, which offers subscribers access to over 200 data bases and plans to add thirty each year in the near future. The present collection contains over 100 million records, with citations to articles in 10,000 different journals. The largest sample of media databases is maintained by Nexis, one of Mead Data Central's products, which contains the full texts of new stories and articles from the major wire services, ten newspapers, and forty-eight magazines, among other items. The list goes on and on.

The emergence of international networks and global access to wide-ranging information resources reflects a growing interdependence of worldwide economic activity. The importance of networking from an international trade perspective is that it provides an efficient channel for trade in services. Bechtel's use of information technology to tie together its far-flung operations represents international trade in engineering, consulting and management services. Citibank's use of information technology to link its global branches to corporate treasurers results in international trade in financial information services. Lockheed's use of information technology to provide access to data bases represents still another type of trade in information services.

THE ROLE FOR TRADE POLICY

Just as information technology has dramatically affected the production of goods and services and the operation of multinational firms, it has also created new issues of concern to trade policymakers. Trade policymakers have been confronted with questions such as the right to plug equipment into a communications network, the use of networks to deliver services, the transfer of information across borders, and access to information stored in foreign computers. Information technology has given a new dimension to trade policy.

To a large extent, the future competitiveness of both manufacturing and service firms will depend on access to the latest telecommunications equipment and information networks as distribution systems for the electronic delivery of information products or services. Trade policy can be a useful tool in ensuring that business opportunities are not lost because of discriminatory government restrictions in these areas.

Questions regarding barriers to trade in up-to-date telecommunications equipment and services are very much at the forefront of U.S. government concerns about foreign trade restrictions. Such concerns are frequently the subject of bilateral trade consultations. Over the past year, we have addressed a broad range of issues in this area, including the restrictive effects of computer decrees in Mexico and the Republic of Korea, informatics legislation in Brazil, policies concerning purchases of telecommunications equipment by NTT, the Japanese telecommunications monopoly, and regulations by Bundespost, the German telecommunications monopoly. Trade in telecommuncations equipment is also being discussed in the General Agreement on Tariffs and Trade (GATT), the international trade organization. The current review of the GATT Government Procurement Code, for example, will include a discussion of procurement practices by telecommunications monopolies.

Trade policy officials have also been drawn into discussions on the establishment of value added communication networks (e.g., in Japan), and the right to use such networks for the delivery of services (Japan and Germany). The business community has also expressed concern about new regulations being considered by various foreign authorities that could hamper international flows of intercorporate, intracorporate, or private data. In light of these concerns, the United States proposed in 1982 that the twenty-four developed countries of the OECD adopt a political-level commitment to minimize barriers to the flow of information. The proposal was patterned after the Trade Pledge adopted by OECD countries in 1974, which was designed to minimize the use of trade barriers in solving trade problems created by the oil crisis. Such a "data declaration"—now known as the "Declaration on Transborder Data Flows"—was adopted by OECD ministers in April 1985 at their annual meeting. It commits OECD governments to minimize barriers to the international flow of data and to develop cooperative solutions to any problems created by the introduction of new communications and data processing technologies (OECD 1985).

A third set of issues that has been addressed through trade policy channels concerns policy measures that limit the range of telecommunications equipment that can be plugged into international communications systems. Some government communications monopolies have restricted the ability of users to connect input and output devices to the communications network. While governments should have the sovereign right to assure that equipment plugged into the system does not adversely affect the system, if such actions are taken for the admitted or unadmitted purpose of limiting the sale of foreign services or equipment, then trade policy questions arise. A number of countries have been negotiating a so-called Interconnect Agreement under the auspices of the GATT, which would establish new rules in this area.

The current international trading rules of the GATT do not apply to services issues in general, nor do they deal with many of the specific trade problems cited above. To rectify this situation and lay the groundwork for the future expansion of trade in services, the United States has proposed that the GATT initiate negotiation of a framework of contractually binding rules and principles that will help liberalize trade in all service sectors. The framework would facilitate the reduction of trade barriers by establishing a set of groundrules for addressing trade problems through bilateral consultation and multilateral negotiations.

The following principles might be included in a framework agreement on services:

- *Transparency:* Laws and regulations whose purpose it is to protect domestic services industries would be notified by the parties to the agreement with the opportunities for cross-notification by other countries who view certain provisions as trade distortive.

- *National Treatment:* All parties to the agreement would assume the obligation of national treatment for those laws and regulations not notified as barriers or any future rules that would be implemented.
- *Due Process:* Countries would assure that new laws and regulations applying to services are made public with the opportunity for comments by interested parties prior to their implementation.
- *Public Monopolies:* A public monopoly involved in the provision of services would adopt an arms-length relationship between its own monopoly activities and its activities as an international competitor, a competitor domestically in other services, and as a supplier of services.
- *Dispute Settlement:* Provision would be made for dispute settlement procedures, including consultation and compensation.
- *Subsequent Commitments:* Procedures would be established for the negotiation of subsequent commitments dealing with the reduction of trade barriers, including provisions laying out these commitments and the re-balancing of concessions made.

Negotiation of an umbrella agreement would be followed, at a later stage, by negotiations designed to reduce existing barriers to trade in individual service sectors (Office of the U.S. Trade Representative 1983).

CONCLUSION

Growth prospects for the domestic service economy and for international services trade rely on the continued availability of modern communications technology and access to information resources and delivery systems. Trade policy can help ensure future growth prospects by addressing specific barriers that limit services trade opportunities and by formulating general principles, rules and procedures to govern international services trade in the future.

NOTES

1. Drawn from interviews between the authors and private sector representatives, 1984–85.
2. Based on discussions between the author and members of the Societe Internationale de Telecommunications Aeronautique, 1984–1985.
3. Based on discussions between the authors and U.S. member banks of SWIFT, 1984.

REFERENCES

General Motors Corporation/Saturn Corporation. 1985. Press releases (February 4, July 29). Detroit, MI.

Office of the U.S. Trade Representative. 1983. *U.S. National Study on Trade in the Services*. Washington, D.C.

Organization for Economic Cooperation and Development (OECD). 1983. *Transborder Data Flows in International Enterprises: Based on Results of a Joint BIRD/OECD Survey and Interviews with Firms*. Number DSTI/ICCP/82.23. Paris.

Organization for Economic Cooperation and Development (OECD). 1985. *Declaration on Transborder Data Flows*. Press release, PRESS/A(85)30 (April 11). Paris.

Seligman, Davis. 1985. "Life Will Be Different When We're All On-Line." *Fortune* (February 4).

Spero, Joan. 1985. *International Trade and the Information Revolution*. Cambridge, MA: Harvard University Press.

U.S. Council of Economic Advisors (CEA). 1985. *Economic Indicators February 1985*. Washington, D.C.

DISCUSSION OF CHAPTER 5
Donald A. Hicks

Feketekuty-Hauser offer clear illustrations of a variety of impacts of new forms of information-based international trade in the services. These diverse impacts include at least four major ones. The first three are generally familiar and significantly interrelated; only their dimensions are new to us. The fourth impact raises disturbing issues largely because of its novelty.

First, the *range* of tradeables has been expanded enormously. Today, research and development, data processing, and the whole panoply of services tied to expertise of one type or another—for example, management, legal, and financial services—are able to be traded in international markets.[1] Second, new technologies have expanded the *scale* of trade relationships so dramatically as to eliminate what once appeared to be "natural" barriers to long-distance trade. Twenty-four-hour trading illustrates clearly the way in which the constraints imposed by older time-distance relationships are being swept aside; the work day and work week are losing their ability to organize economic activity as new applications of existing technology wring the diurnal cycle out of services trade. Third, the *speed* of trade has increased dramatically as the exchange of new services now piggybacks on the speed of light. And finally, the *reach* of new technologies and their new combinations challenges traditional conceptions of privacy and accessibility. As data bases proliferate, files can be easily merged to reconstruct increasingly fleshed out profiles of individuals, firms, and other units of analysis. This data pooling capacity poses as yet poorly understood threats to our traditional conceptions of privacy, freedom, and property rights. The rapid development of such synthetic data bases for commercial reasons raises further issues concerning restricted access to proprietary information sources for examination of public interest issues.

Together, these impacts lend proportions to information-based services trade that have the power to intimidate. There is broad agreement that something that expansive, that telescopic as well as microscopic, that disregarding of time and space must be a threat! But is it necessary to view the newest form of information-based services trade as a species apart? Probably not. It may be worth reminding ourselves of the many important ways in which what we are experiencing is really not a radical departure from what we have known for a long time.

REWIRING INDUSTRIAL PROCESSES AND PLACES

The rise of information-based services trade represents at best simply one—and perhaps not the most consequential—form of adjustment to ongoing industrial change. From this perspective, much-heralded new information technologies can be viewed as simply reinforcing a number of ongoing advanced industrial developments. First, the new services trade illustrates the continued mechanization of services. Increasing capital intensity, dependence on special labor inputs, and the rise of new markets near and far indicate a growing interdependence, rather than an antagonism, between goods and services production. The reconstructed and rewired central business districts that have sprung up in major cities around the nation since the late 1970s offer a physical illustration of changing ways in which the "city" itself serves as a production technology—and not simply as a situs for other technologies—for an evolving industrial economy.

Second, the corporation itself is a form of technology that has adapted to a global economy through the rise of multilocational/multinational firms. The significance of this development rivals—and predates—that of the diffusion of computer-based communication technologies. As a result, new products, new markets, and even new capacities for production itself dispersed, thereby bringing entire regions into the industrial mainstream.

I come from the South, which has long been viewed as the land of branch plants and inferiority complexes, and I cannot resist noting that the new trade in the services evokes the long-familiar issue of the "extended workbench" that, at the regional level, has been accompanied by the persistent concern that ever greater portions of industrial activity would be siphoned off to the South and West. This search for lower labor cost environments was expected seriously to undercut our industrial core regions. Increasingly extended and complex production arrangements since before World War II have indeed transformed the South dramatically into what today is the locus of the bulk of the nation's total output, manufacturing, and population. What was once a remote low-cost production platform for the industrial North and Midwest is now recognized as an arc of regional economies capable of incubating the greatest part of their new industrial development rather than being dependent on spinoffs from other regions.

In this context, the impacts of new information technologies may be as much the consequence of larger changes in the economy as the cause of them. For example, today Dallas hosts perhaps the world's largest cluster of telecommunications firms, a large and rapidly expanding computer software and data processing services complex, and the third largest and fastest growing high-technology sector in the United States. This capacity has been developing all through the post–World War II period, and today the bulk of the resulting employment is tied to older and larger firms. Places like Dallas have developed into industrial assets rather than simply industrial appendages.

MAGNIFYING THE ROLE OF SMALL BUSINESS

Advanced industrial development not only broadens the industrial base in a geographic sense, but also amplifies the contributions of firms whose size was once a major impediment to the scale and scope of their activities. Information technologies permit even the newest and smallest of businesses to participate in a global economy. Using Texas as an example again, a third of the Dallas area's high-tech firms have been established during the 1980s alone. Yet, a fifth of these firms have an explicit international trade orientation (see Table 5D–1). While this tendency appears to be less pronounced in the business services (SIC 73) in general, a growing body of research indicates that the expanded scale of new small firms in selected high-tech service sectors such as

Table 5D-1. International Export Orientation of High-technology Firms in the Dallas–Forth Worth Regional Economy.

Sic	Industry	Total Number of Firms	Number of Exporting Firms	Percent Exporting
28	Chemical and allied products	15 (1.9%)	1	6.7%
35	Non-electrical machinery	20 (2.5)	4	20.0
36	Electrical and electronic equipment	222 (28.1)	59	26.6
37	Transportation equipment	8 (1.0)	3	37.5
38	Instruments and related products	156 (19.8)	60	38.5
73	Business services	369 (47.7)	31	8.4
	TOTAL	790 (100.0%)	158	20.0%

Source: Hicks and Stolberg (1984).

computer services (SIC 737) is increasingly commonplace. Figure 5D–1 reports that nearly one fifth of the computer services firms in the state of Texas report international target markets for their major product.

NATIONAL BORDERS AND INFORMATION-BASED TRADE

Information-based technologies and the trade they facilitate appear to be more evolutionary than revolutionary from this perspective. Given the rate and scale of the diffusion of the underlying technologies, the resulting trade is invisible and instantaneous. Consequently, it is also regarded as disorderly. Existing trade balances, statuses, and relationships become volatile and unenforceable viewed from the perspective of nation-states. As a result, policy questions arise that revolve around how to define comparative advantages in information-based services trade. Once defined, how do we maintain them? And what are the distortions in trade resulting from protectionist impulses?

While the adjustment difficulties of national governments are predictable, they are not to be discounted or casually dismissed. Rapid diffusion of technology can lead to a climate in which ongoing investment in

Figure 5D-1. Computer Software and Data Processing Services (SIC 737): Target Market for Major Product.

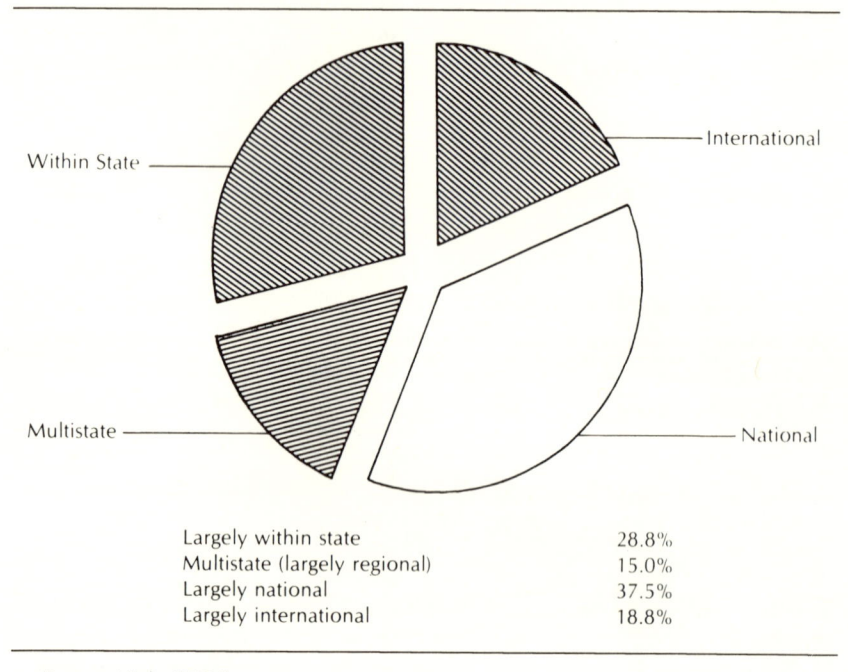

Largely within state	28.8%
Multistate (largely regional)	15.0%
Largely national	37.5%
Largely international	18.8%

Source: Hicks (1984).

innovations can be inhibited. Accelerated product cycles can undercut the expected returns on research and development by industry so drastically that new investment may be dampened. When the products are intangible and able to be traded globally via information flows, the result can look like disorder. What balance can be struck between maintaining our competitive advantages in information-based services trade without imposing explicit or subtle barriers either to that trade or to the continued development and application of technologies on which this trade is based? Perhaps there are useful insights to be gained by examining early international exchanges involving innovations in goods production more than a century ago.

LESSONS FROM THE PAST?

In the mid-nineteenth century, we were the Japan of our day, depending heavily on rapid adoption and imitation. In London in 1851, the

Crystal Palace was set up by Queen Victoria and Prince Albert to showcase state-of-the-art manufactures in the wake of industrialization. Americans were eager visitors. Two years later in 1853, the Crystal Palace in New York City attracted a British delegation to study what looked to them to be "the American system of manufactures." They were evidently blind to the fact that much of what they saw was borrowed from Europe originally! The factory system, interchangeable parts, and the division of labor constituted the new industrial infrastructure of this mass production revolution.[2] The key to our success with mechanized production was the widespread application to a variety of industries. It was this early "trade" in ideas that led to the subsequent explosion of goods production in the United States. As was to be the case at the interregional level a century later, the industrial development of the United States did not come at the expense of the industrializing nations of Europe as much as it was a healthy extension of it.

DISTINGUISHING TECHNOLOGY DIFFUSION FROM INNOVATION

Today, it is widely noted that our competitive advantages lie more in our capacity to innovate than in the trade that flows from innovation, yet this may be only partly true. In information-based services trade, just as in the early development of a goods production capacity, comparative advantages hinge on the pace and range of new applications of existing technologies. The capacity to spur diffusion may be every bit as imporant as the fostering of innovation.

In several important respects, new forms of services trade are not as novel or unfamiliar as they are often portrayed. Indeed, we have always had an information-based services economy. Originally, the linking technologies of transportation and communication were inevitably combined. It was not until the rise of the pure communication technologies during the nineteenth century that the message could be sent without the messenger. Yet, the marvelous and even awesome impacts of technology that so command our attention today are more wisely regarded as reflections of their diffusion, rather than their innovation.

In recent decades, it has been the *diffusion* of new communication capabilities throughout the economy that arguably has been at least as important to the rise of information-based goods and services production as have been new technological innovations themselves. The wider application of telecommunications to new industries, the resulting integration via "networking," and the synergy provided by feedback from consumers are principally the consequences of this widespread diffusion. That this capacity now permits transborder services flows may have the larger impact of broadening the base of advanced industrial economies throughout the world.

Nations must retain the capacity and incentives for creative application and commercialization of existing technologies. And that process may be greatly impeded by attempting to make new forms of information-based trade abide now largely irrelevant national borders. In the end, the innovations that result in tomorrow's technologies and trade are rooted in today's open exposure to new ideas and demands. Continued efforts to negotiate a free and open trade environment in information-based services probably offer the best opportunity for the gains made by our trading partners to supplement, rather than supplant, our own.[3]

NOTES

1. Nevertheless, this expansion has been accompanied by a declining trade surplus in services as well as a modest contraction in the U.S. share of world services trade in recent years. As Shelp has correctly noted, however, recent efforts to identify and negotiate the dismantling of barriers to services trade abroad do not obviate the need to allocate greater resources to vigorous export promotion of services. See Shelp (1984).
2. For a series of excellent discussions of the ways in which new technological capacities shaped early goods production in the United States, see Mayr and Post (1981).
3. To a considerable extent, frustration with the fact that other nations are exploiting our policy of open services trade has not led to increased support among major U.S. services firms for retaliation or the adoption of restrictive trade policies by the United States. For the results of a 1983 Price Waterhouse survey of 220 companies from among the Fortune Services 500 companies having foreign operations, see "Business Views on International Trade in the Services" (1984).

REFERENCES

"Business Views on International Trade in the Services." 1984. In *The Service Economy and Industrial Change*. Hearing before the U.S. Congress Joint Economic Committee (April):93–249.

Hicks, Donald A. 1984. "Computer Software and Data Processing Services: Development Characteristics of a High-Technology Service Industry in Texas." (Governor's Office of Economic Development and the Texas Computer Industry Council, Austin, Texas) Center for Policy Studies, University of Texas–Dallas (July).

Hicks, Donald A., and William H. Stolberg. 1984. "The High-Technology Sector: Growth and Development in the Dallas–Forth Worth Regional Economy 1964–1984." Center for Applied Research, University of Texas-Dallas (October).

Mayr, Otto, and Robert C. Post. eds. 1981. *Yankee Enterprise: The Rise of the American System of Manufactures.* Washington, D.C.: Smithsonian Institution Press.

Shelp, Ronald K. 1984. "The Service Economy Gets No Respect." *Across the Board* (February):49–54.

DISCUSSION OF CHAPTER 5
Gérard Pogorel

New information and communication technologies (NICT) are having a great impact on both the manufacturing and the service sectors of the world economy. New products have been created. Efficient management procedures are implemented, coordinating the activities of highly complex organizations (especially matrix form, which combines vertical and horizontal links). The new technology calls into question the division between markets and hierarchies, multinational enterprises (MNEs) and small businesses, large and small nations. The strategies of a few worldwide corporations promoting the use of NICT is assuming a major importance.

The information and communication sector, in particular, is undergoing an industrialization process that is characterized by differentiation and specialization. A division of labor is taking place that is international in scope. The process is capital intensive, substituting capital for labor. It is complementary to changes in production processes in manufacturing and favors the full-scale application of an efficient factor allocation.

WHAT ARE THE BEARINGS OF NICT IN THE PRESENT WORLD SITUATION?

NICT offers the world opportunities but are perceived by many countries as a major threat: These technologies can very easily bring changes in the location of activities and losses in employment. The liberalization in the trade in goods has been accompanied by large flows of international investment. MNEs have relied, at least partially, on a strategy of local production. Whatever reactions may have arisen, employment opportunities are still a strong argument for governments to invite foreign companies to establish themselves and gain access to more or less protected markets. A local establishment and local jobs are no more necessary for service activities using NICT. A representative of an artists' and comedians' union once told me that screen actors are the only people who can watch themselves working while they are unemployed. Technology creates jobs, but where? In his book *Stolen Memories* an adviser to a French Minister of Industry noted that the economies of scale in existing data banks and related services might deprive all but a very few countries in the world of their own data storage and retrieval capacity (Lorenzi and LeBoucher 1978). The extended use of NICT in the service sector presents the possibility of a delocation process affecting many activities—science and technology, research and development, culture and information pertaining to the social and political system—that many countries consider essential parts of their very being.

These fears may be called into question. No such process is taking place for the moment. As for the cultural argument, it is often simply a disguise for preserving more mundane vested interests. Furthermore, the delocation of activities is no news in economics, and its outcome has often been positive.

The liberalization of trade in services depends on the international negotiations now underway at the GATT. There are many obstacles that will have to be overcome before these negotiations can promote an open and balanced international trade policy system. We will review some of these difficulties and offer an analysis of the attitudes held by some of those involved in the negotiations.

First, liberalization of trade in manufactures took place in a different time. New participants have now to be considered. Currently there are two categories of third world countries: the ones who are developing and all the others. Japan has asserted its position in the world economy. European countries are at a critical point. As a whole, the international economy is more multilateral than it used to be. International negotiating exercises are more complex. Protectionism in services exists at the outset and concerns markets that have long been considered national in their very nature. Although technological change renders this concept obsolete, longstanding attitudes are hard to overcome.

Second, we have to consider the present situation of comparative advantages. American companies have taken proper advantage of the opportunities with which history has provided them. In most sectors they have achieved a dimension unknown to their foreign counterparts. They have combined economies of scale and economies of scope to gain a competitive edge on the world market. Let us take an example on the telecommunications market. GTE Corporation is a relatively small competitor by U.S. standards, yet even before deregulation it had more subscribers than the German Bundespost and the French Telecoms Agency put together. Therefore, Americans and Europeans have opposite points of view. Americans are proud of their achievements, as they should be. They invite everyone to follow their lead and think in terms of market competition. Europeans think in terms of "cooperation" or organized technology transfer. They would like programs to be developed between companies on the European market before competition can take place. An example is the European Strategical Program in Information Technology (ESPRIT), which offers a 1.2 billion dollars community budget (in 1984) for sixty-six cooperative research programs. When high-technology imports from the United States or Japan cannot be avoided, Europeans would like joint ventures to ease their impact.

This may sound terribly heretical to some, especially to those economists trained to believe in the virtues of the marketplace. Yet, we must understand that Europeans perceive a renewed "technology gap," and they believe in the basic superiority of consciously determined social action as a rectifying agent over the uncertainties of the open sea.

This can be referred to as the peculiarity of comparative advantages in service and high-technology activities. They have no root in basic factor endowments (natural resources, cheap labor, or abundant capital). They belong to the category of "dynamic" comparative advantages, so that nearly every country hopes it might achieve such an advantage. This results in renewed advocacy for the infant industry argument, which means many "temporary" trade barriers.

Third, we have to face the fact that the short-term cost of protection in service is very low. We can approximate its order of magnitude by using the X-efficiency approach: The cost of monopolistic structures on any of the big consumer markets amounts to about 1 or 2 percent of the price of the service (Leibenstein 1981). Another measure of the cost is the moderate extra charge to telephone users imposed by a monopoly. By both of these measures the order of magnitude is the same. These are not high costs to pay, especially if one believes that this protectionism contributes to the fulfillment of national objectives and to the preservation of the economic, social, and political order.

But these are only short-term considerations. Higher competition standards are not only meant to bring a 1 to 2 percent price advantage. There is the important long-term impact that the market structure has on the innovative process. Some countries are ready to pay, or have the taxpayers pay, for the flow of their national culture through the new channels.

Finally, countries and international trade policy systems are losing their resistance to sectional policy pressures. Many national economies are functioning, more or less, as generalized corporate systems. Economic sectors are acting as lobbies to protect themselves from foreign competition. Also, the people living in industrialized countries (with no exception) are acting as a kind of lobby to protect themselves from foreign manpower.

We may conclude on an optimistic note. There are a few hints that certain barriers are slowly breaking down. With the prospect of a way out of the world economic crisis, Europeans are gaining the confidence to make changes. In fact, change can be observed at the top levels of government and business. Leaders in Europe, and maybe elsewhere, know that a failure in promoting an open and balanced international trade policy system in the field of new information and communication technology would signal the end of the benefits of the international structure.

REFERENCES

Leibenstein, H. 1981. "Microeconomics and X-Efficiency Theory." In *The Crisis in Economic Theory*, edited by D. Bell and I. Kristol. New York: Basic Books.

Lorenzi, J.-H., and E. LeBoucher. 1978. *Mémoires Volées*. Paris: Economica.

DISCUSSION OF CHAPTER 5
Ronald Kent Shelp

The role of service industries in the development process is one of the most ignored economic questions of the twentieth century. Services have played second fiddle in economic thought to what many consider the more important elements of economic production—manufacturing and agriculture. It is no surprise, therefore, that service technologies have been ignored as well. In fact, the association of services with technology at all has only come about in recent years with the revolutionary advances in the new information technologies.

While there is neither a theoretical nor an empirical basis to support the conclusion that information technologies are essential for economic progress, fascination with these technologies has so captured public imagination that there is little argument that they are. Disagreement does arise, however, over the appropriate role of foreign suppliers of information technology in national development plans.

This fundamental issue is at the core of the current debate over establishing international rules within GATT (General Agreement on Tariffs and Trade) to govern service trade. While trade in information technology is only one aspect of these discussions, to many it is the most important.

TRADE RULES FOR SERVICES

The notion of establishing trade rules for services had its germination in the United States in the early 1970s when American service firms, confronted with a multitude of foreign barriers, began to demand help from government. One result was the inclusion of services in the Trade Act of 1974. Pressed by a coalition of service businesses—construction, airlines, insurance, travel services—Congress took an historic first in trade legislation when it extended most U.S. trade laws to services and urged the administration to negotiate international rules governing service trade.

This launched a twelve-year effort that first bore fruit in November 1984 when the GATT contracting parties established a working group to study services trade. The United States, as the leader of this effort, hopes this working party will conclude that service trade rules are needed. If the industrial nations launch a new round of trade negotiations in the next few years, the United States has demanded, with support from Japan and several European nations, that services be a principal concern in negotiations.

At first glance one wonders why services, a trading activity estimated by the London-based Committee on Invisible Exports to have reached $700 billion in world trade in 1983, is outside the international system of trading rules. One would assume this oversight would be relegated to the past and the fastest growing sector of international trade would be integrated now into the trading system. For several reasons this is not the case.

First, there is a basic conceptual problem with the subject of services trade. Not only has trade theory ignored services, but the broader subject of the economics of services itself has been ignored as well. Colin Clark (1957), the Australian economist, summed it up well when he said, "The economics of tertiary industries remain to be written. Many as yet feel uncomfortable at even admitting their existence."

If a theoretical understanding of service economics is nonexistent, little wonder none exists for service trade. Instead, discussions of service trade seem only to raise a series of tough, unresolvable issues. For example, since the consumer takes part in the production, how can the service be traded—that is, how can a service be produced in one country and consumed in another? Or, since a service cannot be stored, how can it be exported? And, even if some services can be traded, are there benefits from such trade?

In the case of goods and commodities, the theory of comparative advantage is widely accepted as rationalizing the benefits of trade, but there is no such agreement about trade in services. Many ask whether comparative advantage really applies. Even if it does, are not services so linked to other national concerns—cultural pride, national security, individual welfare—that it would be contrary to the national interest to permit them to be traded?

A second basic problem is the dismal lack of data on services trade. Even the United States' data on service trade, which is the best available, is totally inadequate. For example, government commissioned studies indicate that in 1980 United States' service exports ranged somewhere between $60 and $120 billion. Compounding the problem is the lack of disaggregation in the service data that does exist. There is general data by category, but sparse data on the individual industries within a category. Without this, it is very difficult to make decisions on the impact and the benefits of trade liberalization in services.

A third major issue is rooted in the fear of many nations that the United States has an overwhelming comparative advantage in service trade. After all, the United States is the first and largest service economy. The service sector employs 74 percent of the workforce (U.S. Dept. of Commerce 1984) and provides 67 percent of GNP (U.S. Dept. of Labor 1984). Most years, trade surpluses have offset merchandise deficits. The United States' aggressiveness in pushing for international trade negotiations on services has only reinforced these fears.

CHANGING VIEWS OF TRADING NATIONS

When the United States first suggested negotiating trade rules for services, she received little support from other nations. This situation has changed dramatically, especially in the European Community. At first the Community and its individual members were either hesitant or outright opposed to the suggestion that international trade rules for services were necessary. Even the United Kingdom, whose major export is services, showed little interest. This has changed as the Community and its members have come to understand their stake in services trade.

In 1983, the Commission of the European Communities conducted a study on the significance of service trade to both the Community and its member countries. Highlights of its findings were announced by Leslie Fielding, Director General for External Relations of the EC Commission, in a speech in London in October 1983. Mr. Fielding said, "The European Community is the world's largest producer of services, accounting for 36 percent of world exports of services, three times as much as the United States."

Perhaps most startling of the Commission's findings was the fact that three members—France, Germany, and the United Kingdom—each have service exports approximating between 60 and 75 percent of U.S. service exports. The Commission study also discovered what the United States has long known: Services are vital to employment. Of the 19 million jobs created in the 1970s in the United States, 17 million, some 89 percent, were created by service industries (U.S. Dept. of Labor 1984). There has been similar service job creation in Europe, although it has not been as dramatic. Between 1973 and 1981, when 4 million manufacturing jobs were lost in the Community, 3.4 million new jobs were created in "market services"—that is, nongovernment services (Commission of the European Communities 1983).

These revelations have brought about a dramatic change in the views of the European Community. Now it supports "the need to examine the introduction of service trade into the international trading system of rules" (Commission of the European Communities 1983). Not all Community nations share this view. France continues to be opposed. One reason is that the European Community study was unable to determine what services (and what nations) would benefit from service trade liberalization.

Japan on the other hand has been supportive of the United States' position from the beginning. Prime Minister Nakasone was the first head of state to announce support for a service trade negotiation. Cynics attribute Japanese support to the strong pressure Japan has received to reduce its huge trade surplus with the United States and other countries. Since Japan has a deficit in service trade with the United States, it would be to her advantage to be generous in an area of weakness. Liberalization of service trade deflects attention from the merchandise deficit, according to the argument.

Whether this assertion is valid or not, the important point is that the Japanese are serious about services. Prime Minister Nakasone, speaking before the Japan society after the Williamsburg Summit in 1983, said one of Japan's most formidable problems was managing the transformation to a post-industrial economy.

Apparently, there is fierce competition within the Japanese government to address this issue. The Ministry of International Trade and

Investment (MITI), Ministry of Foreign Affairs, and the Japanese Planning Agency have all established service study groups. These agencies have led delegations of Japanese businessmen to the United States and Europe to study services trade. Clearly, Japan has concluded that services, especially information-based services, are high priority activities central to future competitiveness. She is preparing herself to compete in this sector as she prepared herself to compete in traditional and high-tech industries.

DEVELOPING COUNTRY OPPOSITION

Most developing countries have strongly resisted the effort to discuss international trade in services in the international organizations. Brazil has led the opposition with strong support from India. The reasons vary. Brazil has taken a traditional infant industry view towards services. She argues that indigenous service industries, like other industries, should be protected until they are able to compete with foreign service industries. India, which is not as strongly opposed to a services exercise as Brazil, is less precise about her concerns. There seems to be sympathy with the infant industry perspective, as well as a fear that the jobs now provided in India by services will be threatened with foreign competition. The Indians frankly admit that they do not know enough about the subject and that in-depth studies are necessary.

While Brazil and India have spearheaded the opposition to trade in services, with the sympathy of many other developing nations, this block is no more unified on this issue than on most others. Several actually are supportive of an effort to liberalize service trade. Hong Kong and Singapore are service economies already and have prospered through an open service environment. Nevertheless, no developing nation or regional group of developing countries has seen the issues defined in a way that leads them to go against the leadership of the newly industrialized nations like India and Brazil and fight forcefully for the inclusion of services on a GATT agenda.

SERVICE TRADE AND INFORMATION TECHNOLOGIES

While international dialogue about services trade has been underway for ten years, the subject of information technologies has only come to the forefront of these discussions in the last few years. Until very recently the trade barriers faced by traditional service industries—banking, insurance, construction, engineering, transportation, travel, and professional services—have dominated the discussions. But the remarkable technological change that has occurred in recent years has brought about a shift in focus.

The world has become enamored of the new information technologies. Nations as different as France and Brazil have embraced a vision that holds the new technologies as the key to a prosperous future. Those who possess them will be rich and competitive. Those who do not will fall behind. While the term "new technologies" covers a broad range of economic activities, in the popular parlance, "information technologies" has become almost interchangeable with new technologies.

COMPETITIVENESS IN INFORMATION TECHNOLOGIES

While there is little dissent from the international consensus that securing the new information technologies is essential to the national interest of virtually every nation, there is division about the best way to attain these technologies. One view is that the best way to keep up with technological change is to maintain open markets. Countries that encourage the free flow of trade in the products and services related to information technologies are those likely to keep abreast of the latest advancements. Perhaps most characteristic of this philosophy is the United States, a nation having an admitted edge in these technologies.

The other view is that the best way to achieve a national goal of technology competitiveness is to undertake a massive indigenous effort to develop information technology industries. Inherent in this approach is the philosophy that while they are developing they must be protected from outside competition. This is, in other words, a variation of the classic infant industry approach. Brazil, the leading nation in opposition to examining service trade in GATT (or anywhere else), is an example of this attitude. She has implemented a strongly protectionist plan to encourage the development of her informatics sector.

While the developing world is not unified on which approach to take, most would find themselves taking an approach to development that has been characteristic of the developing world. A 1984 meeting of the Trade and Development Board of the United Nations Conference on Trade and Development (UNCTAD) considered the broad subject of service trade for the first time. The Secretariat paper prepared for the meeting was a well researched, extensive, fairly dispassionate treatise on the subject. While it did not make basic policy choices between liberalization or protection, it did observe that services have a little understood role in the development process and recognized that the information revolution will make many previously nontraded services tradable. It also raised the specter of neocolonialism with the warning that transnational companies would be able to dominate service trade and relegate developing nations to the low-skilled aspects of data processing. So, by implication, it leaned towards the traditional approach.

FINDING THE BEST PATH

If there was a theoretical body of knowledge, supported by empirical evidence, that clearly demonstrated the advantages of liberalized trade in the information-based service technologies, it would be much easier to deal with this subject. Regretably, an examination of whether the principle of comparative advantage applies to trade in services, especially information services, has not been undertaken. For developing countries, such an examination must include the basic role of services in economic development.

Although the theoretical literature and empirical evidence is scant, some does exist. For example, the recent book *Service Industries in Economic Development—Case Studies in Technology Transfer* (Shelp et al. 1984) is an interesting examination of this subject, which looks at three companies, American International Group, Bechtel, and Sears, Roebuck and their activities in a variety of developing countries. The book draws some interesting conclusions about this long-ignored subject. It concludes that services play a very positive role in development, a role that has been not only misunderstood but overlooked. While the case studies in this book do not focus directly on the information technologies, clearly all three of these companies utilize these technologies.

More work of this nature must be carried out. I suspect the results of such studies will persuade the developing nations of the benefits of liberalized trade in services just as the European Community study persuaded them. More than likely, empirical research will support the thesis of Jagdish Bhagwati of Columbia University, who argues that the developing nations have a comparative advantage in what he calls the over-the-wire transmission of engineering, medical, legal and other services.

This theory can already be demonstrated by example. Lawyers in Korea receive a request from a New York affiliate in the United States to undertake legal research. Their findings are transmitted by means of a combination of computer and telecommunication technologies to a data base storage facility in the Midwest. From there, the information can be accessed by law firm affiliates in London and Milan.

Developing nations can benefit enormously from such activities. They introduce new technologies, create jobs, and generate revenue.

There is an irony here, however. As the developing nations come to appreciate the benefits of free flow of information and trade in the new information technologies, a counterreaction is likely to occur in the industrial countries, including those that today favor liberalization, such as the United States. As they begin to understand the potential "export of jobs" associated with these technologies, especially those associated with moving the back office function overseas, they may have second thoughts.

This is the price that has to be paid for maximizing the benefits of trade in anything, be it goods, commodities, or services. There are gains and losses on both sides. What at the moment looks like an overwhelming advantage for the United States, and perhaps a few other countries, may prove to be quite different in the long run.

REFERENCES

Clark, Colin. 1957. *The Conditions of Economic Progress.* New York: St. Martin's Press.

Commission of the European Communities. 1983. Unpublished study.

Fielding, Leslie. 1983. Speech to Chamber of Commerce of the North Sea Ports London (October 21).

Nakasone, Yasuhiro. 1983. Speech before Japan Society, New York (May 31).

Shelp, Ronald K.; John C. Stephenson; Nancy Sherwood Truit; and Barnard Wasow. 1984. *Service Industries in Economic Development—Case Studies in Technology Transfer.* New York: Praeger.

U.S. Department of Commerce, National Income Office Bureau of Economic Analysis. 1984.

U.S. Department of Labor, Bureau of Labor Statistics, Employment, and Earnings. 1984.

6 INFORMATION TECHNOLOGY AND THE UNITED STATES ECONOMY: MODELING AND MEASUREMENT

Charles Jonscher

Fritz Machlup published in 1962 a study of the extent to which labor and nonlabor resources were used in the United States for the creation and processing of information as opposed to physical goods. Since then numerous analyses of a similar kind have been carried out—by Peter Drucker (1968), Daniel Bell (1973), Marc Porat (1977), and again Machlup (1980) among others. Although the exact findings depend on how information products or services are defined, the general conclusion emerging is that half of all economic activity in the United States can be attributed to the processing of knowledge or facts rather than physical goods, and that the proportion is increasing with time.

In this chapter we analyze the two major structural changes that have been measured by such studies, and these structural changes are apparent to any casual observer of a modern industrial economy. The first is the increasing demand for information technology as a proportion of demand for all technology. The second is the increasing demand for information or white collar labor as a proportion of demand for total labor.

Even though such structural trends are observed and measured at the macro level, they can properly be modeled and explained only at the

---

I am grateful to Dale Murphy for extensive assistance with the empirical research undertaken for this paper. This work was supported by grants from the National Science Foundation and the Bureau of the Census.

micro level—in terms of increasing demand by individual producing units (firms) or consuming units (households) for information technology and information labor services. In this chapter we will develop a simple analytic framework that will allow the separate sources of these macroeconomic changes to be identified and measured.

In particular, we will use this framework to ascertain whether the trend towards increased use of information resources (information technology and information labor) is primarily a demand-side or supply-side phenomenon. Is it occurring primarily because consumer demand is shifting in favor of goods and services that are in some sense information intensive—such as entertainment, educational, and professional services? Or is it occurring primarily because the technology and organization of economic supply is requiring greater information resources to manage and coordinate production activities? We will find that it is our second question that provides the right answer. The implications of this finding for future trends in productivity and employment are analyzed in another paper by this author (Jonscher 1983).

THE MODEL

The model is based on two kinds of labor occupation—information labor and production labor—and on two kinds of commodity—information services and production goods. Information and production workers produce information services and production goods, respectively. Broadly speaking, an information worker is one whose primary activity is to handle and process information. In this category we find managers, clerical workers, and accountants. Construction and factory workers are examples of production workers whose primary activity is to handle and process material goods. The distinction is roughly the same as the one between white collar and blue collar occupations.

The task of identifying the pattern of labor expenditures on information activities is made practicable by the very high degree of occupational specialization present in modern societies. We use occupational categories as the primary instrument for distinguishing information processing from production activity. If a person is classified in labor statistics as a billing clerk, we may be reasonably confident that his or her primary functions are to prepare and process bills; these are information handling activities associated with the management, organization, and coordination of economic activity. Consequently, a billing clerk is classified as an information rather than a production worker. Conversely, if a person is classified as a sheet metal worker we assume that his primary function is to work sheet metal and not to process economic information; we categorize him as a producer. Sometimes the billing clerk may help to unload a delivery truck (production, not information handling), and the sheet metal worker may fill out timesheets (information handling, not production); but these activities are the exception rather than the rule.

A few worker types are more difficult to classify; in these cases we have to make a (sometimes rather arbitrary) choice. For example, actors and other entertainers do not fit the classification scheme neatly. A foreman is an important instance of an "ambiguous" occupation. While some of a typical foreman's time is spent doing the same job as his subordinates, much of it is spent monitoring, supervising, and keeping time records. Fortunately, for our purposes, the number of occupations for which classification problems of this kind arise is a very small proportion of the total. The great majority, perhaps 95 percent, of the working population can be identified with reasonable confidence as fitting one or the other of our categories. The results of the classification exercise that we have undertaken for this study are presented in the appendix. The first section of the appendix contains a complete list of the occupations we have assigned in the information sector.

As to the classification of commodities, an information service is, by definition, the product of the work of an information worker and a good is, by definition, the product of the work of a production worker. This means that the definition of goods in our model includes certain commodities that are generally defined as services but which do not have the character of information services; examples are the output of an automobile repair shop or a trucking company.

The inputs and outputs of an information worker's and a production worker's activity are illustrated diagrammatically in Figure 6–1. The boxes represent labor activity, and the arrows, flow of goods and services. Throughout this paper, boxes and arrows are drawn with solid lines if they represent production labor and goods, and with broken lines if they represent information labor and services.

In the analysis that follows we will be concerned with the *net* output of goods and information services produced respectively by production and information workers—that is, the output net, respectively, of goods and services used as inputs. We will use the following terminology to describe the inputs and outputs associated with a single information worker:

Figure 6-1. The Inputs and Outputs to Production and Information Labor Processes.

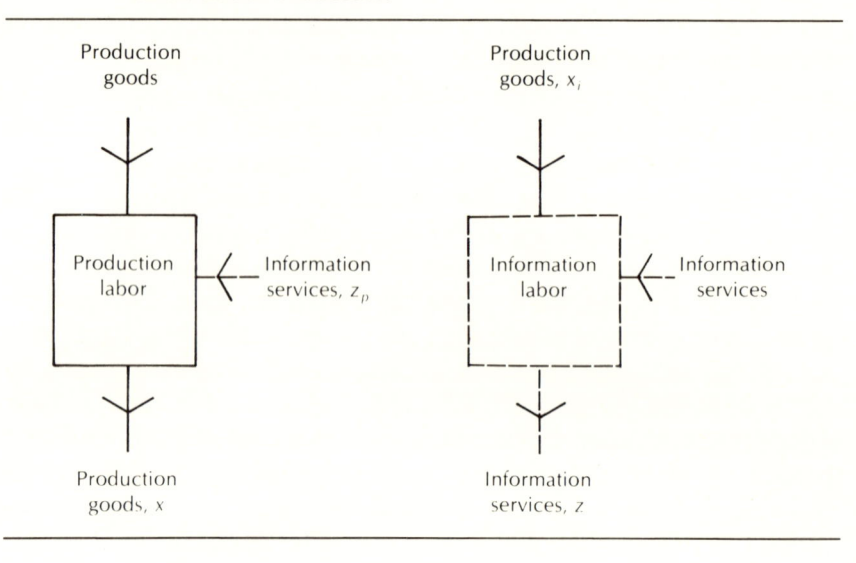

x_i: Input of goods used by information worker
z: Net output of information services (net of all inputs except information labor and x_i).

In the case of a production worker inputs and outputs we will use the following terminology:

z_p: Input of information services used by production worker
x: Net output of goods (net of all inputs except production labor and z_p).

We define the following coefficients linking the levels of input and output of each type of worker:

$$a_z = z_p/x$$
$$a_x = x_i/z.$$

A particularly important category of goods used as inputs by information workers is information technology—goods such as computers, telecommunications systems, and office automation equipment. In the empirical analysis that follows we will identify the flow x_i as the use of information technology by information workers. The coefficient a_x

therefore measures the value of information technology used to produce each dollar's worth of output of information services.

The delivery of a good or service to the final consumer involves a chain of production and information activities, each activity taking as inputs both production goods and information services. Consider, for example, the provision of a production good, such as a manufactured product. The last few steps in the chain leading to that delivery are illustrated in Figure 6–2. Manufacturing is a production activity but uses as inputs both production technology services (e.g., machine tools) and information services (e.g., management and administration of the manufacturing process). The manufacture of machine tools is similarly a production activity using both kinds of input; the provision of management services is an information activity using production good inputs (e.g., office equipment, telephones) and information services (e.g., banking). Throughout the figure a box is drawn with a solid line if it represents production labor; with a broken line, if it represents information labor.

Figure 6-2. Chains of Production and Information Activity: Case 1, A Manufactured Product.

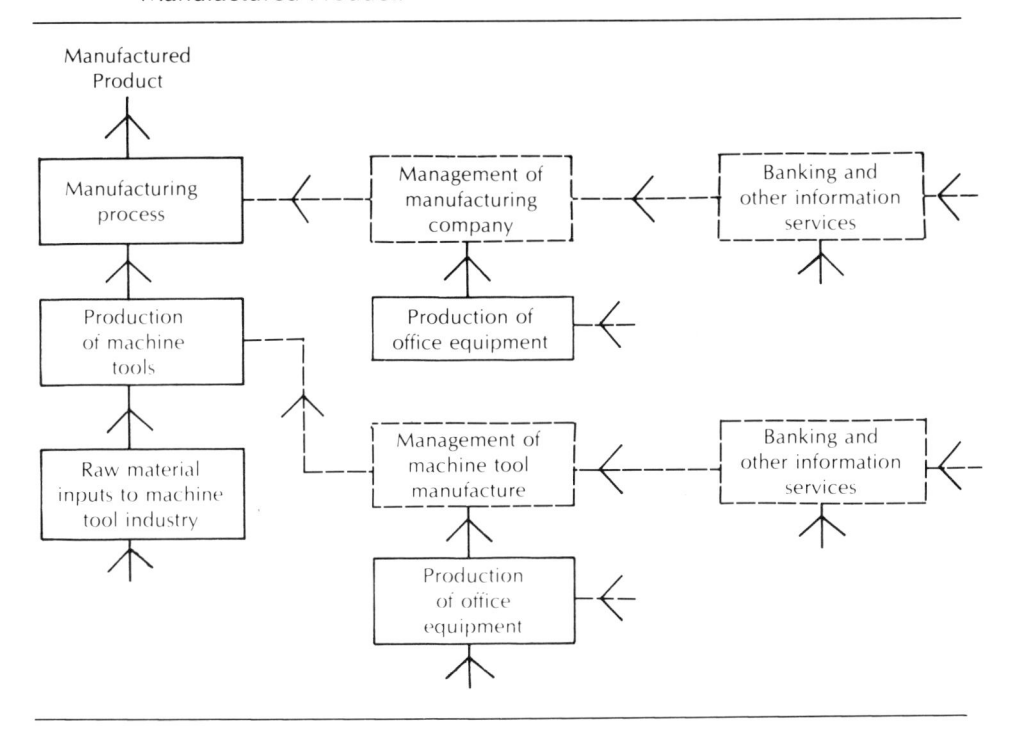

124   SERVICES IN TRANSITION

The output of a solid box is always a solid line (production goods); of a broken box, always a broken line (information services).

Figure 6–3 shows a corresponding chain for the provision of banking services. While the final output is an information service, successive inputs of both production and information labor are required. We note that in a complete diagram of the input-output structure of the economy, Figures 6–2 and 6–3 would be intermeshed: Banking is an input to the manufacturing industry, and manufactured goods are used in banks.

We wish to model the interrelationships between information and production activities in such a way that the pattern of use of the two kinds of resources can be clearly identified. We do this by taking the two kinds of activity we have defined at the micro level (the activity of information workers and production workers) and defining two sectors of the economy at the aggregate level:

1. *An information sector,* comprising the activity of all information workers
2. *A production sector,* comprising the activity of all production workers.

The effect, in terms of the two diagrams in Figures 6–2 and 6–3, can be described as that of moving all the solid boxes to one side, say the left, and consolidating them into one aggregate box representing the

Figure 6–3. Chains of Production and Information Activity: Case 2, Banking Services.

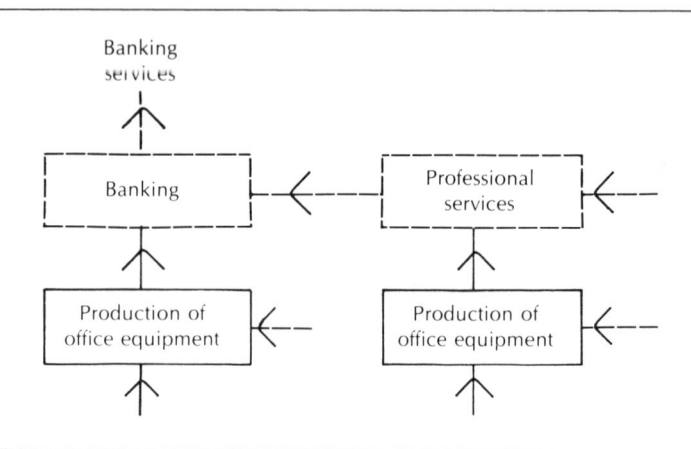

production sector. All the broken boxes are moved to the other side and consolidated into one representing the information sector. All flows of services between the individual elements in Figures 6–2 and 6–3 are retained but consolidated into aggregate flows between and within the two sectors.

We also define two categories of final consumption items, consumed by households:

1. *Production goods and services,* consisting of goods (housing, food, clothing, durables, etc.) and of services associated with the supply of these goods (marketing, retailing, delivery, after sales service, etc.)
2. *Information services and technology,* consisting of services directly provided by information workers (newspapers and broadcast programs, education, legal services, etc.) and information technology associated with the delivery or consumption of such services (telecommunications, TV and radio equipment, etc.).

The result is a framework with two sectors and four flows, as illustrated in Figure 6–4. The figure includes examples of the goods and services comprising each of the flows.

The quantities in the aggregate model illustrated in Figure 6–4 are defined as follows:

I: the total information workforce
P: the total production workforce
Z^F: final (consumer) demand for information services and associated goods
X^F: final (consumer) demand for production goods and associated services
X^I: quantity of information technology provided to the information sector
Z^P: quantity of information services provided to the production sector.

In a closed economy, the relationship between these aggregate or macro quantities and the micro-coefficients a_z and a_x can be calculated as follows:

1. Define X^T and Z^T as the total output, intermediate and final, of all production and information units respectively.

Figure 6-4. A Two-Sector Model of the Macroeconomy.

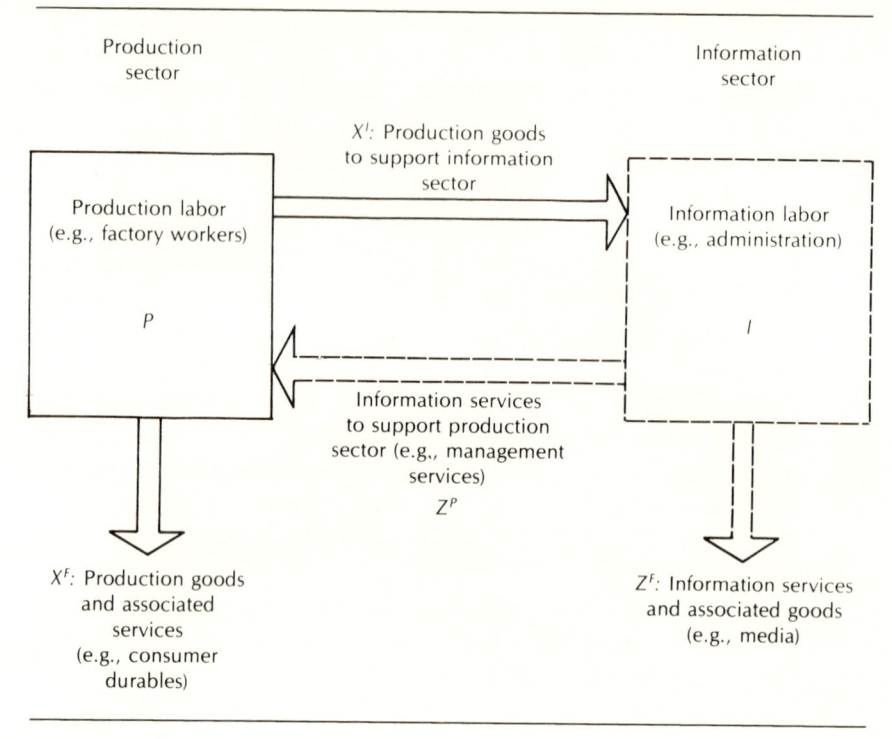

Production sector — Information sector

- Production labor (e.g., factory workers), P
- Information labor (e.g., administration), I
- X^I: Production goods to support information sector
- Z^P: Information services to support production sector (e.g., management services)
- X^F: Production goods and associated services (e.g., consumer durables)
- Z^F: Information services and associated goods (e.g., media)

Source: Jonscher (1983).

2. Consider initially only one step in the chain of successive intermediate stages of production and information activities required to produce given outputs of X^F and Z^F. We label the intermediate production and information inputs required for producing for *final demand only* $X^{(1)}$ and $Z^{(1)}$ respectively. Then,

$$X^{(1)} = a_x Z^F$$

$$Z^{(1)} = a_z X^F.$$

3. Moving one step further back in the production chain, we can define an input requirement vector for the activities producing $X^{(1)}$ and $Z^{(1)}$ (i.e., units two steps back from final demand):

$$X^{(2)} = a_x X^{(1)}$$

$$Z^{(2)} = a_z X^{(1)}.$$

ERRATUM

The equation printed on page 127 should be displayed as follows.

$$X^T = X^F \sum_{i=0}^{\infty} (a_x a_z)^i + a_x Z^F \sum_{i=0}^{\infty} (a_z a_x)^i = (X^F + a_x Z^F)/(1 - a_x a_z)$$
$$Z^T = Z^F \sum_{i=0}^{\infty} (a_z a_x)^i + a_z X^F \sum_{i=0}^{\infty} (a_x a_z)^i = (Z^F + a_z X^F)/(1 - a_x a_z).$$

4. Thus the total required outputs of products and information services, X^T and Z^T, required to product X^F and Z^F of final demand, are then given by:

$$X^T = X^F \sum_{i=0}^{\infty}(a_x a_z)^i + a_x Z^F \sum_{i=0}^{\infty}(a_z a_x)^i = (X^F + a_x Z^F)/(1-a_x a_z)$$

$$Y^T = Z^F \sum_{i=0}^{\infty}(a_z a_x)^i + a_z X^F \sum_{i=0}^{\infty}(a_x a_z)^i = (Z^F + a_z X^F)/(1-a_x a_z).$$

APPLICATION TO UNITED STATES DATA

Figure 6–5 indicates the values, for the United States economy, of the variables marked in Figure 6–4. Data have been obtained for two years, 1960 and 1983. The following points should be made:

1. I and P are measures of "labor value added"—employee compensation plus corporate profits and other proprietors' income. Proprietors' income is considered an overhead on the employee compensation of information and production workers; it is allocated to I and P in proportion to the direct compensation costs.
2. Z^F is calculated at purchase prices, using the product classifications in the appendix (sections 2 and 3 respectively).
3. X^F is obtained by subtracting Z^F from total consumer expenditure.
4. Z^P is obtained by subtracting consumer purchases Z^F from the total cost $I^T + X^I$ of providing information technology and labor in the economy.
5. $P + I$ is equal to total compensation of employees plus proprietors' income. In order to arrive at total value added in the economy (GNP), it is necessary to add the following: capital consumption allowances; rental income of persons; corporate profits; net interest; and indirect business tax and nontax liability, *net* of government subsidies.

From this macro data we can obtain, using the equations at the end of the previous subsection, the values of the input coefficients of information and production activity at the microlevel. These values are given in Table 6–1.

On the basis of the data presented in Figure 6–4 and Table 6–1, we can make a few general statements about the changes in information resource allocation that have taken place in the United States between the

128 SERVICES IN TRANSITION

Figure 6-5. Information and Production Sector Data: United States, 1960 and 1983 (All data in dollars of 1983 value).

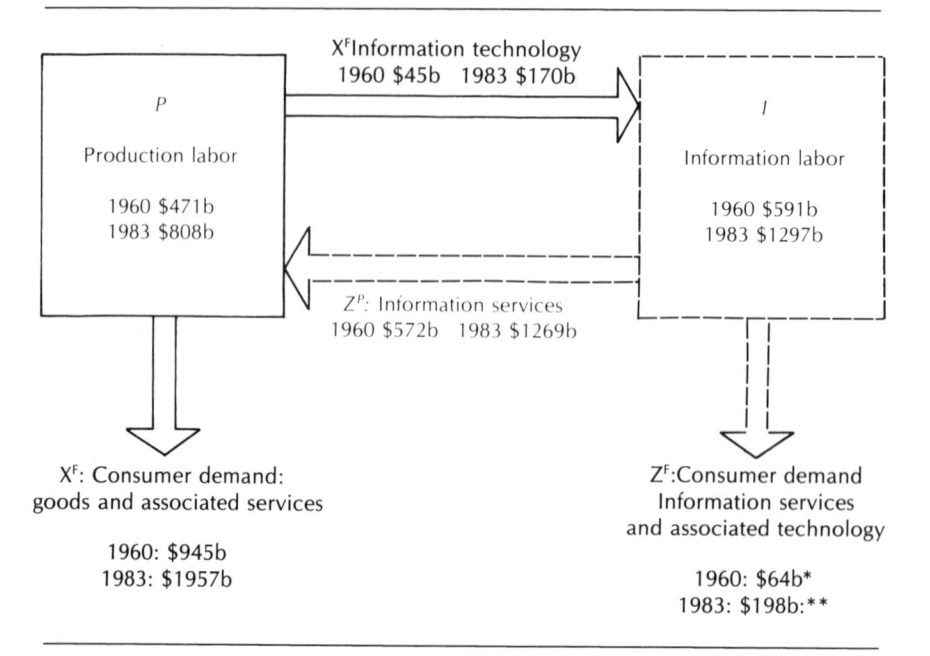

```
                    X^F Information technology
                    1960 $45b   1983 $170b
    ┌─────────────────┐ ═══════════════════════▶ ┌─────────────────┐
    │        P        │                           │        I        │
    │ Production labor│                           │Information labor│
    │                 │                           │                 │
    │  1960 $471b     │                           │  1960 $591b     │
    │  1983 $808b     │ ◀─ ─ ─ ─ ─ ─ ─ ─ ─ ─ ─ ─ │  1983 $1297b    │
    └─────────────────┘                           └─────────────────┘
                      Z^P: Information services
                      1960 $572b   1983 $1269b
            │                                              │
            ▼                                              ▼
    X^F: Consumer demand:                         Z^F: Consumer demand
    goods and associated services                  Information services
                                                  and associated technology
         1960: $945b
         1983: $1957b                                  1960: $64b*
                                                       1983: $198b:**
```

Sources: The following sources were used to derive this data. I, P were obtained by multiplying numbers on information and production workers (calculated by applying the occupational classifications in the appendix to data in the *National Industry-Occupation Employment Matrix*, 1971 and 1981) by average wage data obtained from the *Statistical Abstract of the United States*, 1961 and 1984. X^F, Z^P were obtained by applying the industry classifications given in the appendix to data on final demand for the relevant product categories in the *Detailed Input/Output Structure of the United States Economy*, 1962, 1977. In all cases, data for years not directly available in the sources cited were obtained by linear interpolation from available data. For some product categories, data for 1983 were directly from the *United States Industrial Outlook* 1984.

Note: All product and service flows are valued at purchase prices except Z^P, which is not marketed and is valued at the cost of supply.

* of which $48b is spent on information services, $16b on information technology.

** of which $136b is spent on information services, $62b on information technology.

years 1960 and 1983. We observe immediately from the data in Figure 6-5 the increase that has occurred in the ratio of information to production labor costs in the economy; this grew from 1.25 in 1960 to 1.6 in 1980. These numbers justify the description of the present day U.S. economy as one based on information rather than traditional industrial work as its principal resource using component.

Table 6–1. Information and Production Sector Input Coefficients for the U.S. Economy, 1960 and 1983.

Description	Symbol	1960 value	1983 value
Information technology to information labor cost ratio	a_x	0.076	0.13
Information services to production labor cost ratio	a_z	1.21	1.60

Source: Calculated from data in Figure 6–5; for methodology, see text.

We can see from the diagram and associated table of micro-coefficients that the growth in information resource use is principally driven by changes in production technology rather than consumption patterns. Consumer demand for information services and technology rose from $64 billion in 1960 to $198 billion in 1980, a threefold increase. However, even at the latter date, it accounted for only 14 percent of the total output of information services and technology in the economy. The remaining 86 percent was used as an input to the management and organization of physical production processes taking place in the production sector, or production services delivered to the final consumer (Z^P).

Thus, the demand for information workers has grown in recent years principally as a result of the increased requirement for information services (interpreted in a very general sense, to include management services) by those parts of the economy concerned with physical production. The extent to this increase is indicated by the input micro-coefficient a_z. In 1960 this had the value of 1.21, indicating that the production of each dollar's worth of physical production output in the economy required $1.21 worth of information services to be associated with it; by 1980 cost of information associated with that dollar of final output had risen to $1.60.

The parameter on Figure 6–4 that has increased by the largest proportional amount between 1960 and 1983 is X^I, the production and use of information technology. This grew from $45 billion at the beginning of that period to $170 billion at the end (both figures being quoted in dollars of constant 1983 value). Like the growth in information labor, this increase had two courses, one related to changes in consumer demand and the other to the structure of input coefficients in the supply side of the economy. Consumer demand for information technology increased from $16 billion to $62 billion; this increase is very large in proportional terms but is much smaller in absolute magnitude than the increase in volume of information technology purchases made as an input to the workplace. This latter number grew from $48 billion in 1960 to $136 billion in 1980, and it is largely responsible for the explosive growth in the industries that supply high-technology equipment to the U.S. economy.

APPENDIX
OCCUPATIONAL AND PRODUCT CATEGORIES ALLOCATED TO THE INFORMATION SECTOR FOR THE PURPOSE OF THIS STUDY.

(1) INFORMATION OCCUPATIONS

Engineers, technical
Life and physical scientists
Mathematical specialists
Engineering, science technicians
Computer specialists
Social scientists
Teachers
Writers and artists
Other professional and technical workers
Buyers, sales, loan managers
Administrators, public inspectors
Other managers, officials, proprietors
Advertising agents, sales workers
Stenographers, typists, and secretaries

(2) INFORMATION TECHNOLOGY PRODUCTS

Office, computing, and accounting machinery
Telecommunications equipment (excl. public network equipment)
Telecommunications carrier services
Radio, TV and hi-fi equipment, accessories, and supplies

(3) INFORMATION SERVICES FOR FINAL CONSUMPTION[a]

Banking, insurance, real estate, legal, and brokerage services
Educational services
Postal services
Entertainment services: radio and television broadcasting, cable television, motion pictures
Newspaper, magazine, and book publishing

REFERENCES

Bell, D. 1973. *The Coming of Post-Industrial Society*. New York: Basic Books.
Drucker, P. 1968. *The Age of Discontinuity*. New York: Harper and Row.
Jonscher, C. 1983. "Information Resources and Economic Productivity." *Information Economics and Policy*, no. 1.
Machlup, F., 1962. *Knowledge: Its Location, Distribution and Economic Significance*. Princeton, NJ: Princeton University Press.
Machlup, F. 1980. *The Production and Distribution of Knowledge in the United States*. Princeton, NJ: Princeton University Press.
Porat, M. 1977. *The Information Economy: Definition and Measurement*. OT special publication 77-12 (1), U.S. Department of Commerce.
United States Bureau of the Census. 1961, 1984. *Statistical Abstract of the United States*.
United States Department of Commerce, Bureau of Economic Analysis. 1962, 1977. *The Detailed Input/Output Structure of the United States Economy*.
United States Department of Commerce, Bureau of Industrial Economics. 1984. *United States Industrial Outlook*.
United States Department of Labor, Bureau of Labor Statistics. 1971, 1981. *The National Industry–Occupation Employment Matrix*.

[a] Only the value of those services bought by households is assessed.

DISCUSSION OF CHAPTER 6
Dennis A. Yao

Jonscher's dichotomization of the economy into a production sector and an information sector is a useful perspective from which to analyze the impact of information technology on productivity. A time series comparison of the two sectors shows dramatic increases in the share of information workers, expenditure share of information technologies, and relative productivity of the information sector. None of this is particularly surprising, but it does suggest that Jonscher's perspective on the economy is becoming increasingly relevant.

The problems in operationalizing this vision are common to any endeavor that combines theory with measurement: The links between microtheory and macrobehavior are not well developed and the data, at any reasonable level of disaggregation, is uncollected, if it exists at all. Measurement is further complicated by problems such as finding appropriate measures to accommodate learning-by-doing and in-house software development that are important to consider when examining the productivity effects of information technologies. Conquering these problems will be difficult but should prove rewarding.

Jonscher has made headway in this area in his 1983 paper and in the paper included in this volume. Both of the papers use Jonscher's two-sector model of the economy and share a similar basis in some micro-level theory. The 1983 paper is concerned with establishing this theory while the current paper simplifies the micro-level theory in order to introduce chains of production and information activities into the model. In each case Jonscher fits data to his model and discusses what the data imply about the economy.

At the conference Jonscher discussed the primary result from his earlier paper: The 1980s will see "a reversal in the previous decade's slowdown in economic growth, as information worker productivity rises substantially." Figure 6D-1, taken from Johnscher's 1983 paper, shows the historical track of productivity in the economy as well as Jonscher's extrapolations of future productivity.

A casual examination of the curves makes clear the speculative nature of Jonscher's projection. Given the relatively recent rise to prominence of the information sector, it is not surprising that the projections depart from the previous track of the economy. However, the extent of this departure is worrisome. An examination of Jonscher's model (Jonscher 1983) does nothing to allay fears about the accuracy of the model since the model is built from some assumptions that are not innocent, such as a closed economy and fixed coefficients of production and fixed price–productivity relationships. Such assumptions impose considerable structure on the predictions that Jonscher's model can make and raise questions as to the robustness of Jonscher's results to less restrictive assumptions about the workings of the economy.

Figure 6D-1. Size and Productivity of the Information and Production Sectors, 1950–2000.

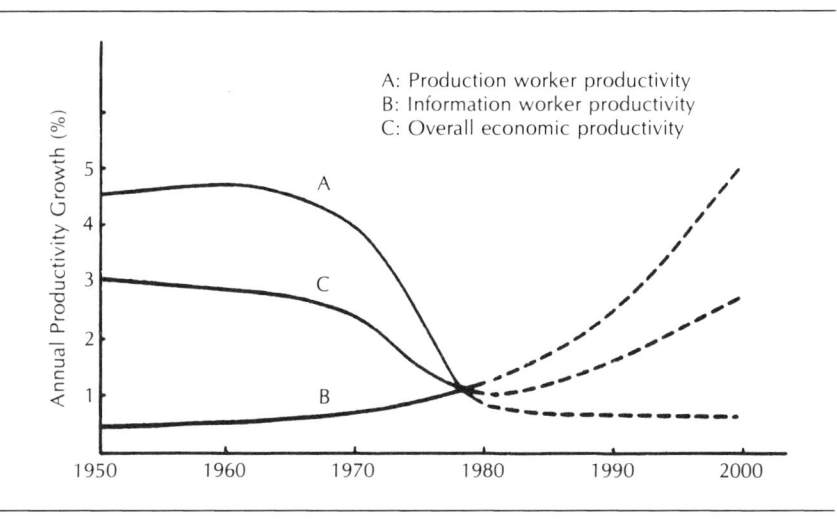

Source: Jonscher (1983).

In his current paper Jonscher calculates information and production sector input coefficients for the U.S. economy in 1960 and 1983 and suggests that the growth in information resource use is "principally driven by changes in production patterns rather than consumption patterns." The latter conclusion seems hard to deny given the magnitudes of the differences calculated by Jonscher. It is important to note, however, that this growth is that of information technology and information labor together: Substitution of information technology for information labor is not explicitly considered. For example, in banking the effects of information technology have been quite dramatic, but Jonscher's model may treat that activity as one in which the change in the use of information resources may be quite modest since technology was substituted for labor.

Jonscher's paper is basically an exercise in accounting. Given his closed economy assumption and the overall balance of inputs and outputs in the economy, flows between his production and information sector can be calculated indirectly through measures of consumer demand for information, compensation to labor in each sector, and so forth. An incorrect estimate for one of these values will ripple through the accounting relationships and affect other estimates. Thus, if the categorization of information labor and production labor is incorrect or if capital flows are not constant over time (since technology is durable and has value in future years), the flows of information technology and information services will be incorrect as well.

Conclusions drawn from Jonscher's results for 1960 and 1983 should be made cautiously for a number of reasons. First, since Jonscher's input coefficients are each based on essentially one data point, the true input coefficients a_x and a_z for the early 1960s and the mid-1980s may be substantially different than those calculated by Jonscher for 1960 and 1983. Second, the criticisms associated with the 1983 model are also applicable here. In particular, the degree to which the economy is closed changes in important ways over the period of comparison. Finally, Jonscher's model does not hold constant the mix of industries in the U.S. economy. Thus, while gross estimates of the change in information resources can be made, an arguably more interesting question, the extent to which existing industries have changed their use of information resources, is not addressed.

One could always say more about the various problems that afflict all attempts to understand complex interactions. However, I will go on to discuss how contributions from the theory of organizations may be useful for understanding the effect of information changes on productivity. In so doing, I will address some of the problems of administrative coordination and point out some issues that are important for an understanding of the impact of information technology on the service sector.

A change in information technology affects productivity in at least two different ways. First, the technology offers a new means for carrying out tasks (e.g., billing or expert systems). Second, it can change the nature of organizational relationships through its effect on the control of decision processes. The first effect is self-explanatory. The second is more woolly, and therefore more difficult to explain; but it is potentially the most important.

I will briefly describe two different views of organization theory and the implications of these views for assessing of the impacts of information technology. The "rational" school of organization theory descends from Max Weber. It offers a view of organization structure as something that is designed to increase an organization's efficiency in meeting its goals. In this view, structure is designed to break complex tasks into subtasks, which are further broken down into smaller tasks, until the task becomes manageable by a single worker. Working backwards, the lowest level individual's output becomes a higher level worker's input, until the overall task is completed (Simon 1976). These relationships are orchestrated through the formal organizational structure and its rules. Thus, in this view, the basic problem of organizational design is to coordinate activities and manage information flows among the units of the organization.

Given the premise that organization design is an instrument of rational management, it is clear that advances in information technology that widen the set of possibilities for coordination and information exchange should lead to changes in organization structure. For example, headquarters can have more control over its regional offices if telecommunications are improved. If communications technologies are adopted, it might be possible to reduce the autonomy of regional offices, assuming such a change is desirable.

The premise that organizations are designed and managed to accomplish the relevant task most efficiently is arguable. For example, an implication of such a premise is that an organization faced with significant environmental change will adapt its structure to the changed environment. However, "population ecology" theorists suggest that individual organizations rarely change in substantive ways, even in the face of considerable environmental change (Hannan and Freeman 1977).

Organizational inertia may result from power and politics within organizations, systematic misperceptions by organizational members, previous investments in plant and equipment, legal and financial barriers constraints on action, or considerations of legitimacy. I will describe the first two factors in more detail since they seem the most compelling and widely applicable explanations for organizational inertia.

Organizational structure determines the power and influence structure within the organization as well as the structure used to achieve organizational goals (Pfeffer 1981). The relationship works in the opposite direction as well: Players with power can determine structure. Thus, managers in power are likely to resist change since it puts their current situations at risk. Those who might benefit most from change are, on average, not in a position to affect decisions about structure. These forces act to bias organizational decisionmaking in favor of the status quo.

A second explanation for organizational inertia is that organization members may misperceive problems and potential solutions to those problems. Organization design and culture affects the way information is transmitted and processed within an organization, which, in turn, affects how people within the organization perceive the internal and external environment. For example, a firm that has spent the last two decades protecting its profits from the regulatory clutches of the federal government may see most of its problems stemming from regulation even when regulation ceases to be a primary factor in the firm's profitability. This occurs because sensitivity to regulatory issues has been institutionalized into the firm's culture and its structure, to the neglect of other factors that affect profitability. Similarly, when a person has learned to perceive a particular problem in a particular way, a tremendous amount of contrary information is required to cause a shift in the person's perceptual paradigm (see Jervis 1976). The same holds true for organizations.

Of course, organizations that do not change in the face of environmental shifts may not survive. The implication of the population ecology argument is that organizational change within an industry comes not as much from adaptation by dominant organizations as through the growth of less dominant organizations or the genesis of organizations that are a better match to the demands of the environment. Thus, new technologies, rather than causing changes within existing organizations as is predicted by the rational organization school, could lead to the growth of less established organizations at the expense of more established organizations.

Advances in information technology are likely to result in changes that improve productivity in organization structure; however, our earlier discussion indicates that it is unclear from the theory whether these changes will occur rapidly within existing organizations or will come about as new organizations displace the inertia-bound older organizations. Such uncertainties have troubling consequences for researchers who attempt to measure the impact of information technology on the economy. The effect of information technology involves both the simple use of the technology and the rearrangements of organizational structure that such a new technology may allow. To incorporte the organizational effect in measurements of productivity, researchers will need to learn how to identify changes in organizational form and how to link these changes back to the more conventional measures such as investment and labor force size.

REFERENCES

Hannan, M.T., and J. Freeman. 1977. "The Population Ecology of Organizations." *American Journal of Sociology* 82, no. 5:929–64.

Jervis, R. 1976. "Perception and Misperception in International Politics." Princeton, NJ: Princeton University Press.

Jonscher, C. 1983. "Information Resources and Economic Productivity." *Information Economics and Policy* 1:13–35.

Pfeffer, J. 1981. "Power in Organizations." Marshfield, MA: Pitman.

Simon, H. 1976. "Administrative Behavior." New York: The Free Press.

7 INFORMATION TECHNOLOGY, DEMOGRAPHICS, AND THE RETAIL RESPONSE

George Sternlieb
James W. Hughes

This chapter is organized into three broad sections. The first details the demographic matrix of 1995; America will be a much more mature nation, a middle-aged society predominantly "paired and nested." The era of explosive labor force growth will have passed—a period of labor force shortage will have arrived. Decentralization and deconcentration trends will continue at regional and metropolitan levels, but older regions—presently typified by New England—may secure increasing vigor. And the demographic and economic parameters of the 1990s indicate a far more receptive environment for technological innovation.

The second section highlights a much more difficult task—forecasting technological impact. The demographic matrix of the balance of the century is relatively "certain" within general boundaries, but there are relatively few technological imperatives with such vigor as to support instant judgment. An overview of the evolution of retailing in America provides an insightful example of the complexities at work.

The concepts of stasis and inertia versus the forces of change unleashed by technological innovation are the subject of the final section. Journey to work—the linkage between residence and workplace—is evaluated, along with the notion of the "electronic cottage." The impact of the information era may portend households free of spatial ties as they work at their dispersed electronic residences—with information commuting, not people. But just as shopping malls flourish in the face of electronic retailing, so too will the office remain viable. People will not want to be isolated from other people. Thus the impact of technology must be viewed through a matrix of societal elements that will shape its eventual spatial distribution—and settlement patterns as well.

DEMOGRAPHIC PARAMETERS

The confusion between sequence and causation is a hazard of the social sciences. We are dependent upon past relationships for forecasting the future. When these relationships alter—or if they are coincidental in time rather than descriptive of immutable linkages—the predictive failure can be very costly indeed. We are much more competent as historians than as futurists.

This stipulation is essential as we project demographic realities to come. It is made even more significant when we attempt to interpret the applications of communications and information technology both present and anticipated.

In the first domain, for example, it is chastening to observe the demographic forecasts of yesteryear. In the depths of the Depression, the consensus of learned forecasters, typified by the 1933 Hoover Commission Report, envisioned a population peak of 145 million people in the United States in the 1980s (President's Research Committee on Social Trends 1933).

The post–World War II baby boom (1946 to 1964) was completely unanticipated in both its scale and its longevity. The rapid increase in reproduction was matched only by its precipitous decline. The subsequent baby bust of the post-1964 years was equally unforeseen. We have moved from national population projections for the year 2000 of more than 300 million to a consensus of 265 to 270 million (Sternlieb, Hughes, and Hughes 1983). The former was a function of the fertility rates of the 1950s; the latter, of their abrupt reduction in the 1960s and early 1970s. In retrospect, the tendency for straightline extrapolation based on "clear trends" among the nominally learned is all evident.

There are, however, three basic demographic phenomena that can be forecast with a reasonable degree of certainty. They revolve around the powerful dominance of the baby boom cohort moving through its life cycle with enormously consequential societal repercussions; the maturing baby bust generation, introducing the concept of shrinkage at each stage of its life cycle; and the rise of the elderly—as yet much more a function of longevity than of a unique size of cohort. These three phenomena will dominate our population change through the balance of the century. Anticipations of their future ramifications feed back even now to our vision of social issues to come.

From an *areal* perspective, there are also three seemingly immutable processes of our time: decentralization, particularly evident in the dominant settlement artifacts—the major industrial cities—of a century we now realize ended with World War II; suburbanization and exurbanization, which has resulted in a continuous broadening of the concept of metropolitan areas; and regional shifts—that is, the transfer of population and economic activity typically from the Northeast and Midwest to the South and West. So consequential has this last element been, as to raise a number of statistical anomalies—that is, the rise of cities and metropolitan areas as the new growth areas thicken up, and of vast conurbations, perhaps mislabeled metropolitan areas, growing in size while their older forebears decline.

Bounding these elements—and at one and the same time both dependent on them and serving as accelerants as well—are transformations of the American labor force, and technological/economic functions as well. The demographic dynamics, summarized subsequently, set the basic stage for the future.

The Population Context

The United States is passing through the pressures exerted by the enormous increments of population growth that have characterized the post–World War II era. From 1950 through the mid-1980s, our population increased by nearly 60 percent (Sternlieb, Hughes, and Hughes 1983), but this is a process that is now slowing. The baby boom upsurge of the 1950s, marked by an 18.5 percent population increase nationally between 1950 and 1960, gave way to the baby bust era of the 1960s and 1970s, with decade population increases on the order of 13.4 and 11.4 percent respectively. The dynamics set in motion over these last three decades will dominate the demographics of tomorrow. *Much of the adaptation and receptivity to new technology and information systems will be shaped by them.*

The stress points of the 1970s are illustrated in the age structure data of Table 7–1, which highlights the reduction in the absolute number of children under the age of fourteen years in the 1970s (the baby bust

Table 7-1. Total Population Age Structure, U.S. Total Population (Including Armed Forces Abroad): 1970 to 1983 (Numbers in thousands).

	1970	1980	Change: 1970 – 1980 Number	Change: 1970 – 1980 Percent	1983	Change: 1980 – 1983 Number	Change: 1980 – 1983 Percent
Total	205,052	227,704	22,652	11.0%	234,496	6,792	3.0%
Under 5 years	17,166	16,457	− 709	− 4.1	17,826	1,369	8.3
5 to 13	36,672	31,080	− 5,592	− 15.2	30,116	− 964	− 3.1
14 to 17	15,924	16,139	215	1.4	14,633	− 1,506	− 9.3
18 to 24	24,717	30,347	5,636	22.8	30,148	− 199	− 0.7
25 to 34	25,324	37,593	12,269	48.4	40,334	2,741	7.3
35 to 44	23,150	25,882	2,732	11.8	29,492	3,610	13.9
45 to 54	23,316	22,737	− 579	− 2.5	22,342	− 395	− 1.7
55 to 64	18,682	21,756	3,074	16.5	22,219	463	2.1
65 years and over	20,107	25,714	5,607	27.9	27,384	1,670	6.5

Sources: U.S. Bureau of the Census, *Statistical Abstract of the United States: 1984* (104th Edition), Washington, D.C., 1983; U.S. Bureau of the Census, Current Population Reports, Series P-25, No. 949, *Estimates of the Population of the United States, by Age, Sex and Race: 1980 to 1983*, U.S. Government Printing Office, Washington, D.C., 1984.

generation), with a decline of more than 6 million; and the enormous growth of young adults in the twenty-five to thirty-four years of age range (the maturing baby boom), who increased by half. Indeed, nearly all of the population increment of the 1970s was in the twenty-five to forty-four years-of-age sector (20.6 million out of 22.7 million). The growth in older Americans barely compensated for the loss of the young.

The three basic propulsive forces were thus made evident in the 1970s: the sheer size—and now the aging—of the baby boom generation; the continued growth in the elderly; and a relative dearth of new, young adults on the horizon. While the baby boom echo, as a function of the sheer size of the cohort at risk, is illustrated by the resumed growth in the under-five years of age population between 1980 and 1983, it is but a shadow of the earlier vitality that produced its parents.

Presented in Table 7-2 are the age structure shifts projected from 1983 to 1990 and then through 1995. By that terminal date, the demographic profile of America is dominated by the aging of the baby boom generation. Over 73 million Americans will be between thirty-five and fifty-four years old—a dramatic expansion without parallel in our past. Its companion—a shrinking number of young adults—is indicated by the relatively small increments in their historic absolute number. And the much-feared accession rate to the elderly will be substantial, but it will really only become dominant in the next century.

America of 1995 will be a much older nation, with its population concentrated in middle-aged to near-middle-aged groups. It will be much less dominated, at least from a numerical point of view, by the youth orientation of past decades. It should be noted in this context that, subject to changes in immigration flow, population projections to 1995—at least for people over the age of ten—are relatively secure in scale. The demographic matrix of the next decade has already been set in place.

Regional Population Shifts

Of considerably less certainty are future regional settlement patterns. In the 1970s, accelerated population growth in the South and West on a national scale brought with it a new vocabulary, of Sunbelt and Frostbelt, to the general media. But more significantly, it represented the visible product of the long-term pyramiding of successive technological innovations.

Before the turn of the century, F.J. Kingsbury (1895) isolated three factors portending significant changes in the population distribution

Table 7-2. Population Projections by Age, U.S. Total Population (Including Armed Forces Abroad): 1990 and 1995 (Numbers in thousands).

	1983	1990	Change: 1983 – 1990 Number	Change: 1983 – 1990 Percent	1995	Change: 1990 – 1995 Number	Change: 1990 – 1995 Percent
Total	234,496	249,731	15,235	6.5%	259,631	9,900	4.0%
Under 5 years	17,826	19,200	– 1,374	– 7.7	18,616	584	3.0
5 to 13	30,116	32,183	2,067	6.9	34,443	2,260	7.0
14 to 17	14,633	12,940	– 1,693	– 11.6	14,071	1,131	8.7
18 to 24	30,148	25,777	– 4,371	– 14.5	23,684	– 2,093	– 12.0
25 to 34	40,334	43,506	3,172	7.9	40,489	– 3,017	– 6.9
35 to 44	29,492	37,845	8,353	28.3	41,994	4,149	11.0
45 to 54	22,342	25,391	3,049	13.6	31,378	5,987	23.6
55 to 64	22,219	21,090	– 1,129	– 5.1	20,951	– 139	– 0.7
65 years and over	27,384	31,799	4,415	16.1	34,006	2,207	6.9

Note: Census Bureau Middle Series Projection.
Sources: U.S. Bureau of the Census, Current Population Reports, Series P-25, No. 922, *Projections of the Population of the United States: 1982 to 2050* (Advance Report), U. S. Government Printing Office, Washington, D.C., 1982; U.S. Bureau of The Census, Current Population Reports, Series P-25, No. 949, *Estimates of the Population of the United States, by Age, Sex and Race: 1980 to 1983*, U.S. Government Printing Office, Washington, D.C., 1984.

between the city and its surrounding countryside—the trolley, the bicycle, and the telephone. Each of these entrants into American life was seen as expanding the periphery of urban settlement. Kingsbury perceptively suggested that alterations in society's course are often underlaid by the pyramiding of seemingly unimportant and inconspicuous developments into forces of major consequence.

Current modifications of America's demographic evolution have been facilitated by the same general categories of technological innovation recognized by Kingsbury—public and private transportation and communications. Advances in air transport and dry-bulk cargo shipping, the Interstate Highway System, and the increasing sophistication of place-independent computer linkages—have served substantially to homogenize time and space, and radically alter patterns of connectivity.

Predecessors of these innovations gave impetus to the suburbanization process in earlier decades. In the 1970s they advanced to the national scale and facilitated increasing disparities in interregional population growth. And the processes at work have propelled themselves into the 1980s. In Table 7–3 we have shown the changes in the regional distribution of America's population from 1980 through 1984. The conventional wisdom of population shifts to the South and West at the cost of the Northeast and Midwest is still valid. Roughly 90 percent of all of America's population growth in the first four years of the 1980s was in the former areas; the latter, at least from an aggregate demographic perspective, remained virtually static.

The pattern of change from mid-1983 to mid-1984 indicates a potential break from the past. The slowing down of the natural resource economy—of the mineral base of Texas and the Rocky Mountain areas—introduces new uncertainty. Wyoming, for example, actually lost population, but this may be only a recession-borne blip. The new information economy, however, may be much less resource-dependent than its predecessor. The world economy that it makes possible further deepens the problems of those domestic areas whose raison d'etre rests on suddenly challenged bases. The copper states are depressed by both fiber optic cables and alternative mineral exploitation throughout the world.

The future will hold equally significant and equally unanticipated developments. In the early 1970s, New England was still considered an economic laggard, depleted by the loss of its historical industrial mainstays over the preceding half century. Spearheaded by new innovations, the information and technological era has reversed New England's economic fortune. Although its 1980 to 1984 population growth still lags the nation, a base for future growth has been established.

Table 7-3. Estimates of the Resident Population of States, July 1, 1983 and 1984 (Including Armed Forces Residing in Each State) (Numbers in thousands).

Region, Division, and State	Estimate July 1, 1984 (provisional)	Estimate July 1, 1983	April 1, 1980 (Census)	Change, Number	1980-84 Percent
United States	236,158	234,023	226,546	9,612	4.2
Northeast	49,728	49,502	49,135	592	1.2
New England	12,577	12,486	12,348	228	1.8
Middle Atlantic	37,151	37,016	36,787	364	1.0
Midwest	59,117	58,890	58,866	251	0.4
East North Central	41,601	41,478	41,682	-81	-0.2
West North Central	17,515	17,412	17,183	332	1.9
South	80,576	79,637	75,372	5,204	6.9
South Atlantic	39,450	38,852	36,959	2,491	6.7
East South Central	15,028	14,931	14,666	362	2.5
West South Central	26,098	25,854	23,747	2,351	9.9
West	46,738	45,994	43,172	3,565	8.3
Mountain	12,553	12,348	11,373	1,180	10.4
Pacific	34,184	33,646	31,800	2,385	7.5
New England					
Maine	1,156	1,145	1,125	32	2.8
New Hampshire	977	958	921	56	6.1

Vermont	530	525	511	18	3.6
Massachusetts	5,798	5,763	5,737	61	1.1
Rhode Island	962	956	947	15	1.6
Connecticut	3,154	3,139	3,108	47	1.5
Middle Atlantic					
New York	17,735	17,663	17,558	177	1.0
New Jersey	7,515	7,464	7,365	150	2.0
Pennsylvania	11,901	11,889	11,864	37	0.3
East North Central					
Ohio	10,752	10,736	10,798	−46	−0.4
Indiana	5,498	5,472	5,490	8	0.1
Illinois	11,511	11,474	11,427	84	0.7
Michigan	9,075	9,050	9,262	−187	−2.0
Wisconsin	4,766	4,746	4,706	60	1.3
West North Central					
Minnesota	4,162	4,144	4,076	86	2.1
Iowa	2,910	2,904	2,914	−4	−0.1
Missouri	5,008	4,963	4,917	91	1.9
North Dakota	686	681	653	34	5.2
South Dakota	706	699	691	15	2.2
Nebraska	1,606	1,596	1,570	36	2.3
Kansas	2,438	2,426	2,364	74	3.1

Table 7-3. continued

Region, Division, and State	Estimate July 1, 1984 (provisional)	Estimate July 1, 1983	April 1, 1980 (Census)	Change, Number	1980–84 Percent
South Atlantic					
Delaware	613	606	594	18	3.1
Maryland	4,349	4,299	4,217	132	3.1
Dist. of Columbia	623	623	638	−16	−2.4
Virginia	5,636	5,556	5,347	289	5.4
West Virginia	1,952	1,962	1,950	3	0.1
North Carolina	6,165	6,076	5,882	283	4.8
South Carolina	3,300	3,256	3,122	178	5.7
Georgia	5,837	5,732	5,463	373	6.8
Florida	10,976	10,742	9,746	1,229	12.6
East South Central					
Kentucky	3,723	3,713	3,661	62	1.7
Tennessee	4,717	4,676	4,591	126	2.7
Alabama	3,990	3,961	3,894	96	2.5
Mississippi	2,598	2,581	2,521	77	3.1
West South Central					
Arkansas	2,349	2,325	2,286	63	2.7
Louisiana	4,462	4,440	4,206	257	6.1
Oklahoma	3,298	3,310	3,025	273	9.0
Texas	15,989	15,779	14,229	1,759	12.4

Mountain				
Montana	824	815	787	37	4.7
Idaho	1,001	987	944	57	6.0
Wyoming	511	516	470	42	8.9
Colorado	3,178	3,416	2,890	288	10.0
New Mexico	1,424	1,399	1,303	121	9.3
Arizona	3,053	2,970	2,718	335	12.3
Utah	1,652	1,618	1,461	191	11.0
Nevada	911	897	800	110	13.8
Pacific				
Washington	4,349	4,302	4,132	217	5.2
Oregon	2,674	2,658	2,633	41	1.6
California	25,622	25,186	23,668	1,955	8.3
Alaska	500	481	402	98	24.4
Hawaii	1,039	1,018	965	74	7.7

Source: U.S. Bureau of the Census, *Commerce News*, CB 84-233, Public Information Office, Washington, D.C., December 28, 1984.

Will a similar path be open to other aging industrial regions? The Sunbelt-Frostbelt disparities of the 1970s were linked to shifting energy costs and the obsolescence of the industrial infrastructure of the past. But the age of energy "shortfalls"—and with it the rush to Texas and the mountain states—may be over, raising questions as to the long-term pulling power of these areas. The new information era has not only resurrected New York City as the national—and now worldwide—financial capitol, but it has also given it much greater potency, challenging the role of the "regional cities." The inertia of past spatial demographics will be continually challenged as the future economy unfolds.

Long-term shifts of population—and with them, jobs, residence place, entertainment facilities, and all the infrastructure of modern-day life—render obsolete old facilities in left-behind areas and demand an accelerated level of new capital provisions in the high-growth areas. With them comes the capacity—at least the potential—for crest-of-the-wave innovation, for the employment of new means of communication and transportation that do not face the competition of the already-in-place infrastructure of the older sections of the nation. One out of four houses built in the South dates from 1970 or later—the equivalent for the Northeast is one in ten (Sternlieb, Hughes, and Hughes 1983).

Central City Population

The subject of population change and the concomitant alteration of economic functions in central cities is an enormously complex one. In our own estimation, we do not see the pattern of population decline, shown in Table 7-4 for selected cities from 1950 to 1980, altering markedly in the future. The long-term nature of the forces underlying this decline makes this evident.

The development of the horse-drawn streetcar in the late nineteenth century was the initial instrument that stretched the city beyond its circumscribed pedestrian limits. The ability to transmit electricity from a central power station to a moving vehicle, and the development of an efficient electrical streetcar motor, further accelerated movement to the countryside. The diffusion of the telephone and advances in the transmission of electricity economically, including the switch from direct to alternating current, also facilitated population decentralization. At the same time, they also permitted *employment* centralization, increasing the number of people who could be gathered at a central locus within a fixed period of time.

Table 7-4. Population Change, Selected Cities—1950 to 1980.

City	1950[a]	1970[b]	1980[c]	Change: 1950–1980 Number	Change: 1950–1980 Percent	Change: 1970–1980 Number	Change: 1970–1980 Percent
Boston	801,444	641,071	562,994	−238,450	−29.8	−78,077	−12.2
Buffalo	580,132	462,768	357,870	−222,262	−38.3	−104,898	−22.7
Chicago	3,620,962	3,369,357	3,005,072	−615,890	−17.0	−364,285	−10.8
Cincinnati	503,998	453,514	385,457	−118,541	−23.5	−68,057	−15.0
Cleveland	914,808	750,879	573,822	−340,986	−37.3	−177,057	−23.6
Detroit	1,849,568	1,514,063	1,203,339	−646,229	−34.9	−310,724	−20.5
Minneapolis	521,718	434,400	370,951	−150,767	−28.9	−63,449	−14.6
New York City	7,891,957	7,895,563	7,071,030	−820,927	−10.4	−824,553	−10.4
Newark	438,776	381,930	329,248	−109,528	−25.0	−52,682	−13.8
Philadelphia	2,071,605	1,949,996	1,688,210	−383,395	−18.5	−261,786	−13.4
Pittsburgh	676,806	520,089	423,938	−252,868	−37.4	−96,151	−18.5
St. Louis	856,796	622,236	453,085	−403,711	−47.1	−169,151	−27.2

Sources: U.S. Bureau of the Census. *County and City Data Book, 1956* (A Statistical Abstract Supplement), U.S. Government Printing Office, Washington, D.C., 1957; and U.S. Bureau of the Census, *Commerce News*, "Three Cities of 100,000 or More At Least Doubled Population Between 1970 and 1980, Census Bureau Reports," CB81-92, Public Information Office, Washington, D.C., June 3, 1981.

[a] April 1, 1950 Census.
[b] April 1, 1970 Census.
[c] April 1, 1980 Census.

The advent of widescale automobile ownership after World War II merely accentuated the suburbanization process. It permitted the working-out of long-standing social desires that had been evidenced in the late 1920s. The data of Table 7–4 were virtually preordained by the technological introductions of a half century before.

At present, despite much publicity, the often-heralded return of older suburbanites and Yuppies to the central city simply has not occurred; future demographics, particularly the slowing growth of household formation, are a distinct negative. *The homogenization of space—and increasingly of time—available through information technology has made much of the historical functions of the older core areas obsolete or, at best, opened them to very substantial and increasingly successful competition.* The major dynamics of dispersion and decentralization made possible by the technology of yesterday can only be accentuated by future innovation; within this latter context, there is little, at least on the horizon, that is unique and specific to central cities and might provide them with a new surge of competence and pulling power.

Household Change

The impact of technology is a function of the societal matrix that serves as a shaping device. Within this context, the shifts in America's household configurations are particularly important. The 1970s were the years of nominally unorthodox households—singles and "mingles"—and a relatively slow growth in traditional married couples. Overall, however, there was an enormous expansion in the number of American households. Housing buying power, at least in the beginning of the 1970s, was relatively high—a variety of household types, therefore, had the capacity to seek out independence. The future, however, in our own estimation, will be quite different.

In Table 7–5 we have projected household growth increments by age, type, and tenure, from 1983 through 1995. (The 1983 and 1995 totals are presented in Tables 7–6 and 7–7.) The pattern is one that reflects the maturing of America. First and foremost is a decline in the scale of household formation—absolute household growth will average only 1.2 million per year in the early 1990s as compared to 1.7 million in the 1970s.

Secondly, and equally evident, is the continued dominance of ownership. Again, this has significant ramifications for the adoption of new

Table 7-5. Projected-Household Growth Increments: By Age, Type and Tenure: 1983 to 1995 (Numbers in thousands).

		OWNER HOUSEHOLDS				
		Family Households			Nonfamily Households	
			Other Family			
	Total	Married Couple	Male House-holder	Female House-holder	Male House-holder	Female House-holder
All Households	11,038	8,005	251	1,031	624	1,124
Under 25 years	− 184	− 117	− 13	− 12	− 30	− 15
25 to 34	44	34	− 1	11	15	− 16
35 to 44	4,742	3,809	114	448	250	120
45 to 54	3,839	3,011	105	389	164	171
55 to 64	− 609	− 439	− 21	− 44	− 21	− 84
65 years and over	3,206	1,709	67	238	244	948

		RENTER HOUSEHOLDS				
		Family Households			Nonfamily Households	
			Other Family			
	Total	Married Couple	Male House-holder	Female House-holder	Male House-holder	Female House-holder
All Households	3,417	1,247	96	734	563	778
Under 25 years	− 811	− 318	− 17	− 118	− 192	− 166
25 to 34	39	57	− 12	2	2	− 10
35 to 44	2,089	854	74	539	414	209
45 to 54	1,155	460	46	228	231	191
55 to 64	− 146	− 55	− 11	− 11	− 38	− 31
65 years and over	1,092	249	17	94	146	585

Source: CUPR Household Projection Model.

technology. On the one hand, owners may be more desirous—or perhaps even more capable—of long-term capital investment in their domicile. A second, and perhaps less salubrious (from the viewpoint of technological innovation, at least), element is the decline in renter households. While not precisely coterminous with multifamily housing—it is

Table 7–6. Owner and Renter Households by Age and Type, U.S. Total: 1983 (Numbers in thousands).

OWNER HOUSEHOLDS

	Total	Family Households			Nonfamily Households	
		Married Couple	Other Family Male Householder	Other Family Female Householder	Male Householder	Female Householder
All Households	54,494	38,853	1,195	4,427	3,513	6,507
Under 25 years	1,097	759	47	80	163	49
25 to 34	8,985	7,060	162	553	872	338
35 to 44	11,149	8,895	263	1,103	589	299
45 to 54	9,525	7,499	240	929	401	456
55 to 64	10,519	7,709	210	777	440	1,383
65 years and over	13,219	6,929	273	986	1,048	3,982

RENTER HOUSEHOLDS

	Total	Family Households			Nonfamily Households	
		Married Couple	Other Family Male Householder	Other Family Female Householder	Male Householder	Female Householder
All Households	29,423	11,055	821	5,043	6,001	6,504
Under 25 years	4,597	1,670	152	727	1,071	977
25 to 34	10,119	4,377	254	1,812	2,175	1,501
35 to 44	4,871	1,997	178	1,222	970	504
45 to 54	2,829	1,109	111	588	553	468
55 to 64	2,555	893	74	346	562	680
65 years and over	4,451	1,009	51	348	670	2,374

Source: U.S. Bureau of the Census, Current Population Reports, Series P-20, No. 388, *Household and Family Characteristics: March 1983,* U.S. Government Printing Office, Washington, D.C., 1984.

indicative of relatively modest increments in large-scale, physically integrated housing configurations—this may have some limiting impact in adoption of large-scale, centrally located innovation.

Unlike the 1970s, household growth will be dominated by married couples—typically two-worker households—concentrated in the thirty-five to fifty-four year old householder age segment. At least in historic

Table 7-7. Household Projections by Age, Type, and Tenure of Households, U.S. Total: 1995 (Numbers in thousands).

	OWNER HOUSEHOLDS				
	Family Households			Nonfamily Households	
		Other Family			
	Total	Married Couple	Male Householder	Female Householder	Male Householder	Female Householder
Under 25 years	913	642	34	68	135	34
25 to 34	9,029	7,094	161	564	887	322
35 to 44	15,891	12,704	377	1,551	839	419
45 to 54	13,364	10,510	345	1,318	565	627
55 to 64	9,910	7,270	189	733	419	1,299
65 years and over	16,425	8,638	340	1,224	1,292	4,930
TOTAL	65,532	46,858	1,446	5,458	4,137	7,631

	RENTER HOUSEHOLDS				
	Family Households			Nonfamily Households	
		Other Family			
	Total	Married Couple	Male Householder	Female Householder	Male Householder	Female Householder
Under 25 years	3,786	1,352	135	609	879	811
25 to 34	10,158	4,434	242	1,814	2,177	1,491
35 to 44	6,960	2,851	252	1,761	1,384	713
45 to 54	3,984	1,569	157	816	784	659
55 to 64	2,409	838	63	335	524	649
65 years and over	5,543	1,258	68	442	816	2,959
TOTAL	32,840	12,302	917	5,777	6,564	7,282

Source: CUPR Household Projection Model.

terms, these are people moving into the peak income-earning years, with a greater capacity for capital investment. Time will tell whether they have as much desire for crest-of-the-wave "electronics" as they exhibited in the 1970s. At least the more youthful among them are children of the electronics age, already shaped by casual ease of access to the computer; this, combined with personal means, may yield a much greater level of adaptation to the era of high technology than we have yet seen.

Labor Force Constraints

Changes in the labor force may well be the most important manifestation of the demographic matrix, both in terms of the economy of tomorrow and of technological adoption as well. The United States from 1970 through 1982 was unique among its principal overseas trading partners in terms of total civilian employment growth (Table 7-8). While it expanded in the brief twelve years by more than 25 percent (almost 21 million jobs), it was actually declining in Germany and Great Britain. Even Japan's performance—an 11.6 percent growth rate (6 million jobs)—was dwarfed in comparison.

The level of capital investment in production facilities in the United States was severely impacted by this phenomenon. The costs of money in the 1970s increased very substantially; at the same time, labor was relatively freely available—and, particularly at unskilled levels, relatively cheap. The temptation to maximize the use of the latter—and minimize the former—was pervasive.

Table 7-8. Total Civilian Employment in the U.S., Four Largest European Nations, and Japan: 1970 to 1982[a] (Numbers in thousands).

	1970	1982	Change: 1970 to 1982 Number	Percent
United States	76,678	99,526	20,848	26.5
Four largest European countries, total	89,290	88,920[b]	− 370	− 0.4
France	20,320	20,980[b]	660	3.2
Germany	26,100	25,090[b]	−1,010	− 3.9
Great Britain	23,780	22,460[b]	−1,320	− 5.6
Italy	19,090	20,390	1,300	6.8
Japan	50,940	56,857[c]	5,917	11.6

Sources: Norwood, Janet L. 1983. "Labor Market Contrasts: United States and Europe." *Monthly Labor Review* 106, no. 8 (August): 3–7 (for U.S. and Europe); OECD, *Labor Force Statistics: 1969 to 1980*, Paris, 1982, and Quarterly Supplements (for Japan).

[a]Includes self-employed, other non-payroll, and agricultural employment.
[b]Preliminary.
[c]Third Quarter.

Table 7-9. Civilian Labor Force, by Sex, Age, and Race, 1970–1982, and Middle Growth Projection to 1995.

	Labor Force (in thousands)				Participation Rate				
	1970	1980	1982	1990	1995	1970	1980	1982	1990	1995
Total, age 16 and over	82,771	106,940	110,204	124,951	131,387	60.4	63.8	64.0	66.9	67.8
Men										
16 to 24	51,228	61,453	62,450	67,701	69,970	79.7	77.4	76.6	76.5	76.1
16 to 19	9,725	13,606	13,074	11,274	10,573	69.4	74.4	72.6	74.7	74.5
20 to 24	4,008	4,999	4,470	4,123	4,043	56.1	60.5	56.7	62.3	62.9
25 to 54	5,717	8,607	8,604	7,151	6,530	83.3	85.9	84.9	84.4	84.1
25 to 34	32,213	38,712	40,357	48,180	51,358	95.8	94.2	94.0	93.8	93.4
35 to 44	11,327	16,971	17,793	19,569	18,105	96.4	95.2	94.7	93.7	93.1
45 to 54	10,469	11,836	12,781	17,469	19,446	96.9	95.5	95.3	95.6	95.3
55 and over	10,417	9,905	9,784	11,142	13,807	94.3	91.2	91.2	91.3	91.1
55 to 64	9,291	9,135	9,019	8,247	8,039	55.7	45.6	43.8	37.4	35.3
65 and over	7,126	7,242	7,174	6,419	6,311	83.0	72.1	70.2	65.5	64.5
	2,165	1,893	1,845	1,828	1,728	26.8	19.0	17.8	14.9	13.3
Women	31,543	45,487	47,755	57,250	61,417	43.3	51.5	52.6	58.3	60.3
16 to 24	8,121	11,696	11,533	10,813	10,577	51.3	61.9	62.0	69.1	71.6
16 to 19	3,241	4,381	4,056	3,788	3,761	44.0	52.9	51.4	56.8	58.2
20 to 24	4,880	7,315	7,477	7,035	6,796	57.7	68.9	69.8	78.1	82.0
25 to 54	18,208	27,888	30,149	40,496	44,852	50.1	64.0	66.3	75.6	78.7
25 to 34	5,708	12,257	13,393	16,804	16,300	45.0	65.5	68.0	78.1	81.7
35 to 44	5,968	8,627	9,651	14,974	17,427	51.1	65.5	68.0	78.6	82.8
45 to 54	6,532	7,004	7,105	8,718	11,125	54.4	59.9	61.6	67.1	69.5
55 and over	5,213	5,904	6,073	5,941	6,008	25.3	22.8	22.7	20.5	19.9
55 to 64	4,157	4,742	4,888	4,612	4,671	43.0	41.3	41.8	41.5	42.5
65 and over	1,056	1,161	1,185	1,329	1,337	9.7	8.1	7.9	7.4	7.0

Source: Fullerton, Jr., Howard N., and John Tscheller. 1983. "The 1995 Labor Force: A Second Look." *Monthly Labor Review* 106, no. 11 (November):5.

158 SERVICES IN TRANSITION

The situation is very different, however, as we turn to the future. The Bureau of Labor Statistics projects a total labor force growth from 1982 to 1995 of only 21 million (Table 7–9). Thus, we will move from a pattern of labor force expansion that in the 1970s averaged 2.4 million participants a year, to 1.8 million in the 1980s, and to 1.3 million in the first five years of the 1990s—barely one half that of the 1970s. The technological imperative—assuming that we have passed through the era of economic shocks—is evident. *The 1970s, from a demographic point of view, were far from a salubrious era for technological implementation—the 1980s are much more positive—and the 1990s, drastically more so.*

Table 7–10. Total Civilian Employment in the U.S., Selected European Nations, and Japan, by Economic Sector: 1970 to 1982.[a] (Numbers in thousands).

	United States	France	Germany	Great Britain[b]	Italy	Japan
Agriculture[c]						
1970	3,567	2,821	2,262	782	3,839	8,860
1981	3,519	1,800	1,402	647	2,731	5,570
1982	3,571	(d)	1,371	(d)	2,525	(d)
Goods Producing[e]						
1970	26,080	7,917	12,465	10,531	7,586	18,190
1981	28,995	7,208	10,885	8,038[f]	7,722	19,700[g]
1982	27,070	(d)	10,480[f]	(d)	7,594	(d)
Service Producing						
1970	49,031	9,605	11,442	13,071	7,656	23,890
1981	67,883	11,968	13,261	14,373[f]	10,003	30,540
1982	68,888	(d)	13,251[f]	(d)	10,277	(d)

Sources: Norwood, Janet L. 1983. "Labor Market Contrasts: United States and Europe." *Monthly Labor Review* 106, no. 8 (August): 3–7 (for U.S. and Europe); OECD, *Labor Force Statistics: 1969 to 1980*, Paris, 1982, and *Quarterly Supplements* (for Japan).

[a] Small adjustments made to the overall employment data in Exhibit 8 could not be made to certain sectoral data. Includes self-employed, other non-payroll, and agricultural employment.
[b] Includes Northern Ireland.
[c] Not available.
[d] Not available.
[e] Manufacturing, mining, and construction.
[f] Preliminary.
[g] Includes utilities.

America—subject to changes in immigration—is going to be short of labor. This will be manifested in a broad variety of areas. One has only to glance at the increment in individuals over the age of sixty-five, from 20 million in 1970 to 34 million in 1995, to see one reflection of the increased demand for personal services—and this in the face of a drastic shrinkage in the labor force. Technological innovation will be the key to closing the gap.

It will be services, judging from past trends both here and abroad, that will dominate employment growth. As shown in Table 7–10, even the success stories of the 1970s—Germany and Japan—showed little increment in goods-producing employment; indeed, Germany actually had a small decline. It is the service sector throughout the advanced industrial economies that represent the future.

While the exhortations for growth in productivity necessary for survival in an increasing competitive world economy have been directed toward manufacturing, services have been the real productivity laggards. As labor shortfalls loom—and as a byproduct, labor costs increase—the imperatives of mechanization in the service sector are evident. Demographic and economic parameters strongly suggest a far greater degree of receptivity to new technology—borne of necessity. Predicting its impact, however, is far more problematic.

PREDICTING TECHNOLOGICAL IMPACT

While we have suggested the level of uncertainty in forecasting demographics, much less is our capacity to envision the technological future—and perhaps even more strikingly the levels and pace of adaptation to the alternatives that it makes possible. It is not yet a generation since the concept of the computer utility dominated technical literature with a vision of super high speed central computers whose capacities were so unique as to require relatively few of them—with users tied in via dedicated wire networks.[1] Project Multics, the principal effort in this regard, cost the General Electric Company its taste for competing in the computer field—and this despite enormous levels of financing and a massive input at MIT.[2] At least as of this writing, the free-standing small scale computer linked as a peer to a broad network—with no necessary central point—is now being viewed as the pattern for the future.

The uproar on video games as a defiler of youth—with commercial versions absorbing somewhere on the order of 25 billion quarters in 1982 and even greater market penetration predicted with new technological lures—has moved to the land of the hula-hoop. The best selling toys of 1984 were not computers—they were not even electronic—but rather the Cabbage Patch doll and its incident number of accessories and knockoffs. Modernity fell out, dolls fell in.[3]

But technological innovation can have far-ranging ramifications, changing our folkways. Dedication to location was evidenced in the past by the vast network of baseball leagues. Does anybody still go to the Class A League Albany Senators? The memory of the Newark Bears and the Jersey City Giants has passed into legend, but they have been replaced by new TV loyalties, seemingly independent of place. The Dallas Cowboys are now advanced as "America's Team" in football.

In a recent suburban garden apartment study conducted by the Rutgers University Center for Urban Policy Research (Horowitz 1983), respondents tended to describe their location in terms of highways and shopping centers, not municipalities. Areal orientation remains; its axes and artifacts, however, are altered. The immediacy of the local movie theater and its accompanying handful of stores in small town America has largely disappeared, but the regional shopping centers have become "teenage villages." Adaptation has many forms; there are relatively few technological imperatives with such vigor as to support instant forecasts. Retailing provides an insightful example of the complexities at work.

The Retailing Evolution

The ambivalent nature of technology in altering areal patterns and organizational formats is exemplified by retailing. The pattern of communications of a hundred years ago revolved around major city wholesalers who concentrated the products of small-scale manufacturers, and/or imports, and in turn maintained traveling sales forces that serviced the decentralized pattern of small merchants located at every crossroads location, U.S.A. As so ably pointed out by Chandler (1977) in *The Visible Hand,* prior to the Civil War, with the exception of the industries that rose to service the railroads, manufacturing was conducted in very small, individually owned facilities. The railroads provided the transit facilities for the drummers, and for delivery of goods. The communications lines typically were the mail service—again typically carried by the railroads—as well as the telegraph, which commonly used the same rights of way.

Given the seasonal character of a largely agricultural society, credit provision was central, both from retailers to consumers—and from wholesalers to retailers as well. Despite the early rise of advertising, its media and potency were relatively limited. Quality was essentially locally certified, and this was increasingly the case as individual retailers grew in scale. As late at 1910 a minority of Americans lived in urban areas, with localism a dominant. The rise of cities was accompanied—and perhaps aided as well—by a synergistic relationship between the expansion of local newspapers and local retailing. The growth that ensued permitted the development of the classic department store, an optimization of the economics of central place that was to continue practically to our own time. The high-speed press fostered this expansion. The newspaper was king, and retailing its most prominent patron.

Certification of quality was a function of having bought at Bambergers' or Lazarus or Altman's or any of the other major downtown facilities. But this dominance of what was in effect local branding, paralleling the equivalent hegemony of local advertising media and communications, was challenged in the years immediately prior to World War II—and has nearly disappeared in recent decades.

While the first rise of national magazines of significant circulation occurred around the turn of the century, the rise of true national brands was a function of the development of radio. There had been pioneers before in exotic consumer goods, such as brands of cigarettes, but soon they were joined in by a broad variety of other nondurable consumer goods. This was the era of Jello and Chase and Sanborn coffee.

For the upscale market the national magazines had increasing style/brand potency, and with it centralization of manufacture. Just prior to World War I, for example, there were more than a thousand individual manufacturers of pianos in America. Steinway and Baldwin, in tune with *Vanity Fair* and the early version of *The Saturday Evening Post,* soon signaled a very substantial curtailment, with an equivalent process taking place in automobiles. To make a genius of the obvious, this was just the beginning as we moved into the television era, which provided a much broader spectrum of information, of dynamic visuals, and national—and increasingly international—brands. The role of local retailers as certifiers of quality gave way before the rise of these national entities whose very scale permitted the development of technology. The relationship was an enormously dynamic one. Color television without the potential availability of advertising dollars would at the very least have waited for another generation—and perhaps forever.

What was the impact on retailing? In the very act of providing brand certification, the goods in question became commodities. The package of services, of aura, and most of all credibility given by the local retailer was subsumed by the manufacturer and certified by national media. The Good Housekeeping Seal was alive implicitly before it was formalized. Grocery stores might decry the very low markups available and lack of price protection on national merchandise, but they had to carry the goods—they were literally pulled through the channels of distribution. The rise of the discount house and other forms of reasonably efficient distribution left the old mechanisms—and their historic areal distributions—in disarray. *Where you bought something became much less important than what you paid for it. The definition of staples/commodities was enormously broadened by the new communications channels.* And Main Street America became obsolete.

Paralleling this development, and to a certain degree contravening it, was the rise of the chain store operations. These called for a rigorous standardization of operation, an assumption of replicability of market and location, and the capacity to merchandise and administer from a central node. Again coming to full vigor roughly around the turn of the century, their dominance of the urban scene was epitomized by Sinclair Lewis's *Main Street* with the presence on every Main Street in America of Thom McAn, A&P, JCPenney and the like. And the scale of these operations—without the abilities of our new high technology—was considerable indeed. JCPenney's, for example, prior to its current consolidation, had more than 1,600 units—A&P at its peak more than 30,000 (Moody's Investor Service Annual).

The technologies involved were all in place three generations ago: rail and then truck shipping, telegraph and telephone for communications, and dependable mail service both for parcels and unit-control purposes (i.e., detailed information on a daily base of items sold, stock needs and the like, forwarded to a central location for information processing and response). While chain store dominance of small town America has been decried, it permitted a substantial broadening of market centers, which flourished as a function of—and undoubtedly facilitated—the thickening of urban America which so vigorously characterized the 1920s.

None of these institutional developments can be characterized simply as either centralizing or decentralizing in their nature. There is strikingly little in current technology that so far has altered that generalization. Machine-readable unit-control tickets were envisioned in the 1920s

—and came into being in the beginning of the 1950s. So far they have merely replicated the information available utilizing flocks of clericals. At least in the United States, videotex shopping has been notable by its failures. A more vigorous effort in this regard under government auspices is being promulgated in Western Europe, particularly in France. Again, however, the vision of shopping at home, while continuously reinforced by the vigor of mail order, has not significantly altered the broad spectrum of retail merchandising. The modern suburban shopping center, in its replacement of Main Street, is much more a tribute to the national highway program (and, if anything, a belated tribute) than it is to communications or information technology.

The influence of technologies and informational processing *past* is evident in the retailing configurations *present*. These in turn certainly have impacted on the areal distribution of economic activity and population concentrations as well. As of the moment, while there is much in the way of new information/communications technology that could produce significant shifts in the near-term future, there is little in the way of market success. Even the computer has facilitated but not basically altered extant functions.

Mail order, which a generation ago was viewed as a leftover remnant of an understored, rural America, has expanded. In substantial part this is a tribute to the speed, cost efficiency, and excellence of reproduction made possible by modern color printing mechanisms particularly when linked with the consumer targeting and partitioning made possible by the computer.

Videotex, which would be the next logical development in nonstore retailing, is certainly technologically feasible. As of the moment it requires the equivalent of a Sarnoff, with the level of commitment and fiscal competence that was required to deliver color TV. The threshold conditions are so substantial as to have defeated the several entrepreneurial groups that have assaulted it in this country. Even at its most grandiose, it is difficult to believe that it would serve as a passive surrogate for present-day shopping—so much of it is particularly in the suburban shopping center, a tribute to a recreational/social outing as much as it is for exclusively retail purposes.[4] The two-worker household may lean more heavily on nonstore marketing, but the heft of sales is traditional.

The prepunched computer control tag has replaced some of the clericals, hard-wired sales registers linked to computers have abated some of the problems of sales audits, and new self-service fixturing combined with brand identification has limited the expansion of sales help; and these and similar elements clearly will be implemented in the future. Similarly, warehouses have given way to the distribution center with concomitant declines in the carrying costs of inventory. This is linked with a far greater capacity to limit costs and target merchandise or short order with real-time information processing. And it has altered labor force requirements and the loci of employment.

Credit

The subject of the provision and sources of credit over time deserves much more attention than we are able to give it. The old pattern of credit provision by wholesalers to retailers and, in turn, by them to individual customers of a century ago gave way in time to a bifurcation: Small retailers continued this pattern—the larger ones went into the credit business on their own. By working directly with manufacturers and depending only upon normal trade terms—indeed sometimes paying cash—they were able to bring down price. In turn they extended credit to their consumers based on their own fiscal competence and became increasingly dependent on the profitability of consumer credit per se. The range of price, merchandise offerings, and credit certified the unique position of the central city retail giants. They, in turn, assured the pulling power and dominance of the cities they occupied.

Each institution individually provided credit to the same customers; the amount of credit checking and general paper work was enormously redundant. The rise of central credit facilities (i.e., American Express, Visa, and their equivalents) represents a very substantial compaction of this process. Enormously more credit transactions can be undertaken with a reduction of staff per transaction as a function of centralization and the automation of procedures that it permits. While precise data on this point are lacking, it is clear that the competence of the new information technologies has permitted an enormous expansion of credit. While person power per transaction has been reduced, the sheer growth of the operation has provided even more in the way of jobs than would otherwise be the case.

Not the least important reflection of the centralization of credit (even some of the major department stores are foregoing the exclusive use of their own credit cards) has been a lifeline extended to relatively small-scale operations. Local vendors now can be represented in shopping centers and other high transient areas—where they do not know their customers—but still extend credit based on central information processing. *Personal knowledge gives way to formalized centralized information processing. The former is coterminous with sales place, the latter relatively independent.* The rejuvenation of decentralized retailing is in part a reflection, therefore, of the centralization of consumer credit. The back room of the local retailer—once devoted to unit control, to credit files, and perhaps as well even to payroll and sales audit—now can be transported through hardware to an infinite range of locations; and along with them, the jobs that are involved.

The Retail Dynamic and the Limitations of Technology

Perhaps the most consequential innovation of the last fifty years in retail distribution has not been a function of technology, but rather conscious or unconscious systems analysis. This has revoled around the substitution of the customer as order picker for paid labor. Beginning in the depths of the Depression, this was pioneered by the early supermarkets. Clerks behind counters who served as order pickers gave way to bulk stocking (initially in packing cases with, at most, primitive fixturing). The customer served as order picker. The results in terms of efficiency of distribution, largely as a function of the reduction of labor costs, were truly revolutionary.

Efforts at high-tech approaches to the same functional juncture—such as going from wholesale lots (cases) to individual orders—have failed (because of the low costs made possible by self-service). Thus, as early as the 1920s, there were efforts to mechanize order picking with primitive electromechanical devices. Similarly, in the 1940s and 1950s, Grand Union failed with the same approach. Home delivery of foods, attempted in Sweden through centralized warehousing and customer-telephoned orders—accompanied by some measure of electronic gadgetry—foundered on the same rock. Customer self-service is tough to beat in cost. The development of the shopping cart was much more consequential than the new code marking—and the laser registers that have come in its wake. At this writing, the latter innovations have made possible the use of lower class labor (or is it the same class of labor with poorer educations and less arithmetic capacity?) but are dwarfed in consequences by the much more basic systems change. Customer order picking has been so efficient that it is now used in a variety of nonfood areas, as witness the fixturing of the modern-day liquor store, hardware store, home improvement center—and increasingly soft goods merchandise emporiums as well.

As we have indicated earlier, information technology has been more significant in providing access to broader based, areally dispersed selective networks of specialized consumers. This has been fostered by specialized publications—the *Radio Controlled Modeler, The American Orchid Review*—and literally thousands of other media. It is complemented on a broader base by the increasingly sophisticated utilization of census data for specialized mailing—that is, the *Sharper Image* catalog and the ready-to-wear offerings of rugged clothing for the "*L.L. Bean*-ized" urbanite. The total scale of these special mailing efforts has been enormously facilitated by the rise of credit mechanisms independent of specific retailers.

STASIS AND INERTIA

The basic locomotion devices employed in the journey to work have been relatively little changed in a half century. As far back as 1929, the United States turned out as many cars per capita as it did last year;[5] and while the trolley has given way wholly to the bus, the commuter railroads have altered little or at all.

The revolution of suburbanization, we would suggest, has been as much a function of affluence as of technological revolution. Within the latter domain, it is much more a tribute to the national highway program than to communication devices, at least in its first generation (roughly through 1970). It was the Depression of the 1930s, plus five years of wartime constraint, that inhibited the complementary dispersion of population and economic function that was the appropriate complement of the information and transportation innovations of the 1920s, principal among them the telephone. The omnipresence of this incredibly inexpensive device as a facilitator of both centralization and decentralization has often been cited—its prominence is worthy of reiteration.

But even given the constraints of the 1930s and World War II, there was a very long gap between technological competence and societal reaction. The first major enclosed suburban mall dates from the early 1950s, but the large-scale suburban shopping center really did not come into full blossom until the succeeding decade (Sternlieb and Hughes 1981).

It was not until the mid-1970s that the major part of office construction moved out of the central city (Sternlieb and Hughes 1984).

There is a powerful flywheel of custom that leads to inertia. This is particularly the case when it is linked with the enormous sunk costs and slow replacement cycles that characterize American society. We have both the conservative virtues and demerits of long-term affluence and development. A good housing year is one in which starts are roughly equal to 2 percent of the extant stock, portions of which go merely to replace facilities that are scrapped. In New York City, for example, over the last ten years new housing starts have averaged on the order of 10,000 units a year. Given a base of nearly 2.8 million, this would suggest a building replacement cycle on the order of 300 years. While equivalent data on industrial facilities suffers from changes in their nature over time, the average age of the gross stock of fixed nonresidential business capital hovers around the 10-year mark (U.S. Bureau of the Census 1984a). *Thus there can be a much more abrupt response to changes in information technology on the part of production facilities than holds true in terms of settlement patterns.* The latter are complicated by the enormously potent role that housing plays in the United States as a source of personal savings. More than 60 percent of the equity of Americans is frozen in personal housing ownership (Federal Reserve 1984). The conflict between these two elements—the first with a fifty-year "replication cycle," the latter with one only a fifth as lengthy—is particularly striking as we move toward the end of the twentieth century. It has served as a stabilizer of older settlement patterns. Much of what we see as suburbanization or regional shift is a belated response of the latter to new economic spatial imperatives.

Journey to Work and the Electronic Cottage

The journey to work data available from the 1980 Census illustrates in considerable detail the growing congruence between work and residence place. Journey to work times have not expanded; indeed, there is some indication of their contracting. The central city as the major focal point clearly has given way to peripheral, point-to-point, commutation, and with this, a growing dominance of private means of transport as against public conveyors.

The incongruity between the vast amounts of funding that the latter are absorbing versus their declining utilization raises some very real issues as to their continuance. The degenerative spiral of declining usage leading to increased fares, and declining maintenance/service leading to further patronage declines, seems to characterize our older facilities. These tend to set up frictions in commuting to places that are dependent upon public transit—particularly rail transit.

The prototype is New York City. As the commuter linkages begin to generate much more in the way of friction (costs, timetables, and comfort), there is a split in response. On the one hand we have those who can afford to live proximate to the workplace—typically Manhattan—doing so. The long-term decline of Manhattan's population—a process that has nearly seventy years of antecedent—now seemingly has, at the very least, plateaued. But a growing proportion of its job base is maintained by commuters—and there is some indication that their faithfulness to this process has been and will be reduced in time (Stegman 1985). Thus the rise in peripheral locations (northern New Jersey being a premier example) of competing office facilities yields a shift to closer proximity of workplace and residence place. Just as the cutting and styling and selling operations of New York's garment center lofts can remain there while the sewing shops moved to cheaper locations with linkages of interstate trucking, so we see back room office facilities moving peripheral to the city—and sometimes at far greater distance. This latter process in information handling has its equivalent technological enabling mechanisms: the era of the computer—and high-speed communications linkages. Clearly the end of this dynamic is not at hand.

In 1983, with roughly similar sized populations, New Jersey secured four times as many new housing units—and northern New Jersey by itself alone twice as much office space—as New York City. While final data for 1984 are lacking at this writing, current estimates suggest an equivalent disproportionate development. And jobs are increasingly footloose. They can follow as well as lead people.[6]

The close linkage of workplace and residence place is exemplified by journey to work patterns.[7] In 1980, there were approximately 75 million workers sixteen years of age and over resident in metropolitan America. Of the 29 million of them who lived in central cities, fully 25 million worked inside the SMSA of their residence, but barely three million of them in the central business district of their central city. The combined total of those working inside another SMSA—or working outside SMSAs—barely exceeded the million mark.

This is confirmed when the data on workers living outside the central city is viewed. Fully 38 million of the grand total of 45 million for whom data is available worked inside the Standard Metropolitan Statistical Area (SMSA) of residence—but only a third within the central city. The basic technology of communications and information processing now being implemented have been available for at least twenty years. The lag again caused by the fly wheel of custom leaves a gap between technological competence and market fulfillment, but this is rapidly receding into the past.

The absolute measure of this spatial dispersion is most difficult to quantify. The extremes may well be the export of the task of updating mailing lists to the English speaking parts of the Caribbean, or the much noted shift of Citibank's credit facilities to the Dakotas, or of Philadelphia's Sun Oil's credit operation to the South and the like.

There are countervening forces at work as well. Estimates by Regina Armstrong at the Regional Plan Association, for example, suggest that roughly one-half million jobs in the New York region are dependent upon foreign investment. And more than 100,000 of these jobs stem from foreign firm operations in Manhattan (Armstrong). A tribute to this hegemony is the new wave of national centralization of banking, brokerage, and insurance facilities within that city. The World Trade Center may have been a premature title—it is now representative of a potent reality.

While covered more fully elsewhere it is evident that information technology has subverted localism in terms of banking. Despite the scar tissue of legislation left over from the Depression, the defacto nationalization of banking is at hand. It is evidenced by the Bank of America consolidating 2,000 employees in New York City; its international equivalent is revealed by the enormous flow of foreign establishments into the city.

Question must be raised in this context, as to what happens to the old regional centers with the rise of a national and world economy. Philadelphia, at least in banking, is becoming a branch city. Even Chicago is threatened by the same fate.

Some measure of the rise of the new dominance of New York in this context is shown in Table 7–11, which indicates the flow of international phone calls from various major cities in the United States. New York City alone accounted for more than 20 percent of them. "More than twice as many overseas message units were generated by New York City as by Los Angeles. When New York City, northern New Jersey, Long Island, and the four New York State counties north of New York City are added together, the New York metropolitan region accounts for almost 30 percent of the total" (Moss 1984). While some of this flow

Table 7-11. Overseas Message Units.

AREA CODE	
New York City 212	22,718,027
Los Angeles 213	9,310,028
San Francisco 415	4,535,474
Chicago 312	4,028,709
Northern New Jersey 201	4,639,122
Connecticut 203	2,129,146
Westchester, Putnam, Orange and Rockland Counties (NY) 914	1,897,576
Nassau-Suffolk, Long Island (NY) 516	1,705,740
Total (USA)	115,001,763

Source: AT&T Communications. Secured from Mitchell L. Moss. 1984. "New York Isn't Just New York Anymore." *Journal of the International Institute of Communications* 12, no. 4/5 (July/September).

undoubtedly represents nonbusiness calls—proportionate to New York's enormous ethnic population—there is no question of its uniqueness.

The ambiguous role of new information technology with regard to centralization or decentralization is exemplified in the growing challenges to the monolithic role of utility companies, which had central places as their focal point. The new technology is much more spatially ambiguous. For example, NYNEX (the Northeast's regional phone company) derives a disproportionate share of revenues from its largest business customers, with 3 percent of them providing a third of its business revenues; one percent of New York Telephone's business customers generate 25 percent of its revenues. Fully eighty-five out of one hundred top revenue producing customers of New York Telephone Company are located in Manhattan; the borough in and of itself contains 46 percent of New York Telephone's business access lines and contributes 35 percent of its total revenues.[8]

The very scale of the major customers however, permits them to develop bypass operations for their own proprietary use and/or to participate in alternative inexpensive approaches geared to large-scale users. An example is the New York Teleport being built by Merrill Lynch, Western Union, and the Port Authority of New York and New Jersey.

This is a communications complex nearing completion on Staten Island designed to connect customers in the New York metropolitan area with all outside calling points. The customers in turn are linked directly to the Teleport by fiber cable rather than through New York Telephone facilities. Heavy line users were once substantially tied to central city, but how close to the central "exchange" does one have to be in order to take advantage of these efficiencies of scale?

Present technology involving laying of cables, interestingly enough, is following the rights of way of the railroads. Does this suggest office development will be areally defined by the railway line disposition put in place nearly a century ago? Or is there a greater measure of freedom even within today's parameters, much less those of tomorrow? Cable television, for example, provides a second bypass threat to the New York Telephone Company. Commercial data transmission services will soon be available connecting directly to New York and the American Stock Exchange with link to the Teleport, thus enabling subscribers to bypass the local loop completely.

On the one hand, we can envision this type of development as permitting large-scale firms to stay in what is a high-cost location—and making permanent its job base and related settlement pattern as well. But even if technology is so limited as to require this close proximity—the potential feedback on the cost structures of those firms that are not able to take advantage of the new elements must be viewed with some trepidation. Telephone service (and indeed many other elements of New York) is a very high fixed cost operation. A reduction in the user base could require catastrophic increases in the pro-rated charges to the balance of the utility's customers. This in turn could speed decentralization.

These possibilities are far from unique to New York. We would suggest, however, that they are most potent in our older metropoli with fixed capital costs that are particularly sensitive to reduction in usage. This has already been evidenced in the case of the subways and public transit in general—and these may only herald things to come.

As pointed out by Mitchell L. Moss (1984), however, there are requirements imposed by a world economy that may have a very serious feedback, given the limitations of New York City as a whole—and Manhattan in particular. The 24-hour business day is premier among them. The very costs of infrastructure, and the requirements for providing services and information on a worldwide base, impose equivalent staffing requirements. And New York City is not an easy place within which to provide required security. The trans-Hudson City of Manhattan—

northern New Jersey—may play a much more imposing role in the future in this regard. Security difficulties may impose limitations on the growth of Manhattan and the other boroughs as well.

The perfection of communications opens up a variety of alternative locations. The very cost structures of the city and its limited capacity to provide housing for middle management constricts crucial labor force flows. The elite can buy space proximate to work while youthful aspirants are willing to accept very poor housing conditions in order to be close to the dynamo. Other less affluent or less flexible homeseekers are, however, driven away.

Amidst an enormous flow of plenty seen by visitors to New York is the harsh reality of median 1983 renter household incomes under $13,000—and of median homeowner (including co-ops and condominiums) incomes of $25,000 (Stegman 1985). A thin veneer of the rich glamorizes the eye and distracts it from a rather broad spectrum of the poor. However, the sheer animal vitality of the city and its increasing focus—as pointed out very presciently more than a dozen years ago by Eli Ginzberg (1973)—on production services, provides a rare base of opportunity. Even here, however, there is some indication that an increasing proportion of this growth is going to commuters. In 1979 roughly 6 percent of Manhattan's jobs were held by New Jerseyans. Estimates by the Port Authority of New York and New Jersey (1985) indicate that approximately 23 percent of the growth in jobs in that borough over the last five years have flowed to New Jerseyans. Ultimately the jobs will follow the people.

New forms of coaxial cable, optical fiber, and microwave transmission facilities—and as yet unknown and unseen mechanisms—will be put in place. What they suggest is an increase in bifurcation: of centralization of functions on the one hand, and a capacity to spread them out on the other. *In this context we would suggest that technology is an enabling element rather than a determinative one. The impact of technology must be viewed through a matrix of societal elements that shape its ultimate areal resolution—and settlement patterns as well.*

Nowhere is this requirement more evident than in predictions of a society of "electronic cottages." The pinnacle of industrial urbanization was the central city that emerged in the nineteenth century, built on massed population, productive power, and industrial technology. In contrast is the view that the end point of the communications revolution is the electronic cottage. The information era will bring decentralization, just as the industrial era wrought centralization. Households will be free of spatial ties as they work at their dispersed residences—information will commute, not people. A vision of post-industrial cottage industries is raised; knitting is replaced by information work.

The reality to come will not be nearly so extreme. Just as the regional shopping center flourishes despite the potentials of electronic retailing, so too will the office remain a viable workplace. People will still want to be with people. As Naisbett has suggested, the more technology we pump into society, the more people will seek the "high touch" of the office and shopping mall. "The gee-whiz futurists are always wrong because they believe technological innovation travels in a straight line. It doesn't. It weaves and bobs and lurches and sputters" (Naisbett 1982).

NOTES

1. See Security and Exchange Commission (SEC) Registration for C.W. Adams Associates, 1961.
2. See Organick (1972) for background on this point. See also Brooks, Jr. (1979).
3. The data cited here were secured from a series of investment research reports prepared by Goldman Sachs & Co.
4. For a more positive view, see Gordon (1984).
5. This conclusion is based on automobile production and population data secured from Motor Vehicle Manufacturers Association (1979) and the U.S. Bureau of the Census (1984a).
6. Data secured from the New Jersey Department of Labor, Trenton, New Jersey.
7. The data in the following two paragraphs were secured from U.S. Bureau of the Census (1984b).
8. Data obtained from Goldman Sachs (1984) report on NYNEX Corporation.

REFERENCES

Armstrong, R. "The Future of New York in the World Economy." Unpublished paper, The Regional Plan Association, New York City, New York.
Brooks, Jr., F. 1979. *The Mythical Man-Month*. Reading, MA: Addison-Wesley.
Chandler, A. 1977. *The Visible Hand: The Managerial Revolution in American Business*. Cambridge, MA: Harvard University Press.
Federal Reserve. 1984. "Survey of Consumer Finances, 1983." *Federal Reserve Bulletin* (September).

Ginzberg, E. 1973. *New York is Very Much Alive: A Manpower View.* New York: McGraw-Hill.
Goldman Sachs & Co. 1984. *NYNEX: An Investment Report.* New York: Goldman Sachs & Co.
Gordon, W. 1984. "Electronic Retailing: Trends and Implications." *Urban Land* (October).
Horowitz, C. 1983. *The New Garden Apartment.* New Brunswick, NJ: Center for Urban Policy Research, Rutgers University.
Kingsbury, F. 1895. "The Tendency of Man to Live in Cities." *Journal of Social Science* 33 (November).
Moody's Investor Service. Annual. *Moody's Industrial Manual.* New York.
Moss, M. 1984. "New York Isn't Just New York Anymore." *Journal of the International Institute of Communications* 12, no. 4/5 (July/September).
Motor Vehicle Manufacturers Association. 1979. *MVMA Motor Vehicles Facts and Figures '79.* Detroit, MI.
Naisbett, J. 1982. *Megatrends.* New York: Warner Books.
Organick, E. 1972. *The MULTICS System.* Cambridge, MA: MIT Press.
[The] Port Authority of New York and New Jersey. 1985. *The Regional Economy: 1984 Review, 1985 Outlook for the New York-New Jersey Metropolitan Region,* New York.
President's Research Committee on Social Trends. 1933. *Recent Social Trends in the United States.* New York: McGraw-Hill.
Stegman, M. 1985. *Housing in New York City: 1984.* New Brunswick, NJ: Center for Urban Policy Research, Rutgers University.
Sternlieb, G., and J. Hughes. eds. 1981. *Shopping Centers: U.S.A.* New Brunswick, NJ: Center for Urban Policy Research, Rutgers University.
Sternlieb, G., and J. Hughes. 1984. *Income and Jobs: U.S.A.* New Brunswick, NJ: Center for Urban Policy Research, Rutgers University.
Sternlieb, G., J. Hughes, and C. Hughes. 1983. *Demographic Trends and Economic Reality: Planning and Markets in the 1980s.* New Brunswick, NJ: Center for Urban Policy Research, Rutgers University.
U.S. Bureau of the Census. 1984a. *Statistical Abstract of the United States: 1985.* Washington, D.C.
―――. 1984b. *Census of Population: 1980. Journey-to-Work: Metropolitan Commuting Flows.* Washington, D.C.

DISCUSSION OF CHAPTER 7

Peter Linneman

The authors have written a readable and provocative essay on how future demographic patterns will alter the adoption and impacts of technological innovations. One of the most enjoyable aspects of the paper is their efforts to "gaze into the crystal ball" and make forecasts about both demographic and innovation patterns. These projections, while fascinating in their own right, are most interesting because they highlight the historic failing of the social sciences to predict very far into the future with any degree of accuracy. Although their projections for the most part seem absolutely sensible, the cynical reader knows with close to certainty that they will be wrong—but not *why* they will be wrong! Examples of this type of problem abound in the literature. For example, no one foresaw the economic shock of upward spiralling oil prices in the 1970s, or the almost equal downward spiral in these prices (in real terms) in the 1980s. One cannot help but wonder what unexpected economic shock will ruin the authors' forecasts and projections.

In their analysis of the future regional population forecasts, the authors adopt the traditional view that the northeastern Standard Metropolitan Statistical Areas are suffering because they have experienced much lower population growth rates (often static or even slightly negative). These patterns, however, may reflect simply that these more mature areas have already achieved something akin to their optimal size (in terms of the trade-offs between positive and negative externalities).

The notable dimension in population growth patterns may well be that other areas of the country are finally moving towards more optimal sizes.

In evaluating the growth of the Sunbelt in the past two to three decades, I feel that the authors underemphasize the contribution of technological advances in facilitating this growth. One tends to forget how innovations in air navigation and air transportation have reduced the costs associated with traveling to and from the Sunbelt, particularly for the middle class. Similarly, technological advances in irrigation, land management (including land reclamation), pest control, indoor climate control, and telecommunications, to name but a few, have enhanced the "livability" of the Sunbelt. For example, the advent of satellite disks, VCRs, cable television, and "superstations" have transformed many of the more remote areas of the Sunbelt from "cultural wastelands" to offering the same (and often greater) television choice as major urban centers such as New York. This is not to deny the importance suggested by the authors of the interstate highway system in this process, but rather to indicate the importance of technological innovations to the development of the Sunbelt.

The authors present a very thorough description of the historic evolution of the retailing industry's response to technological forces. Their argument that as centralized credit analysis was enhanced by technology, the need for centralized shopping facilities was diminished is particularly insightful.

The authors predict that technology will continue to effect employment patterns. They also foresee that the labor force will increasingly be employed in the service sector. For this reason, the authors argue that technological advances will be particularly needed in the service sector. While not denying the logic of these arguments, it is important to remember that much of the employment in the service sector reflects "face-to-face" interactions between customers and service providers. While lawyers, doctors, hair stylists, and the like can certainly gain more effectiveness from technological advances, many of the services they offer are truly personal in nature. For example, no matter what technological advancements occur, baseball (as we know it today) will still require nine players for each team. The service sector is well advised to realize the importance of personal interactions before it tries to replace them with technological interaction. The very low response rate for "computerized" telephone interviews is a current example of this type of problem. Survey respondents are far more willing to hang-up on a machine than a human. This suggests that certain areas of the service sector may be expected to remain relatively immune to technological advances.

Sternlieb and Hughes present a well-conceived and interesting exploration of future possibilities for information technology. I plan to hold onto this paper for fifteen years so that I can evaluate to what extent "economic shocks" cause their forecasts to be wrong.

DISCUSSION OF CHAPTER 7

Mitchell Moss

There are two major schools of thought regarding the effects of information technology on cities. The most widely held view is that new information technologies will ultimately lead to the demise of cities by allowing electronic means of communication to substitute for face-to-face transactions. Advanced telecommunications technologies, in this context, make it possible to obtain all the benefits of urban life, such as access to a diversity of cultural and information sources as well as contact with work and family, without confronting the frictions of urban life—such as commuting, crime, congestion, and pollution. Ronald Abler (1970) was one of the first geographers to suggest that as cities evolved from manufacturing to information centers, the very location of a city could be called into question.

> Advances in information transmission may soon permit us to disperse information-gathering and decision-making activities away from metropolitan centers, and electronic communications media will make all kinds of information equally abundant everywhere in the nation, if not everywhere in the world. When that occurs, the downtown areas of our metropolitan centers are sure to lose some of their locational advantages for management and governmental activities.

The idea that information technology would obviate the need for cities was also raised by urban planners, such as Melvin Webber (1973) who asked: "Could the forthcoming and unprecedented demands for long-distance communication combine with the space-spanning capacities of the new communications technologies to concoct a solvent that could dissolve the city?" (Webber 1973) One writer has even suggested that "telecommunications has done more than anything else, since the invention of money, to reduce the constraints of the physical environment on organization" (Kellerman 1984).

The alternative perspective, drawn largely from the history of the telephone, holds that communications technologies can facilitate both concentration and dispersion of economic activities. As Jean Gottmann (1977) has stated, "The telephone's impact on office location has thus been dual: first, it has freed the office from the previous necessity of locating next to the operations it directed; second, it has helped to gather offices in large concentrations in special areas."

George Sternlieb and James W. Hughes' essay, "Information Technology, Demographics, and the Retail Response," builds upon the Gottmann thesis by examining the way in which economic and demographic forces have contributed to both centralizing and decentralizing trends. The authors believe that technology is an "enabling element rather than a deterministic one. The impact of technology must be viewed through a matrix of societal elements which shape its ultimate real resolution—and settlement patterns as well." They present a detailed analysis of demographic trends in the United States, highlighting the processes of decentralization of cities, suburbanization, and regional shifts from the Northeast and Midwest to the South and West.

Sternlieb and Hughes' principle argument, however, concerns the "homogenization of space," the way in which "information technology has made much of the historical functions of the older core areas obsolete or, at best, opened them to very substantial and increasingly successful competition." Drawing upon a case study of the retailing industry, they demonstrate how communications and information technologies have led to the rise of the national chain stores, the decline of the traditional downtown locally owned retail department store, the growth of computerized credit bureaus, and the end of credit based on personal ties and knowledge.

The interaction of technology with spatial patterns does not often work in predictable ways, as the authors insightfully note: "The rejuvenation of decentralized retailing is in part a reflection, therefore, of the centralization of consumer credit." Indeed, it is one of the great ironies of consumer services that the availability of national credit cards, in combination with the 800 telephone number system, has stimulated retail growth in what are geographically remote stores, such as L.L. Bean's in Maine, Land's End in Wisconsin, and a variety of other specialized establishments. Telecommunications has converted the "mail order" catalogue operation, initially designed for farmers far from cities, into an electronic shopping center—utilizing long-distance telephone, on-line credit verification, and mail-distributed print catalogues—that extends the geographic reach of stores in rural areas to urban and suburban households throughout the nation.

The issues raised by Sternlieb and Hughes highlight the need for a greater understanding of the relationship of information technology to patterns of urban development. Clearly, technology does not, by itself, bring about locational change. Yet new telecommunications systems do open up opportunities for development that were not previously available, and not all cities and regions are able to take advantage of the opportunities presented by technological change effectively. The growth of national banking operations in Delaware reflects the strategic role of state tax and regulatory policy in attracting footloose financial service firms. Where firms once located manufacturing plants near natural resources and transportation networks, the information based services of the 1980s and 1990s will require access to high-speed data networks, a skilled labor force, and a favorable set of residential and educational services—all of which are subject to public intervention.

Moreover, there is growing evidence that the process of technological innovation is quite uneven and that the deployment of new fiber optic systems will occur in large metropolitan centers first, thus giving major urban centers a "technological edge" over small- and medium-size cities (Moss 1986). In fact, despite the popular rhetoric about telecommunications leading to geographic dispersion, advanced producer services are predominantly concentrated in the largest American cities (Noyelle 1983).

Although many firms have moved out of central cities, most of the movement has been to outlying suburban areas and to a handful of cities in the South and West, not to a randomly distributed set of places across the North American continent. Far more attention is given to a locational change resulting from a move out of a central city than to the equally pervasive expansion of financial or management service firms within the central business districts of large world cities. What is perhaps most remarkable about the growth of new information technologies is the fact that we have not yet found a substitute for face-to-face contact. There are far more bits of information transmitted through the business lunch than through the videoconference. The challenge for researchers is to determine how interpersonal contact has been enhanced through the use of advanced telecommunications systems. For example, the "trading room" of an investment bank is designed to accommodate an elaborate telecommunications infrastructure and an equally high level of informal information exchange among the traders who sit "cheek by jowl."

Our knowledge of information technology is far greater than our understanding of how such technologies influence the day-to-day activities and locational choices of individuals and firms. The distinctive contribution of Sternlieb and Hughes has been their analysis of how demographic trends are likely to shape the future use of new technologies. It is not enough, however, to examine one social parameter as a guide for understanding the impact of technology. The use of information technology generates its own set of social and economic consequences. Our intellectual frameworks for studying urban regions need to recognize the dynamic nature of communications technology and its influence on the operations of the manufacturing and service sectors. To date, far more attention has been given to the false prophets who predict the potential impacts of information technology than to the more important task of assessing actual effects of new information technology so that we can formulate an informed and intelligent policy to assure the economic health of cities and large metropolitan regions.

REFERENCES

Abler, Ronald. 1970. "What Makes Cities Important." *Bell Telephone Magazine* 49, no. 2 (March-April):15.

Gottmann, Jean. 1977. "Megalopolis and Antipolis: The Telephone and the Structure of the City." In *The Social Impact of the Telephone,* edited by Ithiel de Sola Pool. Cambridge, Mass.: MIT Press, p. 310.

Kellerman, Aharon. 1984. "Telecommunications and the Geography of Metropolitan Areas." *Human Geography* 8, no. 2 (June):222, citing C. Cherry, "Electronic Communication: A Force for Dispersal." *Official Architecture and Planning* 33:733–36.

Moss, Mitchell I. 1986. "Telecommunications and the Future of Cities." *Land Development Studies.*

Noyelle, Thierry J. 1983. "The Rise of Advanced Services." *Journal of the American Planning Association* 49, no. 3 (Summer).

Webber, Melvin M. 1973. "Urbanization and Communications." In *Communications Technology and Social Policy,* edited by George Gerbner et al. New York: John Wiley, p. 301.

8 INFORMATION TECHNOLOGY AND THE SERVICE SECTOR: A FEEDBACK PROCESS?

William J. Baumol

The explosion of techniques for the acquisition, processing, and transmission of information has had major effects upon every sector of the economy. This is clearly true for the services, though the consequences differ in degree from one service subsector to another. I will try to offer some indication of the magnitude of the explosion in information activities and show that this is by no means a postwar phenomenon—that it appears to go back well into the nineteenth century.

Information provision is itself a service or, rather, a bundle of services. Thus, the information sector contributes to the volume of services, while the service sector is the central source of information. This two-way relationship constitutes the basis for a feedback model that raises disturbing possibilities of oscillatory behavior and of dampened productivity growth. My central focus is this two-way interaction and its implications for future economic activity.

INFORMATION AND HETEROGENEITY OF THE SERVICES

The burst of expansion of computer based activity is the tangible epitome of the incredible growth in information provision activity. Different industries have been affected to varying degrees and the services have perhaps been those whose responses have varied most. At one extreme is telecommunications, which has long been at the forefront of technological advance. Computers constantly communicate with one another by telephone, as is widely recognized. It is not generally recognized that in the last few years computation and telecommunications have virtually effected a merger. However, the telecommunications network has itself been transformed into a giant computer. Switches are no longer the simple objects we once could all describe. Today's "intelligent switches" can quickly determine routes for messages that reduce congestion and queuing problems, and perform a host of other near-miraculous tasks. Office switchboards have become astonishingly versatile and sophisticated, and even telephone instruments themselves come equipped with minicomputers that can record information and act in response to it. It is no wonder that AT&T and IBM have been able to invade one another's territory.

At the other extreme, handicraft services such as live theater, teaching of the humanities, and trash collection have all benefitted from computers that are used for word processing, record keeping, and research. The effects, however, are largely peripheral, and the production process underlying these services goes on fundamentally as it always has. For these services, the cost savings promised by computers have been negligible. This is a contributing factor to their persistently low rate of growth in labor productivity. As we can see, it is very dangerous to lump all services together for analytic purposes for their diversity would prove a likely source of major error.

ON THE GROWTH OF INFORMATION AND OTHER SERVICE ACTIVITIES

Estimates extending well over a century that indicate the course of information and other U.S. service activities relative to manufacturing and agriculture may provide a foundation for our discussion. The figures are highly sensitive to the ways these sectors are defined, and the earlier data must, in any event, be taken with much more than a grain of salt. Nevertheless, these figures, taken from work by Professor J. Beniger, provide a reasonably defensible representation of the facts.

Figure 8–1 shows for the period 1800–1980 the share of the U.S. labor force employed in the various sectors. We see that the transition

Figure 8-1. Shares of Labor Force by Sector, 1800–1980.

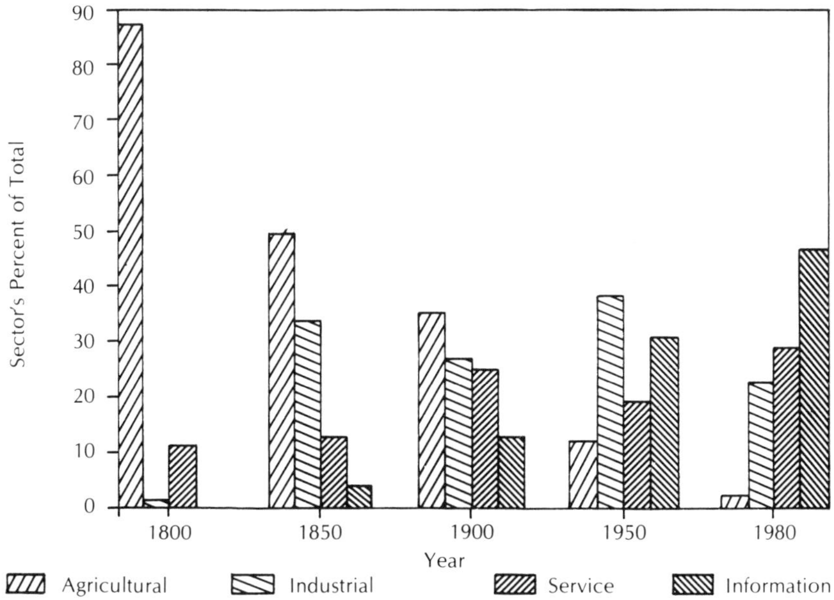

[Bar chart showing Sector's Percent of Total on y-axis (0-90) and Year on x-axis (1800, 1850, 1900, 1950, 1980) with four categories: Agricultural, Industrial, Service, Information]

Source: Beniger (1984).

process has been gradual. Agriculture fell almost linearly from nearly 90 percent of the labor force in 1800 to about 2 percent today. Industrial activity rose steadily until 1950 and then declined sharply in the postwar period to less than 25 percent of the total. Other services rose steadily until 1950 and then, for all practical purposes, levelled at a bit less than 30 percent of the total. Information, however, starting virtually from zero, occupied more than 45 percent of the U.S. labor force by 1980! Clearly the growing urgency of Veblen's "interstitial adjustments" has had its effects.

However, when interpreting these figures, particularly those for industry and services, a crucial caveat must be emphasized. The data in the graph represent relative labor inputs, not relative outputs. The two are by no means proportional. In particular, the long record of productivity growth in industry and its persistent lag in a number of service sectors means that the output of manufactures will not have fallen as rapidly relative to that of the services as has been true of labor inputs. As a matter of fact, data recently assembled by my colleagues and myself (Baumol, Blackman, and Wolff 1985) indicate that there has been no increase in the proportion of U.S. output composed of services. The ratio of number of students graduated, orchestral performances attended, number of tons of solid waste removed, and so forth, to number of watches, shoes, and shovels manufactured has, if anything, been decreasing slightly, despite the rising relative share of the nation's labor time devoted to the former.

The explanation, of course, is the dramatic increase in manufacturing productivity. Since 1870 it is estimated that U.S. output per person hour has increased an incredible twelvefold (Maddison 1982) meaning that the industrial output of 1870 could now be produced with one-twelfth the labor force it then required. With productivity in many services having grown only negligibly, it is clear why the services would have had to absorb an ever expanding share of the manufacturing labor force just to be able to keep up with the growth in manufacturing output.

Similar questions arise about the rate of growth of information outputs, but for more subtle reasons. Many information activities contain a vital component that is essentially handicraft in character—teaching, certain types of research, and production of computer software are examples. If these pure labor components are a very nearly irreducible part of the information activity or are at least resistant to substantial reduction, then the comparative time paths of their outputs and inputs must grow very similar to those in the personal services generally. In other words, the relative increase in information output, however it may be measured, may well be increasing significantly more slowly than its share of the labor force.

More important for our purposes is the implication about the relative prices (costs) of such information activities with comparatively irreducible labor components. As for many of the personal services, the relative prices of these information outputs will grow higher and higher in comparison with those of industrial products. This is clearly true of education, whose ever rising real cost per student day is amply documented. This phenomenon has quite appropriately been dubbed the "cost disease" of educational activity.

More surprisingly, there is also evidence that computation is threatened by similar prospects. As the costs of hardware have plummeted cumulatively in recent decades, they have come to constitute an ever declining share of computation budgets, leaving the remainder to be taken up by software production and other handicraft services. Some estimates suggest that over the decade of the seventies the handicraft component of computation budgets rose from perhaps 20 percent of the total at the beginning of the period to some 80 percent at the end (Baumol, Blackman, and Wolff 1985).

In terms of their budgets, such information activities are asymptotically approaching the structure of what we may call "quasi handicraft activities" such as violin playing and tutoring of students. As that process continues, the relative costs and prices of computation must rise relative to those of industrial products and those rises must compound and culate. Potentially, then, much of the information activity is subject to the cost disease.

This much I have said before on a number of occasions. What I have to add now is the two-way interaction implicit in the process I have just described, and its implications for the future of service activities and for the economy generally.

PRODUCTIVITY AND INFORMATION: THE TWO-WAY RELATIONSHIP

The production and distribution of knowledge (as Professor Machlup described the activities that concern us here) have at least two vital roles to play in our economy: the one relating, roughly speaking, to management; the other, to entrepreneurship. As the interdependencies among different portions of the economy, and even those of individual firms, grow increasingly numerous and complex, information and information processing techniques grow ever increasingly crucial as a means to preserve the health of the requisite interstitial adjustments.[1]

At the same time, information production and dissemination are a prime engine of productivity growth. Indeed, since both basic research and R&D are included within the production of information, it is hard to think of any other comparable and systematic source of growth in total factor productivity.

This is certainly true even of the services most resistant to productivity growth. Here, too, violin playing provides my favorite example. Clearly, the mass media have increased the productivity of the violinist in terms of the number of listeners provided with an hour of music per hour of performance labor, and the dependence of the mass media's productivity—indeed, of their very existence—on the knowledge industry is equally patent. Even live performance is dependent on the flow of knowledge for productivity improvement. Just think of a violinist living in New York who is engaged to perform in San Francisco. The knowledge industry is responsible for the availability of jet aircraft and for the continuing effectiveness of operation of their passenger transportation network. These days our violinist arrives at his work site in a small fraction of the time that it took him before, say, World War II.

Similarly, the emergence of evermore powerful information technology has increased productivity in services as diverse as food catering, retailing, telecommunications, and even research itself. This is the first half of our feedback relationship. Put rather roughly but not misleadingly, we may say that an increase in the outputs of the information activities tends to lead to increased productivity in manufacturing and in other services. This much is obvious, and it is unlikely to be questioned by anyone.

It is the second half of the feedback relationship that is rather more subtle. It tells us that increased productivity growth elsewhere in the economy tends to impede the expansion of information activities by increasing their relative price through the agency of the cost disease. Although information activities encourage productivity, if my contention is valid, the latter tends to impede the former. While there is some time lag involved in the process, this description is sufficient to constitute the completed feedback relationship.

HOW PRODUCTIVITY GROWTH CAN HAMPER INFORMATION ACTIVITIES

To explain how productivity growth elsewhere in the economy can serve as a handicap to the activities of the information industry let us take computation as our illustration. I have already indicated why computation (in contradistinction to computer hardware) may be increasingly (asymptotically) subject to the cost disease. But the source of the cost disease of any economic activity is to be found in the relative lag in productivity growth of that activity compared to what is true of the economy as a whole. Over the centuries live violin playing has risen spectacularly in cost relative to watchmaking because in the course of three hundred years the number of watches producible per person year has risen more than one-hundredfold while, despite jet flights to San Francisco, neither labor productivity nor total factor productivity in violin playing is likely even to have doubled in this time.[2] It is primarily activities with quasi irreducible labor components that have suffered from the cost disease, and they have suffered from it precisely because the presence of that labor component has by definition prevented rapid rises in their labor productivity.

Now, the relative rise in the prices of the outputs of activities that are laggards in productivity growth is more rapid the greater is the relative rise in productivity in the remainder of the economy. If watch productivity had risen ten times as fast as it did in fact, the relative cost of concerts—that is, the number of watches that are exchangeable, say, for a subscription to a concert series—would be proportionately greater than it actually is today.

Thus, as the outpouring of products of the information industry stimulates productivity growth in the economy, it simultaneously raises the relative prices or products of laggard activities, in the comparative dynamics sense of the term. Computation shows just how this happens. Increased productivity in the economy stimulated by a flow of information decreases prices and costs in many areas, the prices of computer hardware among them. This only serves to reduce the share of the overall computation budget accounted for by such products of technology, so a greater proportion of that budget must be devoted to the quasi handicraft portions of computation activity (e.g., software, machine maintenance) with the latter threatening to take over almost all of that budget. As that happens, computation costs tend to be driven up along with those of the quasi handicraft services.

In sum, information activity stimulates productivity growth throughout the economy, but that tends to raise the relative price of computation and other activities. This is almost the end of the story behind the second of our feedback relationships. There is one more step: Products of information activities must be recognized as just another set of inputs into the production process of any firm and, hence, of the economy in general. Virtually all inputs have substitutes, so that when the relative price of any input rises, its use will decrease or will at least not grow as rapidly as it would have otherwise.

For example, consider a procedure that uses computers to schedule production more efficiently, thereby reducing the number of machines needed for the job. If computation is sufficiently cheap relative to the price of one of the machines, it will be profitable to adopt this process. However, if computation is relatively expensive it will be more profitable to schedule production the old-fashioned way, thereby substituting machines for computation.

While the explosion of information is likely to continue, the cost disease has the power, in this way, to reduce the rate of growth of information inputs into other activities below what it would have been otherwise.

HOW THE FEEDBACK PROCESS WORKS

The description of the two basic pieces of the feedback model is now complete. Information flows stimulate productivity growth while productivity growth inhibits the production and dissemination of information. The nature of the feedback loop is clear. It is the mechanism of a sequential process in which today's information flow determines (or at least affects) tomorrow's productivity growth and that in turn affects the next day's prices of information products and their equilibrium output quantities.

Up to a point the mechanism works in the same way as a cobweb model and has the same capacity of yielding a time path that is oscillatory and is either convergent or explosive. It is easy to demonstrate this formally with the aid of a simple difference equation. It is equally easy to describe the process intuitively. The following would be a typical scenario. Let us start our observations, say, in a period in which the outflow of information has grown (relatively) rapidly. In the second period this will increase the rapidity of productivity growth in the sectors of the economy that are not handicraft or quasi handicraft in character. In the third period the relative price of information services (among other such prices) will rise and the output of such services will be restricted correspondingly below what it would otherwise have been. In the fourth period the previous reduction in information outflow will decrease productivity growth below its previous trend; and, in the fifth period, that in turn will hold back the relative price and so stimulate the output of information services.

Clearly, such an oscillatory process can continue indefinitely, and the data show that this conclusion is not entirely farfetched. Figure 8-2 shows year by year growth rates of total factor productivity in the United States for the better part of a century, calculated from data supplied by Kendrick (U.S. Bureau of Census 1973). (His data on labor productivity exhibit a very similar pattern.) The extraordinary frequency of the oscillations is striking. They seem far more frequent than the economy's business fluctuations. Part of the explanation may lie in a process such as the one I have just described, and others like it.

The model has other implications. If the oscillations were really linear, they would tend to dampen out or explode, but neither intuition nor the data I have just shown support such a view. This leads to the inference that the feedback process we are discussing is characterized by nonlinearities—a possibility that is plausible in any event.

Figure 8-2. U.S. Total Factor Productivity Annual Growth, 1884-1969.

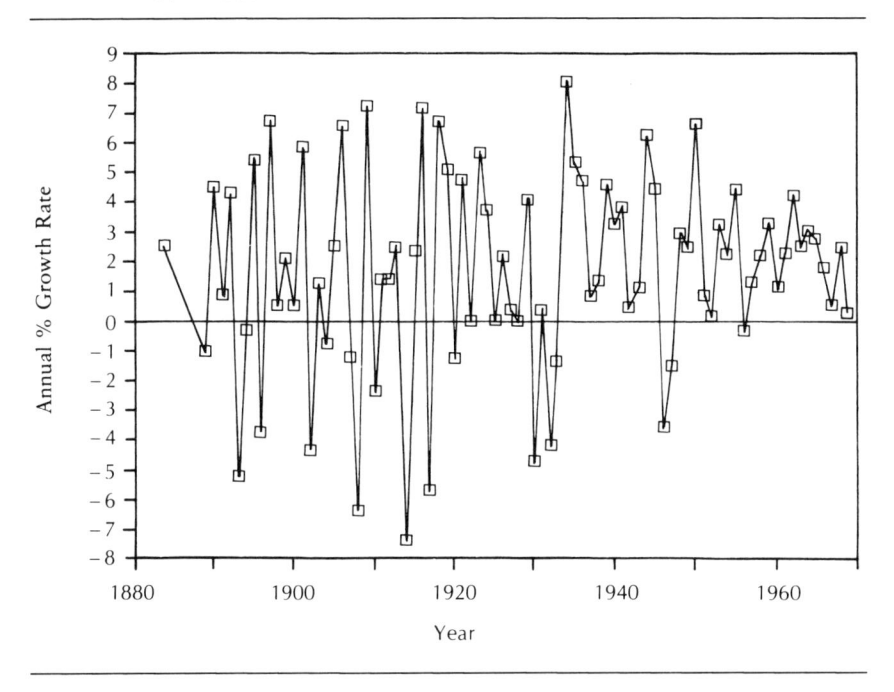

Source: U.S. Bureau of Census (1973).

Nonlinearities have a number of implications that I will merely mention. They may produce stable limit cycles that can go on forever or at least until the underlying mechanism changes. More disturbing is the possibility that they can introduce a regime of what is referred to as "chaotic behavior" in the difference equation literature. This behavior involves deterministic time paths that give all the appearance of being subjected intermittently to very severe random shocks, and which are so sensitive to tiny changes of parameter values as to render virtually hopeless any prospect of estimation of the parameter values of the underlying model by means of statistical observation or, of producing estimates that offer a prayer of robust estimates of the future.

Finally, and perhaps most disturbing, it is possible to show that a process such as ours may well constitute an ever increasing impediment to information flow and, hence, to productivity growth in the economy in general and in the services in particular. If so we may be dealing with a process that is self-terminating or which would tend to terminate itself in the absence of suitable public policy measures. The nature of such policy measures is far from clear at this point.

CONCLUDING COMMENT: IMPLICATIONS FOR THE SERVICES

I have recently been preoccupied with long-term economic data on such subjects as productivity, the composition of the labor force, unemployment, and other variables. These have taught me how dangerous it is to generalize from a brief span of observations. Indeed, the long series have caught me out in a number of embarrassing (published) misapprehensions whose details I would much rather leave undescribed here. I can easily produce cases in which thirty years of continuous decline in some key variable must have suggested that the community had entered a period of irreversible decline, only to have the decline suddenly come to a halt. Similarly, periods of what seem to constitute permanent growth also have a way of being terminated suddenly, with little warning.

The services have for decades been benefitting from the explosion of information products that are themselves, to a considerable degree, services. Surely this has been the characteristic theme of this volume. I have described some of the relationships that may, perhaps, underlie this phenomenon. If the analysis is correct it shows that the phenomenon is not necessarily immune from all dangers. It also suggests a formal structure that can help us to think through the policy options so we can determine what it may be sensible to do in order to deal with these dangers.

NOTES

1. This is the central point in Beniger's unpublished manuscript, which traces the history of the phenomenon and draws out its implications most illuminatingly.
2. Aside from the fact that I collect watches and know something about their technological history, it is hard to think of any other technologically sophisticated consumers' good that has been available and in continuous use before, say, the middle of the nineteenth century. This observation, which may be astonishing when one thinks of it, is another indication of what the information industry accomplished in just one century.

REFERENCES

Baumol, W.J.; S.A. Blackman; and E. Wolff. 1985. "Unbalanced Growth Revisited: Asymptotic Stagnancy and New Evidence." *American Economic Review* 75 (September):806–17.

Beniger, J.R. 1984. "The Control Revolution: Technological and Economic Origins of the Information Society." Unpublished paper, Princeton University.

Maddison, Angus. 1982. *Phases of Capitalist Development.* New York: Oxford University Press, p. 212.

U.S. Bureau of Census. 1973. *Long-term Economic Growth, 1860–1970* (June).

9 CONCLUSION
William J. Baumol

The very fact that this volume has been able to devote so many papers of such substance to the consequences of the information revolution for the services is an important message in itself for it counters the widespread impression that the services, or at least a substantial subset of the services, are inherently resistant to technological change. We realize now that even the most handicraft-like of service activities have undergone the intrusion of computers, of other electronic devices, have benefitted from the forms of transportation introduced by the twentieth century, and have been modified in a variety of other ways, sometimes fundamentally, by the march of technology. That this is so is established beyond question. Even the live performance of dance benefits from computerized control of its lighting and food services profit from improved scheduling of their activities.

While this is established, many questions naturally remain for future research, most of them having been brought out implicitly or explicitly by the papers in this volume. The most obvious and most central question is whether the innovation centering about the advent of the computer has affected the technology of the services in a fundamental manner or whether it has merely altered its periphery. Here we do know something about the answer, and it is obviously very mixed. That is to say, it varies enormously from service to service. Health care, we have been told here, has benefitted from the computerization of bookkeeping and billing, but the intrusion of the computer into the practice of medicine itself has been rather slower. Its help in diagnosis is apparently limited so far, and the day in which surveillance and treatment of a patient will be largely automated is still far away—if it will ever come. Live performance by a string quartet benefits by the availability of jet transportation, which is itself highly dependent on computers and which has tremendously cut the performer time expended in providing concerts in two widely separated locations, but technological change has hardly affected the manner of live performance itself. On the other hand, services such as telecommunications and computation itself have obviously undergone fundamental metamorphosis.

There is no difficulty, then, in documenting such differences in the degree to which technological change has modified the different services at the core of their technology. What is not yet understood, despite their significance, is the explanation of these differences. What is it that renders one service but not another, at least in the short run, impervious to fundamental change in response to information innovations? Once we begin to grasp the answer we will be in a better position to attack the impediments and to prepare ourselves in advance for the prospective developments that the analysis suggests.

A second critical issue raised in this volume but calling for further research is the exportability of services. We have seen that computers and associated technological changes have increased the international exchange of services that previously fell virtually completely within the domestic domain. Even the drawing of blueprints, we have been told here, can now be contracted out to the country that can provide them with greatest cost effectiveness, for transmission to the user without delay. The point here is that if comparative advantages in industrialized activities shifts away from the nations that were previously the leaders in this arena, increased exportability of services can help to provide the substitutes that cushion the economic consequences. Thus, it is important to understand analytically the attributes of the services and of the technological developments that can facilitate their export.

A third issue requiring further research relates to employment in the services. There is strong and consistent evidence indicating that the shift of the United States and other economies toward the services involves this sector's absorption of an ever greater share of the economy's *inputs* but not of an increasing proportion of its outputs. Deflation of the value of service outputs by appropriate sectoral price indexes indicates that, if anything, the share of real GNP composed of services has been falling slightly. This means, tautologically, that the increase in relative employment in services can be attributed to only one thing—relatively lagging productivity (i.e., to a lag in the ratio of outputs to inputs). The share of service employment has grown precisely because (some of) the services have not benefitted from labor-saving innovation to the degree that other activities have. This immediately leads one to inquire whether that relationship can be expected to continue. If the technological developments discussed in this volume do in fact presage rates of productivity growth, even in the laggard services, more slowly relative to those in industry, one may well ask whether the services can continue to serve as a prime refuge for that portion of the labor force that technical change might otherwise render redundant.

Next, this volume suggests it is essential to explore more fully the socioeconomic consequences of technological change in the services. The economy of the central cities is a prime case in point. It seems clear that much of the trauma U.S. urban areas have undergone in recent decades is attributable to the decline in suitability of the city as a manufacturing center, a decline in turn ascribable to technological developments in transportation and in manufacturing itself. The center of the metropolis is now devoted increasingly to the provision of services, for which it still possesses a variety of advantages. The main question here is whether the new technology threatens also to erode the comparative efficiency of the city as a supplier of services—particularly whether increased sophistication of computers and telecommunications will call for increased decentralization of services just as it has of manufactures. The implications for the future of our cities are obviously substantial.

A fifth basic issue for further research that is suggested by this volume is the effect of technological advances in the services on the constraints that beset the execution of government policy. We have been shown how such advance constantly enhances the available types of near monies and in the process threatens to undercut the effectiveness of monetary policy. There are obviously two sides to this story. Technological progress enhances the effectiveness of government activity but it simultaneously assists those who would evade it. "Love laughs at locksmiths" may be taken as a metaphor for the technological moves and countermoves of the two protagonists. Technological advance may yet provide a substantial contribution to the forces of laissez faire, making it increasingly difficult for governments to interfere effectively in the workings of the market mechanism. This startling possibility may yet prove a far more tenable and powerful impediment to policy intrusion than are those pointed out by the literature of rational expectations.

Thus, a variety of crucial issues emerge from the papers in this volume. In each case these papers take us at least a substantial first step toward the requisite analysis, but they also constitute the fertile basis for crucial research undertakings that will no doubt occupy our colleagues for decades to come.

Let me close by proposing a few additional issues (going beyond the contents of this volume) for further research relating to what may be among the primary consequences of the emerging technology of the services. The writings in this book have stressed the role of information as a service that itself serves other services as well as manufacturing. But the growth of information output has profound implications for long-run productivity growth, for the evolution of living standards, and for the relative standing of the world's industrialized economies.

The pertinent data are dramatic. According to data supplied by Maddison (1982) and others, per capita real income in the United States has increased by something like 600 percent in a bit more than a century. This means that the real income of an average American in the 1870s was comparable to that of today's resident of Egypt or the Philippines. Such a growth rate in economic welfare is totally unprecedented in history. At the same time, this period was characterized by rapid and persistent convergence in the productivity growth rates of the industrialized countries. The sixteen countries included in Maddison's data set have narrowed their productivity gap by some 75 percent since 1870. Whereas the output per work hour in the most productive to the least productive country in this set was approximately eight to one in 1870; by 1979 that ratio had fallen to about two to one. As a corollary, it follows that the industrialized countries that were furthest behind the leader in 1870 have necessarily grown most rapidly since, and the data confirm that this has indeed been so.

Both these crucial macro developments—the unprecedented growth in productivity and living standards, and the convergence in the productivity levels of the leading industrialized countries—must critically depend on the expansion and expanding capacities of their information services. The available evidence strongly indicates that innovation *and its dissemination* played a central role in the spectacular growth of productivity that made possible such unprecedented rises in living standards. Moreover, the convergence phenomenon obviously must rest to a considerable degree on increasing ability of a productivity laggard nation to learn of and to learn to adopt the emerging technology of the leaders.

In these ways developments in information technology and the supply of information services exercise a profound influence upon the fate of nations. These are long-run phenomena, and their importance is obviously critical. One of the pertinent attributes of such long-run issues is that if they require any attention by those who design policy, that attention must usually be provided early, well before the relevant consequences begin to merge, when it may well be too late. Yet, it is the fate of practitioners to have their attention constantly diverted by the need to fight fires, leaving them little time to devote to the long run. The responsibility then devolves upon the academic researchers; for if they ignore the long-run issues, there is no one else who will take their place. The information services are crucial not only because they are absorbing an increasing share of our economy's personnel, as is reported elsewhere in this volume, but because to a considerable degree the long-run fate of that economy will be influenced by what those services provide.

REFERENCE

Maddison, Angus. 1982. *Phases of Capitalist Development.* New York: Oxford University Press.

AUTHOR INDEX

Abler, R., 178
Armstrong, R., 169
Arnett, R.H.; Cowell, C.S.; Davidoff, L.M.; and Freeland, M.S., 10

Baumol, W.J.; Blackman, S.A.; and Wolff, E., 186
Bell, D., 119
Beniger, J.R., 184
Benway, S.D., 17

Carpenter, C.J., 14
Carter, G., and Ginsburg, P.B., 28
Chandler, A., 160
Clark, Colin, 111
Commission of the European Communities, 112, 113

Dawes, R., 46
Drucker, P. 119

Eralp. O., and Rucker, B.B., 7
Ermann, D., and Gabel, J., 11

Federal Reserve, 167
Fielding, Leslie, 112–113
Fox, P.D.; Goldbeck, W.B.; and Spies, J.J., 10

Gabel, J., and Ermann, D., 11
General Motors Corporation/ Saturn Corporation, 87
Ginzberg, E., 10, 172
Gottmann, J., 179
Gurley, J.G., and Shaw, E.B., 51

Hannan, M.T., and Freeman, J., 135
Hillman, A.L., and Schwartz, J.S., 24
Horowitz, C., 160

Jervis, R., 136
Jonscher, C., 120

Kellerman, A., 179
Kinsbury, F.J., 143–145
Koehn, M., and Santomero, A., 68

Leibenstein, H., 108
Lindberg, D.A.B., 9
Lohr, K.; Brook, R.; Goldberg, G.; Chassin, M.; and Glennan, T., 28
Lorenzi, J.-H., and LeBoucher, E., 107

McFarlan, F.W., 45
Machlup, F., 119, 187

AUTHOR INDEX

Maddison, A., 186, 198
Marshall, Alfred, 50–51
Moody's Investor Service Annual, 162
Moss, M., 169, 171, 180

Naisbett, J., 173
Nakasone, Y., 113
Nicholas, J.P., 14
Noyelle, T.J., 180

OECD, 89, 95
Office of the U.S. Trade Representative, 96

Packer, C.L., 9
Pfeffer, J., 136
Porat, M., 119
President's Research Committee on Social Trends, 140
Pyle, D., 65

Ruby, G., 17

Samors, P.W., and Sullivan, S., 10
Santomero, A., 65
Santomero, A., and Warson, R., 68

Scheffler, R.M.; Yoder, S.G.; Weisfeld, N.; and Ruby, G., 10
Shelp, R.K.; Stephenson, J.C.; Truit, N.S.; and Wasow, B., 116
Simon, H., 135
Spero, J., 85
Stegman, M., 168, 172
Stern, R.S., and Epstein, A.M., 28
Sternlieb, G., and Hughes, J., 166, 167
Sternlieb, G.; Hughes, J.; and Hughes, C., 140, 141, 150
Stiglitz, J., and Weiss, A., 68

Tobin, J., 51, 57

U.S. Bureau of Census, 190
U.S. Council of Economic Advisors (CEA), 83
U.S. Department of Commerce, 112
U.S. Department of Labor, 112, 113

Waters, K.A., and Murphy, G.F., 8
Webber, M.M., 178–179
Wennberg, J.E.; McPherson, K.; and Caper, P., 11

SUBJECT INDEX

A&P, 162
Advertising media, 161
Aetna Life and Casualty Company, 41–42
Airline industry, 47, 92
Allstate, 37
American Express, 164
American International Group, 116
Amherst Associates, 17
Asset and liability limitations, 61
AT&T, 18, 184
Automation and insurance industry, 38, 40–41
Automobiles, 152, 161, 166

Bank of America, 169
Banking Act, 60
Banking industry, 91–93, 169
    regulation of, 49–70, 73–75, 76–79
Banks, monitoring of, 61–65
Baumol, William, 1
L.L. Bean, 180
Bechtel, 81, 86, 93, 116
Bhagwati, Jagdish, 116
Blue Cross/Blue Shield, 22, 39
Boeing Computer Services, 90
Brands, national, 161, 162

Brazil, 94, 114, 115
Bundespost (Germany), 94, 108

Career mobility, 3
Chain stores, 162
Chicago, 169
Chicago Mercantile Exchange, 81
Citibank, 81, 93–94
Cities, 150–152, 178, 197
Committee on Invisible Exports, 111
Communication costs, 85
Comparative advantage, theory of, 108, 112
"Cost disease," 1, 186–187, 188–189
Credit, 164–165, 179–180
Crystal Palace, 103
Customer self-service, 165–166

Dallas, Taxes, 100
Data General, 15–16, 17
Data processing (DP) costs in hospitals, 12–13, 23
"Declaration on Transborder Data Flows," 95
Deleware, 180
Department stores, 161

SUBJECT INDEX

Deposit insurance system, 60–61, 66
Developing countries, 114, 115–117
Diagnostic related groups (DRG) system, 11, 14, 22, 23–24, 26–28
Dialog Information Services, 93
Douglas Amendment, 49
Dun & Bradstreet, 39

Electricity, 150
"Electronic cottages," 172–173
Electronic Data Systems Corporation, 87
Electronic Transfer of funds (EFT), 42
Employee Retirement Income Security Act (ERISA), 32
Eurodollar market, 51, 84
European Community, 112–113
European Strategical Program in Information Technology (ESPRIT), 108

FDIC, 66, 67
Federal Funds market, 52
Financial services, 49–70, 73–75, 76–79
First Pennsylvania Bank, 77
Flexible benefit plans, 42
France, 113, 115, 163

Galaxy, 16
Galbraith and Greene, 39
Games and toys, 159–160
GEICO, 37
General Agreement on Tariffs and Trade (GATT), 94, 95, 107, 110, 111, 114, 115
General Electric, 2, 159
Germany, 2, 94, 113, 156, 159
Glass-Steagall Act, 49
GM, 87
"Goodhart's Law," 70 n. 9
Grand Union, 165
GTE Corporation, 108

HBO, 15–17
Health care industry, 7–18, 21–25, 26–29, 195–196
Health information systems (HISs), 8–9, 17

Health insurance, 10, 33, 35, 39
Health maintenance organizations (HMOs), 17
Highway program, 166
Hong Kong, 114
Hoover, Herbert, 4
Hoover Commission Report, 140
Hospitals, profit/nonprofit, 10, 11
Household change, 152–156
Housing ownership, 167

IBM, 2, 13, 14, 15, 17, 18, 84, 90, 184
India, 114
Infant industries, 114
Inflation
   and hospital industry, 24
   and insurance industry, 34, 35, 36
Information access, 4, 28–29
Information-sharing function, 46, 47
Information technology and productivity, 119–131, 184–191, 197, 198–199
Insurance agents and brokers, 36–37
Insurance industry, 31–43, 44–48
Insurance Services Office (ISO), 46
Interconnect Agreement, 95

James, Fred S., 39
Japan, 94, 107, 113, 114, 156, 159

Korea, 94

Labor force constraints, 156–159
Land's End, 180
Life insurance, 36
"Lifeline," 17
Lewis, Sinclair, 162
Lockheed, 93, 94

McDonnell Douglas Automation, 13
McDonnell Douglas Corporation, 83
McFadden Act, 49
Macrae, Norman, 5
Magazines, 161
Mail order business, 162, 163, 180
Main Street, 162

SUBJECT INDEX

Marx, Karl, 1
Massachusetts, 52
Mead Data Central, 93
Medicaid, 9, 22
Medicare, 9, 11, 22, 26–27, 29
Mediflex, 17
Merrill, Lynch, 170
Mexico, 94
MIT, 159
Money, concept of, 50, 51, 55, 77–78
Monopoly power, 45, 47
Multinational enterprises (MNEs), 106, 107

National borders, 4, 101–102, 196
Networking, 91–94
New information and communications technologies (NICT), 106–109
New Jersey, 168, 172
New York City, 150, 167, 168, 169–172
New York Telephone Company, 170, 171
New York Teleport, 170–171
Newspapers, 161
Nexis, 93
Noam, Eli, 5
NOW accounts, 52, 77
NIT (Japan), 94
NYNEX, 170

Occidental Life, 39
Organization for Economic Cooperation and Development (OECD), 89, 95
Organization theory, 135–137

Peer-review organizations (PROs), 29
Penn Square Bank, 77
J.C.Penney, 162
Philadelphia, 169
Piano manufacturers, 161
Pluralistic Economy, 1
Population ecology, 135, 136
Population projections, 140, 141–143
Port Authority of New York and New Jersey, 170, 172

Postal Telegraph & Telephones (PTTs), 5
Preferred provider organizations (PPOs), 11–12, 17, 22
Price Waterhouse, 104 n. 3
Project Multics, 159
Public transit, 167–168

Quality, certification of, 161

Radio, 161
Railroads, 160, 162
RCA, 84, 90
Regional population shifts, 143–150, 175–176
Regulation/deregulation, 5
  of financial services, 49–70, 73–75, 76–79
  of insurance companies, 32
Regulation Q, 52, 77
Reserve requirements, 52, 59–60, 78
Retailing industry, 160–166, 179–180
Rutgers University Center for Urban Policy Research, 160

"Safety and soundness," 50, 60–69, 79
Says Law, 48
Sears, Roebuck, 116
Security, 171–172
Self-insuring, 33–34, 35
Service Industries in Economic Development—Case Studies in Technology Transfer, 116
Services, trade in, 81–96, 98–104, 106–109, 110–117
Shopping malls, 163, 166
Singapore, 81, 114
Small business, role of, 100–101
Smith, Adam, 1, 3
SMS, 13, 16
Societe Internationale de Telecommunications Aeronautique (SITA), 92
Society for Worldwide Interbank Financial Telecommunications (SWIFT), 93
Standard Metropolitan Statistical Areas (SMSAs), 168–169, 175
State Farm, 37

SUBJECT INDEX

States
  health care expenditures, 10
  insurance company regulation, 32
Stolen Memories, 107
Streetcars, 150
Sunbelt, 176
Sweden, 165

Tax policy and insurance industry, 34
Technological impact, predicting, 159–166
Telecommunications, 180
Telecoms Agency (France), 108
Teleconferencing and video conferencing, 41
Telephone service, 150, 162, 166, 169–171, 179
Television, 161
Texas, 100–101, 150
Third party administrators (TPAs), 39
Trade Act, 111
Trade Pledge, 95
Trade policy, 94–96, 197–198
Trade rules for services, 111–112
Transamerica, 39

United Kingdom, 112, 113, 156
United Nations Conference on Trade and Development (UNCTAD) Trade and Development Board, 115–116
United States
  Bureau of Labor Statistics, 158
  health care budget, 10
  per capita real income, 198
  service sector, 1–3, 82–83, 112, 113, 159, 176–177, 196–197
UNIX, 18
Utility companies, 170

Veblen, Thorstein, 1, 185
Videotex shopping, 163
Visa, 164
Visible Hand, 160

Weber, Max, 135
Western Union, 170
Williamsburg Summit, 113
Women, 3
Work trip, 167–169
Wriston, Walter, 4
Wyoming, 145

ABOUT THE SPONSORING ORGANIZATIONS

FISHMAN-DAVIDSON CENTER FOR THE STUDY OF THE SERVICE SECTOR

The purpose of the center is to encourage, support, and sponsor research of the fundamental issues and problems in the service sector of the U.S. and global economy, and to disseminate the results of the research. The center encourages research in services from the disciplines of economics, management, marketing, finance, accounting, law, and others as may be appropriate. Publication of supported work is expected. The center explicitly recognizes that research excellence must be sought in close cooperation with the many sectors, both public and private, that have active interests in the service sector. Research is supported for Wharton School and University of Pennsylvania faculty as well as for visiting research staff from the United States and abroad. A major role of the center is the intermediation of those interests with the research community. Gerald R. Faulhaber is Director of the center.

CENTER FOR TELECOMMUNICATIONS AND INFORMATION STUDIES

The center encourages independent research on economics and policy issues in telecommunications and information. It provides both a New

York and national meeting ground for academic researchers, government policymakers, and private and nonprofit sector experts. The center is the only such entity at a business school, as well as the only one using economics and its allied disciplines as the primary analytical methodology.

Center research is disseminated through working papers and edited volumes. As a complement to published research, the center conducts monthly seminars, workshops, and in-depth conferences where current research is presented and critiqued by professionals in the field.

Eli Noam, Associate Professor of Business, and Michael Botein, Visiting Professor in the Law and Business Schools, co-direct the center. Executive Director is Roberta Tasley, and Ed Singletary is Associate Director.

ABOUT THE EDITORS

Gerald R. Faulhaber is Director of the Fishman-Davidson Center for the Study of the Service Sector and Associate Professor in the Department of Public Policy and Management, the Wharton School. He was previously Director of Financial Planning and Director of Strategic Planning, AT&T; and Research Head in the Economic Modeling and Financial Research Department, Bell Telephone Laboratories, Inc. Dr. Faulhaber has held teaching positions at New York and Princeton Universities. He has published numerous articles and papers and is coeditor (with A. Baughcum) of *Telecommunications Access and Public Policy*. He has served as referee for *American Economic Review, Econometrics,* and *Journal of Political Economy*. He holds an M.S. in Mathematics from New York University and an M.A. and Ph.D. in Economics from Princeton University.

Eli M. Noam is an Associate Professor at Columbia University's Graduate School of Business, where he has taught since 1976, and is Co-Director of the Center for Telecommunications and Information Studies. He has also taught at the Columbia Law School and has been a Visiting Professor at Princeton University's Economics Department and Woodrow Wilson School. He has published extensively in economic journals, law reviews, and interdisciplinary journals on issues of telecommunications and regulation. His books include the edited volumes *Telecommuni-*

cations: Today and Tomorrow and *Video Media Competition: Economics, Regulation, and Technology.* He presently is completing a monograph, *Telecommunications in Europe.* Professor Noam serves on the editorial boards of the Columbia University Press and several journals, including *Telecommunications Policy, Telephone Law and Business, Telematics,* and *Law and Society Review.* He is the general editor of the Columbia University Press book series, "Studies in Business, Government, and Society." He received an A.B. from Harvard College in 1970, and a Ph.D. in Economics and a J.D. in Law from the same university in 1975.

Roberta Tasley is Executive Director of the Center for Telecommunications and Information Studies at Columbia University's Graduate School of Business. Prior to joining the center, she was Program Administrator and Instructor at New York University's Interactive Telecommunications Program where she also directed the Telecommunications Clinic. She has published on questions relating to the social impact of electronic work at home as well as served as a consultant on the subject. Ms. Tasley holds a B.A. in Sociology from San Francisco State University and an M.P.S. in Interactive Telecommunications from New York University.

ABOUT THE CONTRIBUTORS

William J. Baumol is a Professor of Economics at Princeton and New York Universities and has consulted extensively for private firms and government agencies. He graduated from the College of the City of New York and obtained his Ph.D. from the University of London. His latest books are *Contestible Markets and the Theory of Industry Structure* (with J.C. Panzar and R.D. Willig) and *Superfairness: Applications and Theory.*

Mitchell Berlin is an economist in the Banking Section of the Research Department of the Federal Reserve Bank of Philadelphia and teacher of Commercial Banking at the Wharton School, University of Pennsylvania. He has also taught economics at the University of Pennsylvania, St. Joseph's University, and the Fashion Institute of Technology. In addition to research on bank regulation, his current research interests include contract theory, the theory of the banking firm, and the credit card industry. Recent working papers include "Screening, Limited Liability, and the Choice Between Long and Short Term Contracts" and "Banking and Private Information." Berlin received his B.A. from the University of Chicago and will receive his Ph.D. from the University of Pennsylvania.

Geza Feketekuty is Counselor to the United States Trade Representative. As such he has responsibility for the development and coordination of

U.S. trade policy. He played a key role in coordinating U.S. participation in the Tokyo Round of Multilateral Trade Negotiations and in planning the next round of multilateral trade negotiations. He also managed the development of government policies concerning trade in services. Feketekuty was formerly with the Council of Economic Advisers as Senior Staff Economist for International Finance and Trade and with the Office of Management and Budget as an economist and budget examiner. He has also been an instructor in economics at Princeton, Visiting Professor at Cornell University, Adjunct Professor at the School of Advanced International Studies of Johns Hopkins University, special assistant at the First National City Bank of New York, and a consultant and statistical analyst for the Book of the Month Club. He was Editor-in-Chief of *The American Economist* from 1962 to 1966.

Mr. Feketekuty is a graduate of Columbia University, Princeton, and the Advanced Management Program of the Harvard Business School.

Eli Ginzberg is Hepburn Professor Emeritus of Economics and Special Lecturer in Business at the Graduate School of Business, Columbia University; Special Lecturer in Health and Society, Barnard College; Director of the Conservation of Human Resources Project; and Director of the Revson Fellows Program for the Future of the City of New York, Columbia University. Dr. Ginzberg was formerly Chairman of the National Manpower Advisory Committee and the National Commission for Employment Policy and is Chairman Emeritus of the Board of the Manpower Demonstration Research Corporation. He is a Fellow of the American Academy of Arts and Sciences and a member of the Institute of Medicine, National Academy of Sciences. He is a long-term consultant to the federal government and to major corporations and non-governmental institutions. He has written many books, primarily on human resources and manpower, including *Good Jobs, Bad Jobs, No Jobs; Employing the Unemployed;* and *Beyond Human Scale: The Large Corporation at Risk*. He holds a B.A. from Columbia University, and an M.A. and Ph.D. in Economics from Columbia University.

Kathryn F. Hauser is the Director of Strategic Planning for Multilateral Negotiations in the Office of the United States Trade Representative (USTR), Executive Office of the President. She is responsible for coordinating private sector advice, developing U.S. trade policy positions, and formulating the U.S. strategy for new multilateral trade negotiations, which are expected to be formally started in 1986. Previously

Ms. Hauser was the Director of Telecommunications Services Policy at USTR. In this capacity she participated in both bilateral and multilateral negotiations on telecommunications services trade issues, including the first international agreement covering transborder data flows. She also coordinated U.S. participation in the General Agreement on Tariffs and Trade (GATT), managed preparations for the 1982 GATT Ministerial meeting, and conducted bilateral and multilateral negotiations among GATT member countries on an anti-counterfeiting code. She entered government service as a Presidential Management Intern. Ms. Hauser received a bachelor's degree from the University of Southern California, a master's degree from Columbia University, and did graduate work at the Graduate Institute for International Studies in Geneva, Switzerland.

Donald A. Hicks is an Associate Professor of Sociology and Political Economy at the University of Texas (Dallas). His current research interests include industrial-urban impacts of technological change. His latest book *Advanced Industrial Development: Restructuring, Relocation and Renewal* will be published later this year, and he has just completed writing *Technology Upgrading and Industrial Renewal: Adjustment Strategies in the U.S. Metalworking Industry* for the American Enterprise Institute. He is now working on a study of the U.S. computer software industry based on a national survey of software firms he conducted last year. For the past two years he has been directing a project examining the restructuring of the Texas and Dallas regional economies. He holds a Ph.D. from the University of North Carolina, Chapel Hill.

James W. Hughes is Professor, Department Chairman, and Director of the Graduate Program in Urban Planning and Policy Development, Rutgers University. Originally educated as an engineer, Dr. Hughes received his Ph.D. in Urban Planning in 1971 from Rutgers. He has been both a Woodrow Wilson and Ford Foundation Fellow, and in 1984 received the Rutgers Presidential Award for Distinguished Public Service.

Professors Sternlieb and Hughes have jointly authored fifteen books and more than thirty journal articles, ranging from *The Atlantic City Gamble* to the "Changing Demography of the Central City" *(Scientific American)*. Numerous of their analyses on housing, demographics, and economics have been published at the Center for Urban Policy Research at Rutgers.

Charles Jonscher is Associate Director of the Research Program on Communications Policy at the Sloan School of Management, MIT. He is also a Partner with Communications Studies and Planning International, a consulting firm based in New York and London, specializing in the telecommuncations industry. He was formerly with the Harvard University Department of Economics. Dr. Jonscher's current research interest is in the economics of information, and he is conducting a two-year study of this topic under NSF funding. He has an M.A. in Engineering from Cambridge University and a Ph.D. in Economics from Harvard University.

Howard Kunreuther is a Professor of Decision Sciences and Public Management and Director of the Wharton Risk and Decision Processes Center, University of Pennsylvania. He was formerly Task Leader of the Risk Group at the International Institute of Applied Systems Analysis. His current research is concerned with the role of compensation, insurance, and regulation as policy tools for dealing with low-probability events. He is coauthor of *Risk Analysis and Decision Processes,* as well as numerous publications in the area of risk and policy analysis, decision processes, and protection against low-probability events. He has an A.B. degree from Bates College and a Ph.D. in Economics from M.I.T.

Peter Linneman is an Associate Professor of Finance and Public Policy at the Wharton School, University of Pennsylvania. Dr. Linneman's primary areas of current research are the impacts of regulations, antitrust economics, mergers and acquisitions, and urban economics and real estate finance. He has published on a variety of topics including minimum wage laws, rent controls, the homeownership decision, the migration decision, and consumer product safety regulation. He holds a B.A. from Ashland College and M.A. and Ph.D. degrees from the University of Chicago.

Mitchell L. Moss is Associate Professor of Planning and Public Administration at New York University and was formerly Chairman of NYU's Interactive Telecommunications Program. He also serves as Deputy to the Chairman of Governor Cuomo's Council on Fiscal and Economic Priorities. He currently directs a project on the impact of new communications technology on cities. His articles have appeared in *Telecommunications Policy, Urban Affairs Quarterly, Land Development Studies,* and *Intermedia.* He has served as a consultant on telecommunications and economic development to the City of New York, Port Authority of New York and New Jersey, and the New York State Energy Research and Development Authority. Moss is a member of the New York State Urban Development Corporation's High Technology Advisory Committee. He holds a B.A. in Political Science from Northwestern University, an M.A. in Political Science from the University of Washington, and a Ph.D. in Urban Studies from the University of Southern California.

Mark V. Pauly is Professor of Health Care Systems and of Public Management, both at the Wharton School, and of Economics at the School of Arts and Sciences, University of Pennsylvania. He is also Executive Director of the Leonard Davis Institute of Health Economics and Robert D. Eilers Professor of Health Care Management and Economics. One of the nation's leading health economists, Pauly has made contributions to the fields of medical economics and health insurance. He is widely published on issues ranging from physician-patient decisions to the operation of markets of medical care and national health policy formulation, with a prevailing emphasis on the role of economics in the provision of medical care and health services. He serves on the editorial boards of *Public Finance Quarterly* and the *Journal of Health Economics*. Formerly he was visiting research fellow at the International Institute of Management in Berlin and Professor of Economics at Northwestern University. He holds an M.A. from University of Delaware and a Ph.D. in Economics from the University of Virginia.

Almarin Phillips is John C. Hower Professor of Public Policy and Management at the Wharton School, University of Pennsylvania and Professor of Economics and Law at Pennsylvania. He has also held teaching positions at Harvard, the University of Virginia, the University of Hawaii, Warwick (England) University, the London Graduate School of Business Studies, Ohio State University, McGill University, the California Institute of Technology, and Northwestern University. Phillips' fields of specialization are industrial organization, regulation, and the economics of technological change. He has authored, coauthored, and edited seven books and has written many articles for professional journals. Phillips has also had editorial responsibilities for several professional publications and has served on the Board and Executive Committee of the National Bureau of Economic Research and as a Senior Fellow at the Brookings Institution. He has acted in many governmental capacities and is currently Chairman of the Advisory Committee on Information Technology and Financial Services of the Office of Technology Assessment, U.S. Congress. Other activities have included consultative roles with the Board of Governors of the Federal Reserve System, the Secretary of the Treasury, and state banking and regulatory agencies. He holds B.S. and M.A. degrees from the University of Pennsylvania and a Ph.D. from Harvard.

Gérard Pogorel is Associate Professor of Economics, Université de Technologie de Compiégne, France, responsible for the Research Program on new information and communication technologies and international relations. He received honors degrees in Business Administration from the Ecole des Hautes Etudes Commerciales, in Sociology from the Sorbonne, and in Economics from the Université de Paris I. He has been awarded a Fullbright research award and a fellowship by the German Marshall Fund. His research interests have focused on transborder data flows and policies in the area of international communications. He has been a main contributor to the UN report, *Transborder Data Flows: Access to the International Data Market,* and is preparing a report to the French Planning Authority on telecommunication policies in Europe. He has contributed to the economic chapter of *L'Etat et la Démocratie,* Report to the President of the Republic. He has served as a consultant to the OECD, the EEC, and several institutions involved in formulating public policy in France and Europe. Together with Eli Noam, he is co-responsible for a U.S.-France cooperative research project on telecommunications policies.

Richard Scheffler is a Professor of Health Economics and Public Policy and Chair of the Program in Health Policy and Administration at the University of California, Berkeley. He is an affiliated faculty member with the School of Public Policy and also teaches in the School of Business Administration at Berkeley. In addition to his teaching duties, he is the Director of the Research Program in Health Economics in the Institute for Business and Economic Research, School of Business. He has taught at George Washington University and the University of North Carolina, Chapel Hill, and was formerly Director of the Division of Health Manpower and Resources in the Institute of Medicine, National Academy of Sciences. He holds a Ph.D. in Economics from New York University.

Robert Shay is Professor of Banking and Finance at the Graduate School of Business, Columbia University. He is a member of the Governing Board of the Credit Research Center of the Krannert School, Purdue University, and member of the Editorial Review Board of the *Journal of Retail Banking*. He is also a member of the boards of directors of the American Union Insurance Company of New York and Eastern Savings Bank. Professor Shay is Faculty Director of the Management of Financial Services Program and Co-Director of the Commercial Bank Management Program. He has written books and articles on retail banking and consumer finance, and holds B.S., M.A., and Ph.D. degrees from the University of Virginia.

Ronald K. Shelp is a Vice President of Celanese Corporation. Formerly he was Vice President of American International Group, Inc., and Vice President/Director of American International Underwriters Corporation. He has been appointed under several administrations as a member of the U.S. delegation to the Organization for Economic Cooperation and Development (OECD) and was elected Chairman of the Industry Sector Advisory Committee on Service Trade Policy. He chairs the Coordinating Committee of the Coalition of Service Industries and the International Trade Industry Committee to the National Association of Insurance Commissioners. Shelp also serves as a trustee or director of numerous national and international organizations. He is an adjunct associate professor of international business and economics at New York University. His publications include *Beyond Industrialization: Ascendancy of the Global Service Economy*. He holds an A.B. in Political Science and American History from the University of Georgia, and an M.A. in International Relations from the Johns Hopkins University School of Advanced International Studies.

George Sternlieb is Founder and Director of the Rutgers University Center for Urban Policy Research and also Professor of Urban and Regional Planning. He has written numerous monographs and articles and edited a special series of books on housing problems. Formerly an executive with the Bloomingdale's department store in New York, he is currently a director of the Citizens Housing and Planning Council, New York, and trustee of the Urban Land Institute, Washington, D.C. He holds a B.A. from Brooklyn College, and M.B.A. and Ph.D. degrees from the Harvard Business School.

Kenneth E. Thorpe is an Assistant Professor of Public Health and Public Policy at Columbia University. He is also a consultant to the Rand Corporation. He has taught Business and Management at Pepperdine

University and served with the Human Resources and Community Development Division of the Congressional Budget Office and with the Department of Commerce. He holds a B.A. from the University of Michigan, an M.A. from Duke University, and a Ph.D. in Policy Analysis from the Rand Graduate Institute.

Dennis A. Yao is Assistant Professor of Public Policy and Management at The Wharton School, University of Pennsylvania. He was formerly Chief Analyst for the Car Product Planning Group, the Ford Motor Company. His research concentrates on models of the markets for information, competition in defense contracting, and organizational learning. He holds a B.S.E. in Civil Engineering from Princeton University, an M.B.A. from the University of California, Berkeley, and a Ph.D. from Stanford University.

David N. Young is President of PARTNERS National Health Plans, a joint venture partnership between Aetna Life & Casualty and VHA Enterprises that markets, administers, and manages health care plans on a nationwide basis. He worked his way up through Aetna as Employee Benefits Representative, Office Manager, Account Executive, Assistant Manager, and General Manager of the Employee Benefits Division. He has also served as Vice President of Insurance Marketing in Hartford, Connecticut.